Legendary Hunts II

More Short Stories from the Boone and Crockett Awards

Boone and Mountain Lion, 1976 | Oil on Masonite. 20 x 30 inches
by Boone and Crockett Club Member Robert Kuhn
(United States, 1920-2007)

Legendary Hunts II

MORE SHORT STORIES FROM THE BOONE AND CROCKETT AWARDS

Presented by the Boone and Crockett Club Publications Committee
Chairman – Howard P. Monsour, Jr.

Stories selected by the following individuals:
- JIM ARNOLD
- KEITH BALFOURD
- MARK O. BARA
- RICHARD T. HALE
- JULIE T. HOUK
- KYLE C. KRAUSE – EDITOR
- REMO PIZZAGALLI
- JACK RENEAU
- JUSTIN E. SPRING
- MARK B. STEFFEN

Published by the Boone and Crockett Club

Missoula, Montana

2011

LEGENDARY HUNTS II
More Short Stories from the Boone and Crockett Awards

First Edition October 2011
   First Printing

Library of Congress Catalog Card Number: 2011939192
ISBN Number: 978-0-940864-73-3
Published October 2011

Published in the United States of America
by the
Boone and Crockett Club
250 Station Drive
Missoula, MT 59801
406/542-1888
406/542-0784 (fax)
www.booneandcrockettclub.com

THE MISSION
of the Boone and Crockett Club

*It is the mission of the Boone and Crockett Club to
promote the guardianship and provident management
of big game and associated wildlife in North America
and to maintain the highest standards of fair chase
and hunter ethics in all aspects of big game hunting,
in order that this resource of all the people may survive
and prosper in its natural habitats. Consistent with
this objective, the Club supports the use and enjoyment
of our wildlife heritage to the fullest extent by this and
future generations.*

Colorado hunter Edison A. Pillmore (pictured above) was given the Sagamore Hill Award at the Club's Sixth Competition held at the American Museum of Natural History in New York. His typical mule deer has a final score of 203-7/8 points and was harvested in 1949 near North Park, Colorado.

Table of Contents

Legendary Hunts II

More Short Stories from the
Boone and Crockett Awards Programs

Jack Greenwood and his son Jerry packing out his award-winning bighorn sheep taken in Sanders County, Montana, in 2001 .

Robert C. Reeve set a new World's Record when he shot this Alaska brown bear in 1948 near Cold Bay. Reeve was shooting a Model 96 Winchester to harvest the bear that reportedly weighed over 1,800 pounds and measured 12 feet wide and 10 feet tall. The skull is currently owned by the American Museum of Natural History in New York City. Reeve was the first hunter to receive a Sagamore Hill Award from the Boone and Crockett Club.

Sagamore Hill Award

Robert H. Hanson

B&C Regular Member

THE SAGAMORE HILL AWARD IS THE HIGHEST AWARD GIVEN
BY THE BOONE AND CROCKETT CLUB. IT WAS ESTABLISHED
IN 1948, IN MEMORY OF THEODORE ROOSEVELT (FOUNDER AND
FIRST PRESIDENT OF THE BOONE AND CROCKETT CLUB), AND HIS
TWO SONS, THEODORE ROOSEVELT, JR., AND KERMIT ROOSEVELT.

The process of determining a recipient of this prestigious
award is quite rigorous. With respect to big game trophies, a Big
Game Awards Final Judges Panel may, if in its collective opinion there is an outstanding trophy worthy of great distinction,
recommend to the Sagamore Hill Award Committee an Award
recipient. That committee is always headed by the immediate
past president of the Club, with the remainder of the committee
made up of past presidents and the current president. As of this
writing, the Awards Committee is chaired by Lowell E. Baier,
immediate past president and a Regular Member of the Club
since 1980, ably assisted by 10 of the Club's past presidents and
current president, Ben B. Wallace, Jr. Only one Sagamore Hill
trophy may be given in any Big Game Awards Program.

The chair distributes all trophy nomination recommenda-
tions to the full committee for further review, and any decision

SAGAMORE HILL AWARD WINNERS

1948 ROBERT C. REEVE – ALASKA BROWN BEAR
29-13/16 – COLD BAY, ALASKA

1949 E.C. HAASE – ROCKY MOUNTAIN GOAT
56-6/8 – BABINE MTS., BRITISH COLUMBIA

1950 DR. R.C. BENTZEN – TYPICAL WAPITI
441-6/8 – BIGHORN MTS., WYOMING

1951 GEORGE LESSER – WOODLAND CARIBOU
405-4/8 – GANDER RIVER, NEWFOUNDLAND

1953 EDISON PILLMORE – TYPICAL MULE DEER
203-7/8 – NORTH PARK, COLORADO

1957 FRANK COOK – DALL'S SHEEP
185-6/8 – CHUGACH MTS., ALASKA

1959 FRED C. MERCER – TYPICAL WAPITI
419-4/8 – MADISON COUNTY, MONTANA

1961 HARRY L. SWANK JR. – DALL'S SHEEP
189-6/8 – WRANGELL MTS., ALASKA

1963 NORMAN BLANK – STONE'S SHEEP
190-6/8 – SIKANNI RIVER, BRITISH COLUMBIA

1965 MELVIN J. JOHNSON – TYPICAL WHITETAIL
204-4/8 – PEORIA COUNTY, ILLINOIS

1973 DOUG BURRIS JR. – TYPICAL MULE DEER
226-4/8 – DOLORES COUNTY, COLORADO

1976 GARRY BEAUBIEN – MOUNTAIN CARIBOU
452 – TURNAGAIN RIVER, BC

1986 MICHAEL J. O'HACO, JR. – PRONGHORN
93-4/8 – COCONINO COUNTY, ARIZONA

1989 GENE C. ALFORD – COUGAR
16-3/16 – IDAHO COUNTY, IDAHO

1992 CHARLES E. ERICKSON JR. – NON-TYPICAL COUES' WHITETAIL
155 – GILA COUNTY, ARIZONA

2001 GERNOT WOBER – ROCKY MOUNTAIN GOAT
56-6/8 – BELLA COOLA, BRITISH COLUMBIA

2010 PAUL T. DEULING – MOUNTAIN CARIBOU
459-3/8 – PELLY MOUNTAINS, YUKON TERRITORY

to make an award must be approved unanimously and through an anonymous vote. Finally, all Sagamore Hill Awards are reviewed and approved by the Roosevelt family.

A special award may also be presented by the Sagamore Hill Award Committee to a Club member who has made an overwhelmingly unique contribution to the Club that will likely change the Club for better, forever.

To date, Sagamore Hill Awards have been given to 17 worthy recipients, the first such recognition having been accorded to Robert C. Reeve in 1948 for his outstanding Alaskan brown bear. Special Sagamore Hill Awards have been given to eight Club members since the award was established.

I have had the honor and privilege of serving on four Judges Panels, two as a judge, once as Chair of the Judges Panel and once as a consultant. That experience has given me an inside view of how the award process operates.

Once the panel has finished its work, which generally has involved four to five days of intense measuring—often from dawn till dusk—the panel, as its last order of business, gathers to determine if any trophy received during that particular Awards Program is worthy of consideration as a potential Sagamore Hill Award winner. As part of that exercise, the judges review the stories which have been authored by the hunters who have taken high-ranking trophies, and frequently a spirited debate ensues. There is no mandate that a Sagamore Hill Award be given for each Awards Program. In fact, of the four panels on which I have served, only two panels elected to recommend the award. This immediately raises the issue of what criteria are considered by the judges.

A new World's Record for a given species does not neces-sarily assure a positive recommendation. In fact, several World's Records were verified at each of the two panels on which I served which did not make an award recommendation. A review of the

Photo from B&C Archives

Harry L. Swank, Jr., was hunting in 1961 with Perley Jones of the US Army Engineer District and Jack E. Wilson of Wilson's Flyer Service out of Gulkana, Alaska, when he harvested the new World's Record Dall's sheep. With a score of 189-6/8 points, Swank's ram is four points larger than Frank Cook's sheep that had held the top spot since 1956. Both gentlemen received the Club's Sagamore Hill Award based on their extraordinary efforts that resulted in harvesting world-class trophies.

trophy awards that have been recognized over the years reveals that a number of trophies were, to be sure, high-ranking, but not necessarily at the top of the list.

In the case of the two Judges Panels on which I served that did make an affirmative recommendation, one trophy tied the World's Record for its specific category and the other was recognized as a new World's Record in its category. That said, it was not the new World's Record status that convinced the judges to recommend the Sagamore Hill Awards, it was the unique set of circumstances surrounding the hunts that tipped the scales. There was a common thread that ran through both hunting experiences that is worthy of detailing in this introduction. I am sure that earlier Judges Panels applied the same criteria when considering a potential award.

In short, to be worthy of consideration, a hunt must exemplify the sporting values that Theodore Roosevelt championed—fair chase, self-reliance, perseverance, selective hunting and mastery of challenges. Keep these criteria in mind as you read the accounting of the hunts which produced the two most recent winners of the Sagamore Hill Award.

In 2001, the Sagamore Hill trophy was given to Gernot Wober, whose Rocky Mountain goat was submitted to the 24th Awards Judges Panel, which convened in Springfield, Missouri, to perform final measuring and verification of the entry scores of trophies taken during 1998-2000. The score ultimately given to this outstanding trophy tied the World's Record in that category. What persuaded the panel to recommend the granting of the Sagamore Hill Award, however, was not its World's Record status, but rather the sporting values previously noted. Readers of the first edition of *Legendary Hunts* will doubtless recall the wonderful story authored by Wober.

He and his hunting partner started their hunt at sea level in

Gene Alford had been in the Selway-Bitterroot Wilderness for 24 days when his hound Scratch treed this cougar. With one shot from his .357 Smith & Wesson at 10 yards, Alford harvested the number two cougar ever recorded by the Boone and Crockett Club. Alford was presented the Sagamore Hill Award at the Club's 20th Big Game Awards Program in 1989.

Bella Coola, British Columbia, and in the space of eight hours, had climbed 5,000 feet, while each packed close to 60 pounds of gear. Wober, a bow hunter, missed a shot at a good goat when his arrow was deflected by a tree. On two more occasions he had equally bad luck.

Before returning to their truck to regroup and replenish their supplies, they spotted a huge goat, which they immediately named "Mr. Big." When they returned to the high country, Wober opted to exchange his bow for his hunting partner's .270. As luck would have it, they once again spotted Mr. Big, and Wober urged his partner to shoot it with his bow.

After a long stalk, fighting slide alder and wet rocks, his partner could not see the goat and asked Wober if he could still see him. When Wober answered affirmatively, his partner yelled, "Just shoot him" (which became the title of the story in Legendary Hunts). One shot from the .270 put the goat down.

All of us who hunt, know the hunt is never complete until the trophy has been caped, skinned, and all edible meat has been carried out. Wober and his partner, fighting tough terrain all the way, demonstrated both their ethics and their persistence in accomplishing this task. The Judges Panel deemed it most appropriate to recommend that the Sagamore Hill Award be given to Mr. Wober.

At the 27th Big Game Awards dinner in Reno, Nevada, in 2010, Paul Deuling, of Whitehorse, Yukon Territory, received the Sagamore Hill Award in recognition of an outstanding mountain caribou he had taken in 1988. However, it was not until 2010 that the score for Deuling's trophy was verified, after which he shipped it to Reno, where the Judges Panel verified its entry score of 459-3/8 points and the new World's Record.

The 2010 Annual Report of the Boone and Crockett Club described the historic hunt as follows:

"Deuling spotted the huge caribou during a 1988 solo hunt for Dall's sheep in the Pelly Mountains of Yukon Territory. He had backpacked six miles across two shallow valleys and a range of hills, all choked with thick, tangled brush. After setting up camp, Deuling climbed a ridge to glass for sheep when he spotted the magnificent bull with a single cow. Deuling later recounted the bull 'appeared to be a black oak tree growing from its head.' A meticulous stalk and a 10-yard shot ended the hunt but began a grueling five-day meat-packing ordeal that would make Deuling temporarily regret his decision to take the trophy."

Eldon L. Buckner, chair of the Boone and Crockett Club's Records of North American Big Game Committee, said, "A Yukon game officer told me that Paul was the only person he knew who would have tackled that job, as the area where Paul killed his caribou is extremely tough country to get around in."

Buckner added, "Along with being a hunter of the highest ethics, Paul is also an extremely modest man. It's a story in itself, but he was finally persuaded to strip the hardened velvet from the antlers and have the caribou measured."

Deuling's full account of his hunt is included in this anthology. It is easy to understand, after reading it, why the Judges' Panel was unanimous in its recommendation to present him with the Sagamore Hill Award.

Parenthetically, I can report that earlier in 2010, also in Reno, at the Wild Sheep Foundation convention, my wife and I had the honor of presenting Paul with the G.C.F. Dalziel Outstanding Guide Award, one of the foundation's highest awards. The committee that recommended Paul for the award noted the many letters it had received, all of which cited Paul's hunting ethics and dedication to the spirit of fair chase.

There will undoubtedly be more Sagamore Hill Awards recommended by future Judges Panels, and it is equally clear that those judges will continue to rely on the values championed by the Club's founder—fair chase, self-reliance, perseverance, selective hunting and mastery of challenges.

ABOUT THE AUTHOR: *Robert Hanson is the secretary of the Boone and Crockett Club (1992–1997 and 2001 to present) and a member of the Club's Board of Directors. An Official Measurer, he is also a member of the Records of North American Big Game Committee, and has served as a panel judge for the 24th and 25th Awards Programs, Chairman of the Judges Panel for the 26th Awards, and consultant to the panel for the 27th Awards. He is an avid North American and African hunter, and lives with his wife, Arlene, also a Club member, on their ranch near Wapiti, Wyoming.*

Bears & Cougar

BLACK BEAR

GRIZZLY BEAR

ALASKA BROWN BEAR

COUGAR

*Black bear, scoring 22-8/16 points,
taken by Elwood W. Maurer in Schuylkill County, Pennsylvania,
in 1997 (pictured with his grandson, Josh).*

Triple Play

Elwood W. Maurer

24th Big Game Awards Program

THE FIRST TIME I SAW THE BEAR I WAS WATCHING THE END OF A CORNFIELD ON THE FIRST MORNING OF ARCHERY SEASON. HE CAME OUT OF THE FIELD AND ENTERED THE OPEN AREA BETWEEN THE FIELD AND THE WOODS. TWO WEEKS LATER ON A MISTY, RAINY DAY, THE WIND WAS JUST RIGHT FOR A STALK THROUGH THE CORNFIELD. I WAS HOPING TO FIND A NICE BUCK BEDDED DOWN FOR THE DAY; INSTEAD, I CAME ACROSS THE BIG GUY ONE MORE TIME. HE WAS SITTING DOWN FACING INTO THE WIND ABOUT 15 YARDS AWAY PULLING AS MANY CORNSTALKS TO HIM AS HE COULD REACH. AS HE FINISHED EATING WHAT HE HAD, HE WOULD SLIDE DOWN THE ROW ON HIS BUTT TO A PLACE WHERE HE COULD REACH MORE.

From the first day of the archery season until the bear season opened, I saw him a total of four times, but I was able to keep weekly tabs on him by checking the end of the field. He made this easy for me because he would spend all day in the field and would come out only to help fertilize the weeds. I never found any bear scat in the field; it appeared he didn't want to contaminate his feeding area.

The field was located on the crest of a steep hill surrounded by hardwoods on three sides. At the bottom of the hill on one side is a native trout stream. The bear had all the requirements of life without traveling more than a quarter mile.

I was lucky to harvest a nice whitetail buck and a fall turkey in the woods adjacent to the field, both with the bow. Could this be my year to take the triple trophy? With the bow?

As the bear season approached I developed my plan. I would sit at the end of the field from first light with my .35 Whelen to see if he would come out or maybe catch him coming back from his nightly jaunt. If I didn't see him until mid-morning, I would take my bow and work through the field looking for him. The day before the season opened, my nine-year-old grandson Josh and I climbed the hill. I wanted to scout the area one more time and give Josh the experience of bear hunting. The next morning about an hour before daylight I parked my truck and began to get my rifle and bow ready for the hike. I was holding both of them in my hand and looking up the hill; I decided to leave my bow in the truck. Mistake. The first light had brought the first snowfall of the season, just a dusting, but enough to keep the wildlife from moving. I soon came to the conclusion that if I wanted this bear, I would need to go in to the field after him.

It was about 8 a.m. when I entered the field. I hadn't gone 60 yards when I looked up a row and there he was about 40 yards away. My Whelen only has iron sights and I couldn't distinguish a vital target. Now what do I do? I decided to slowly approach him. If I got close enough, or if he decided to move, I would be able to tell where to aim. When I got within 20 yards of him I wished I'd brought the bow. He started to raise his head and he was facing away from me into the wind. The bullet took him in the back of the neck and exited through his nose. He traveled only 15 yards and fell about five rows short of exiting the field.

I tagged him and went home to try to get some help to get him off the hill. The only help available was my two daughters, Kim and Jackie. Josh had asked me to get him out of school if I was successful. So the four of us — two girls, a nine-year-old and one excited hunter — climbed back up the hill, took some pictures, and started to roll the bear downhill to the closest place I could get my truck. After an hour and a half we had traveled the 75 yards to the truck. Some carpenters working on a roof nearby came over to help load the big guy on the truck. It took six of us to get the job done. 🦌

Black bear, scoring 22–15/16 points,
taken by Craig D. Martin on Kuiu Island, Alaska,
in 1996.

The Infamous Number 57

Craig D. Martin

23rd Big Game Awards Program

T HE MOST SATISFYING HUNT OF MY LIFE ACTUALLY BEGAN IN THE WINTER OF 1996 WHILE I WAS ATTENDING THE FOUNDA- TION FOR NORTH AMERICAN WILD SHEEP (FNAWS) CONVENTION IN RENO, NEVADA. DURING THE MEN'S LUNCHEON AUCTION, AN ALASKAN SELF-GUIDED SPRING BLACK BEAR HUNT FOR TWO, DONATED BY MIKE JUSTIS, OF BOISE, IDAHO, REALLY GRABBED MY ATTENTION. I FELT AS THOUGH THIS MIGHT BE A GREAT OP- PORTUNITY TO BETTER MY PREVIOUS BLACK BEAR, WHICH SCORED 20-15/16. BESIDES THAT, I KNEW THAT ALASKA'S BLACK BEARS ARE PRIZED FOR THEIR LONG, BEAUTIFUL COATS, SO I DECIDED TO BID.

When the bidding started out slow, I got more excited. But when the donor of the hunt started talking and describing the hunt, the bidding heated up. By the time the price doubled, I found myself holding the highest bid. My excitement over the hunt erased any buyer's remorse I might have had.

The FNAWS convention was a great success with over $3.5 million raised for the foundation and its efforts in "putting sheep on the mountain." I was more than happy to help. I always enjoy the meetings, good company and interesting conversation.

As soon as I returned home to Dayton, Washington, I was

on the phone. Unfortunately it turned out to be bad timing for my regular partner and he decided to pass. I contacted another close hunting friend, Craig Noble of Walla Walla, Washington. He jumped at the offer and said he had another friend, Bill Frazier, also from Walla Walla, who wanted to come. Fortunately, there was room on the boat and Mr. Justis arranged to take the three of us. At the time, I had no idea what measure of success I would find, nor did I know that out on a remote Alaskan island lurked a well-known and much sought-after creature, and that fate would bring us together.

On my birthday, May 1, 1996, we found ourselves on the docks in Ketchikan, Alaska, loading our gear into a Beaver outfitted with floats. It was a 90-minute flight northwest to our destination; a pristine cove nestled in the Tongass National Forest. The cove would be our boat camp location for the next two days. On the day of our arrival, it was bright and warm with not a breath of wind — unusual for the area. After the introductions with the captain and crew of the Rite-Off, we ate a quick meal and got ready for an evening scouting trip.

After loading into a small skiff, we took off to start glassing the miles of shoreline. The waters were filled with sea otters and seals, which we enjoyed watching as they capered in the moonlight, but there were no bear sightings that evening. The clean, brisk Alaskan air made us forget that we had just eaten not too long ago and once back at camp, we were ready to fill up again. This didn't hurt the cook's feelings as we cleaned our plates for the second time that day.

The next couple of days were similar. The weather stayed unusually perfect, warm and clear with no wind. We did see a few bear, but nothing of the size we were hoping for from this area. Jim Bruce, Captain of the Rite-Off, and I talked it over and decided to move camp into another bay to the southwest, which took the better part of the next day.

On the fourth day we started to see more bear. My partners were starting to get itchy while I felt content running the video camera. Craig Noble filled his tag that morning with his first bear ever. It had a long, full coat and was coal black. After lunch, Bill Frazier spotted the bear he wanted. I landed Bill and Craig on the beach downwind of the bruin. Then I paddled the skiff out to where I hoped to get some good video footage of the event. It was fun to watch the two old friends make the stalk together, taking Bill's first black bear.

After we had taken care of Bill's bear, we made a dash across the bay since we still had calm waters for our small hunting craft. As we idled into a small cove, we thought we spotted a large bear at the far end. As we paddled in further for a better look, we could see that this big boar had a thin coat but was probably the biggest bear we had seen thus far. We took some great pictures of him turning over rocks on the beach, and while relishing the solitude of the wilderness, we decided to let him go.

On our way out of the cove I spotted a gleam of black coat through the trees. This was the 25th bear we had sighted so far and he was even larger than the bear we had just passed. He had a big pumpkin-shaped head, but we were disappointed to see a large bald spot on his hindquarters. I took some quick videos of him before we headed out of the cove.

There were only a few hours of light left and as we left the protection of the cove we discovered that high winds had kicked up and the water was too rough for our small craft. We had on our life jackets and a hand-held radio on board for emergencies. We made a call to Captain Bruce aboard the mother ship, asking him to come across the bay and pick us up in the larger, 24-foot fishing skiff. The waters were quite dangerous with white caps peaking over our heads.

It took 45 minutes for Captain Bruce to cross the bay. We transferred into the larger boat and tied the small skiff to the stern, and proceeded back to the Rite-Off. We moved slowly because of the hazardous rocks in the shallow water. I was standing next to the captain when he said, "Is that a dead seal floating out there?" I pulled up my binoculars and could see that it was a large bear. We motored past the bear at 100 yards and stopped to see where he would go ashore. The captain killed the engine and we waited. The bear started swimming faster the closer he got to shore. I asked to be put ashore as quickly as possible.

I climbed on the bow of the boat trying to keep an eye on the bear, which was nearly impossible as high winds and shallow water were making our approach to the rocky shore extremely hazardous. I kept signaling to Captain Bruce to get the boat closer. I stretched out trying to make contact with land and looked over in time to see the bruin climbing out onto the shoreline. Seconds later, I made a jump for it and fortunately hit shore to find my bear nowhere in sight. I took off at a quick sprint 70 yards uphill over slippery rocks and seaweed. When I stopped, I was above, looking down on the bear. He had just shaken off and was running for timber. I took a second to look for rub spots, not taking into consideration how huge he looked. My gun came up, I shot and the bear dropped.

I held my rifle over my head and let out a "whoop." Partly to signal the guys and partly to express my joy. The captain and Craig had been watching the whole drama from the drifting boat. I hadn't realized it, but Bill had jumped out behind me and I had left him in the rocks in my rush to reach the bear before he disappeared into the timber.

I signaled the boat to come in for the bear before the winds made it completely impossible. We had to work fast because the tide, the winds and fading light were working against us. We lashed the dingy to a ledge on the shore; then, using every ounce of strength we had, the three of us rolled the beautiful big bear into the small craft. We were all seriously concerned about whether or not the boat would stay afloat since he filled the entire skiff. There was barely room for me to get in with him. The captain came to shore with the bigger boat to pick up Craig and Bill.

We struggled through the waves back to the Rite-Off, worrying the entire time that the dingy would capsize. Even getting him into the Rite-Off with a boom and winch was a nearly overwhelming job. After the caping was finished, I came up with a crude measurement of 23-2/8 inches. I added it up several more times in disbelief. In Petersburg, we took the cape and skull to State Biologist Ed Crain, where he removed a tooth for aging, and sealed the cape and skull. When the report came back, it showed this wonderful creature to be 18 years old. But that wasn't all. It turned out that I had bagged Bear Number 57, a former "dump bear" from Petersburg that had been sedated and transported to Kuiu Island the previous year. This bear, the infamous 57, would be remembered by many.

In 1995, during the relocation procedure, Alaska State Biologist, Ed Crain, mentioned 57 specifically and was quoted in the Petersburg Pilot, "This bear's a freak, he's so big." At that time, 57's live skull measured 22 inches and his weight was estimated at 600 to 650 pounds. That was a guess, since the state's scale topped out at 500 pounds. I brought the skull to Buzzi Cook, an official measurer for the Boone and Crockett Club — he looked shocked. It turned out that he had been planning a hunt to Kuiu Island for this very same bear after hearing about, "the monster," as one newspaper had called him.

I have been a dedicated trophy hunter for over 20 years and it has been a life-long goal of mine to be in Boone and Crockett Club's all-time records book. This hunt was the experience of a lifetime and if capturing this magnificent bear gives me the chance to join Boone and Crockett's list of elite hunters, it will be the one hunt I'll never forget. 🦌

Black bear, scoring 23-3/16 points,
taken by Andrew Seman, Jr., in Fayette County, Pennsylvania,
in 2005.

A Bear to Remember

Andrew Seman, Jr.

As told by Brian J. Seman

26th Big Game Awards Program

A S WE GAZED AT THE ENORMOUS BEAR THAT LAY THERE BEFORE US, WE COULDN'T HELP BUT THINK ABOUT HOW EV-ERYTHING HAD FALLEN INTO PLACE TO MAKE THIS TRULY A DAY AND A BEAR TO REMEMBER. NEVER DID WE IMAGINE, THOUGH, THAT THE BEAR MY BROTHER AJ HAD JUST TAKEN WOULD TURN OUT TO BE A TIE FOR THE LARGEST HUNTER-TAKEN BLACK BEAR IN THE BOONE AND CROCKETT RECORDS.

Though luck certainly played a big part in our success that day, we are far from novice hunters. My brother Andrew Seman Jr. (or AJ, as most call him), and James, David, and I have combined for more than a century of hunting seasons among us, and most of them were in this area of Fayette County, Pennsylvania. In fact, several of us have taken bucks within a hundred yards of where AJ encountered his trophy bear. We have also taken dozens of big game animals through the years in Pennsylvania, West Virginia, Idaho, and Colorado.

As for Pennsylvania bear hunting, we usually hunt in the traditional bear counties of Lycoming and Tioga, and in the Allegheny National Forest, and while we did hunt hard and find plenty of bear sign, those trips were as much preseason deer scouting expeditions than anything else. In recent years, though, we've heard of many good bear being taken here in Fayette County, and we even tracked and trailed bear through the dense laurel thickets and over the steep rocky slopes that we consider our hunting grounds, but never had any of us ever raised a gun on a bear.

We have hunted State Game Land (SGL) 51 for many reasons. Our knowledge, experience, and love of this area have grown through the years and extended through several generations in our family. There is a special feeling to hunt where previous generations walked, hunted, and grew up. In fact, our grandparents {seems to be too recent} grew up in log cabins very near where this great bear lived and died. This area also has a rich American history, with Fort Necessity and Jumonville, and the early centers of iron and coal.

Many have asked if we knew the bear was in the area and if we were hunting it specifically. In reality, we had no idea it was there. The only indication was in seeing a huge bear several years ago while mountain biking in the area, and that may have been this bear. We decided to hunt SGL 51 because of the tracks and other sign we found there the year before. Plus, we have a hunting camp nearby. Recently built on a stone barn foundation, our rustic camp (with no running water or electricity) is an ideal escape from the modern world and a reminder of how life was here not that long ago.

Opening day was uneventful. AJ and Jim posted for the first day. I had come in from Colorado the day before, and was not planning on hunting bears, but after purchasing my regular hunting license I just couldn't resist picking up a bear license, too. Finding a nonresident bear tag locally turned out to be difficult, but contacting the Game Commission region office I learned I could buy one over the Internet.

Thankful for the advances in licensing technology (and for what turned out to be one of the best returns on $36 I'll ever have), I met up with AJ and Jim in the afternoon. Later that evening, after a meal cooked on the wood stove and a few songs strummed on a guitar or two, we planned the next day's hunt.

Jim, slowed down by a recent hip operation, would post in various places throughout the day based on where AJ and I would be hunting. Through the years, with sometimes just a few of us hunting, we developed a method of mini-drives or "coordinated stalking." An alternating walk-and-stop technique, it's worked well for us, especially with small groups, providing all those involved know the area and are familiar with one another. Timing and maintaining the agreed-upon course is key.

With Jim posted, AJ and I began stalking thickets and other areas in a coordinated manner; stalking and stopping every 50 to 100 yards, separated, at times, by up to 200 yards. Every stalk seemed to be working perfectly as far as the timing, wind and other factors were concerned, and we did see very fresh sign of where a small bear had been foraging. We also heard a flock of turkeys.

After covering three or four miles — and seeing several other hunters — we returned to camp for a late lunch. After some warm soup, we met up with Jim and discussed our options. Initially, we decided to head off in different directions. That changed, however, as we kept reminding ourselves that every year we had found fresh bear sign nearby, along some of the old clearcut trails that ultimately wound through very thick laurel patches and rock ledges of the game lands. Because Jim was already planning on posting in the area, AJ and I decided to continue our stalk-and-stop technique in a large circle around his location.

It was thick and tough to cover, especially without snow to aid visibility and quiet the movement. Neither of us really expected to get a shot, but felt Jim had a good chance if we jumped anything. AJ and I mapped out how we would work the area, and where we could visually check each other's progress and realign as necessary. A clearing divided the area we were hunting, and

Jim was posted nearby, watching the clearing. After crossing the open area we planned on moving very slowly because at that point game would likely be pushed away from Jim.

After AJ and I visually checked each other's position in the clearing, AJ was to move in first and stop. Then I would move in and, alternately, we would work through the area. This area had been clearcut in our youth; the giant oaks that shaded the slopes were but a distant memory. Some areas were so thick we couldn't see even 20 feet, but we also figured game would be naturally funneled or concentrated into this area.

After waiting several minutes for AJ to move into position, I started into the thickest part of the old clearcut. After a short distance, I heard a faint snap. Almost immediately after, a shot followed, then another. At first I thought Jim had shot, but moments later I heard AJ indicate he had gotten a bear. The shots had come from his .280 Sako.

I was no more than a hundred yards from him, but could see no more than a few feet. As I worked toward him, I went not even 20 feet before coming across the bear's bedding site. Then, when I saw where AJ had stopped, I realized that a few feet variation in any direction for either of us and we would never have seen the bear.

The time was 3 p.m. as we gathered around AJ's trophy. We seemed to be just keep saying, "Wow, that's a big bear!"

Being the first bear any of us had harvested, we were figured it was just our inexperience that made the bear seem so impressive. After several attempts to move him, we guessed he was at least 400 or 500 pounds. The head was so massive it was difficult to lift it off the ground. We took several pictures and discussed what to do next.

After several unsuccessful attempts to move him, we lashed him to a pole to position him for field-dressing. Thankfully, several young hunters stopped by to lend a hand. After moving him to a nearby logging road, Jim arrived and we tied the pole to the back of his quad and pulled the bear to the clearing. After the problems we had moving him just to that point, we knew we didn't have enough manpower to get the bear up the steep hill remaining. With fresh snow starting to fall, we felt AJ's four-wheel-drive truck was not likely to make it. And, even if we had the truck there, we would never be able to lift the bear into the bed. Then we remembered the four-wheel-drive John Deere tractor with the front-end loader AJ had just purchased. After a brief discussion, it was agreed to be our only option.

Returning with the tractor, we were able to slide the bucket under the bear, lift it and drive it to the truck and then transfer him into the truck bed. Though it was not easy, we had the bear out of the woods within six hours after it was taken.

After calling friends and family, some with more experience with bears than us, it soon became apparent that this was an exceptionally large bear. The taxidermist later supplied the following dimensions: the bear standing would be 92 inches tall; from nose to tip of its tail, 83 inches; neck, 32 inches; girth, 70 inches. At the Game Commission's Southwest Region office in Ligonier, we learned that bear had an estimated live weight of 733 pounds, which turned out to be the heaviest bear taken in during the 2005 season and the eighth heaviest ever recorded! We learned later that the bear was approximately 15 years old.

One of the officers at the check station asked how we got the bear. He mentioned that as bears become older and experienced, they're less likely to bolt from a drive, but like a mature buck, stay in heavy cover. As we reflected on what the officer said, it further confirmed how fortunate it was that all the circumstances came together.

The bear moved with hardly a sound and headed cross wind away from me, then turned with the wind, apparently in an attempt to circle back around and bed down again in the thicket once I passed. This sneak, circle, and bed technique may have helped this bear survive for so many years. It was only one small sound from a broken twig that alerted AJ to the bear's presence.

Going back to the site the following day allowed us to reconstruct what happened. I attempted to walk the path the bear took while AJ determined where he had shot from — he even found his spent shell casings. It was so thick that the only shooting lanes were no more than several inches wide. AJ eventually found that the first shot hit and passed through a small tree. How he hit the bear on the second shot in such cover is amazing.

After the mandatory 60-day drying time, the skull was measured at the Game Commission Southwest Region office by B&C Official Measurer Michael J. Hardison, and witnessed by PA Game Commission Representatives and family. It was officially listed as having a length of 14-09 and a width of 8-10 for a total of 23-03 and will stand as the new state record black bear taken by a hunter.

AJ always mentioned that if he ever got a bear he would have a rug made from it. AJ's wife Susie and others instead convinced AJ that a bear this big and important should be preserved as a life-sized mount. Interestingly, the taxidermist AJ selected, Mike LaRosa, from Acme, took a bear in Fayette County in 1996 that, at 488 pounds and with a skull measuring 20-08, had been the county's largest.

AJ's father-in-law, Joe Habina, who took AJ on his first elk hunt to a favorite place in Idaho, has often been heard to say, "I'd rather be lucky than good." On that first hunt, on the first day, the first elk AJ saw was a large 6x7 bull that he took with one shot. The first bear he ever shot at turned out to be not just a new state record but one that tied for first among all black bears ever taken by a hunter. We could all use that kind of luck. 🦌

Final score chart for Seman's black bear, which
scores 23-3/16 Points.

Black bear, scoring 22 11/16 points,
taken by Donald R. Corrigan in Newaygo County, Michigan,
in 2009 (pictured with his son, Jake).

Hometown Bear

Donald R. Corrigan

27th Big Game Awards Program

IF YOU TOLD THE RESIDENTS OF NEWAYGO COUNTY, MICHI-GAN, THAT THEY HAD A POPULATION OF 300-400 BEARS LIVING IN THEIR WOODS, MOST OF THEM WOULD NOT BELIEVE YOU. I HAVE HUNTED IN THE COUNTY MY ENTIRE LIFE AND HAD NEVER SEEN A BEAR. WHEN THE MICHIGAN DEPARTMENT OF NATURAL RESOURCES (DNR) DECIDED TO OPEN A BEAR SEASON IN OUR AREA, WHICH IS JUST 20 MILES NORTH OF GRAND RAPIDS, I WAS SKEPTICAL. THE LURE OF BEING THE FIRST HUNTER TO TAKE A "LOCAL" BEAR INTRIGUED ME. AFTER LOOKING AT THE DNR RESEARCH AND POSSIBLE HUNTING AREAS, I APPLIED, AND APPLIED, AND APPLIED. AFTER NINE SEASONS, I FINALLY DREW A PERMIT.

With my permit in hand, I called my good friend Mike Perrin, the first person to take a bear in the county, to find out if he knew of any big bears in the area. Turns out he had trail camera pictures of a large bear that had been on his 40 acres for the last two years. He said that with a week of baiting, we should be in luck.

Opening day is always exciting, whether it's for deer, elk, or bear. My ten-year-old son Jake was going to accompany me on opening day, and we could hardly wait. The first night out we had a big bear come to our bait, but it was well after legal hunting hours. The next three days were the same. We saw bears, but they always came in too late. On the fifth night out, Jake suggested we put "bear bomb" scent on the bait pile. He had seen it mentioned on TV, and was confident it would work.

We were hunting in a swampy, wet, wooded area, and the bear suddenly appeared without a sound. I don't remember pulling the trigger when the bear was within 30 yards, but I was confident it was a good shot as the animal crashed away through the swamp. Our hearts were pounding so hard it was almost surreal; it all happened so fast. After waiting in the blind for about 30 minutes, Jake and I walked over to where the bear was standing when I fired to see if we could find any sign. Following a futile search, darkness was fast approaching, so we went back to the truck and called Mike Perrin for help.

Mike arrived after dark with lights and lanterns. We headed into the swamp and found the bear's trail right away.

I looked at Mike and said "you baited the bear, so you go first."

He said "you shot it, so you go first."

After about two minutes on our hands and knees pushing through the heavy undergrowth, pistols in hand, Jake's fear got the best of him and he decided to wait in the truck. Mike and I continued to track the bear and found him 30 yards from where he was shot. A bear's size is hard to judge, but this one looked huge. It took more than three hours to get him in the truck.

Jake was very excited and was sure I had shot a new world's record. Both of us had a hard time sleeping that night. The next day we checked the bear at the local department of natural resources station. The big boar was 7.5 years old and field dressed at 500 pounds. His estimated live weight was over 600 pounds. The bear wasn't a World's Record like Jake had hoped, but with a skull measurement of 22-11 /16, he was the second largest bear ever shot in Michigan. I have a lot of great hunting memories so far in my life, but to be able to take such a quality bear in my hometown with my son tops them all. Jake and I will never forget that cool, cloudy September 22, 2009, night. It truly was a hunt of a lifetime. 🦌

Grizzly bear, scoring 26-1/16 points,
taken by John J. McPartlin near the Inglutalik River in Alaska,
in 1996.

Don't Think About the Bear

John J. McPartlin

23rd Big Game Awards Program

I T WAS THE END OF SEPTEMBER 1995, ONLY TWO WEEKS SHY OF MY 50TH BIRTHDAY, WHEN I BOARDED A FLIGHT FROM ANCHORAGE, ALASKA, TO SALT LAKE CITY, UTAH. FROM THERE I TRANSFERRED TO ANOTHER FLIGHT FOR THE 75-MINUTE HOP TO GREAT FALLS, MONTANA. I AM A REAL ESTATE BROKER, AND LIVE 28 MILES WEST OF GREAT FALLS.

For the past two weeks, I had been hunting with outfitter Bob Hannon. After arriving in Alaska with my brother, Greg, the ever-changing weather kept us stuck in Anchorage for a couple of days. Greg is a former Navy SEAL and four years my junior. When I told him about my plans to travel north to hunt a grizzly, he said, "Count me in." I would do the hunting, while Greg would handle the photographing.

Ever since childhood, I was thrilled at the prospects of hunting for a big bear. Now, I am truly a very lucky guy. I married a beautiful lady who really enjoys the outdoors. Anne has hunted pronghorn, deer, and black bear with me, and most importantly, she understood my desire to hunt a grizzly. Anne and my daughters all felt strongly that I should try and realize my dream. With the total support of my family, I began to search for a reputable outfitter.

Bob Hannon, owner of Big River Hunting and Trapping out of Koyuk, Alaska, had been recommended to me. From my very first conversation with Bob, I liked him. When he informed me that 92 out of 94 hunters had taken a bear in his years of outfitting, my spirits soared. In addition, an impressive number of these grizzlies made the prestigious Boone and Crockett Club's records book, with one of them tied for first place. I didn't have any thoughts of making a records book. I just wanted the opportunity to hunt and harvest a nice, mature grizzly.

Bob cautioned me that the majority of his grizzly bear success occurred during his spring hunt out of Koyuk. He went on to explain that he was booked for the spring of 1996. He then told me his early fall hunt, which is conducted out of his Big River Lodge, was an area where I might have a chance to take a good bear. From Big River, Bob organizes and runs highly successful fall moose, caribou, and black bear hunts. This year there were no bear hunters going into Big River and he told me if I wanted to give it a try, I was welcome. Over the years he had seen some big grizzlies in the Big River area, so I booked my hunt.

As mentioned earlier, after our arrival in Anchorage, Greg and I were forced to wait for storms to clear along the Alaska Range. For two days, we periodically checked with our charter service in Anchorage. Momentary clearing, followed by clouds and fog, raised and lowered our spirits. Finally, on the third day, the boys from Jayhawk Air said it was a go.

The exhilaration of climbing out of Anchorage, as we passed over Cook Inlet heading into the spectacular Alaska Range, made my heart pound. Looking out the window of the light plane, I saw a most welcome sight — no people, no towns, only wilderness. I pinched myself more than once to tell myself this wasn't a dream. I really did.

For 14 nights and 15 days, I had the privilege of sharing a spike camp in the Alaskan bush with Tom Karshekoff. Tommy is an Athabascan native gifted with a truly uncanny knowledge of, and instincts for, big game and big game hunting. He coupled this with terrific eyesight, hearing, and a cool head. I knew I was in competent hands. Unfortunately, the grizzlies were not to cooperate on that trip. We hunted hard. On three separate occasions, we spent enjoyable moments watching a beautiful, blond sow grizzly and her two cubs. We also saw a dark-colored boar that Tommy figured would go 8 to 8-1/2 feet. We saw this bear on two occasions.

The first time we saw him, we were in the middle of stalking a huge black bear when Tommy spotted him. We quickly forgot about the black bear and switched our focus to the big boar. We traveled at a quick pace for 15 minutes, maybe more. When Tommy stopped, a soft curse came from his lips as he looked back up the valley. The boar had been traveling as only a big bear can. He was easily covering lots of ground in that peculiar, deceptive gait that looks like they are just ambling along. While we were going down the valley, the grizzly was coming up. We had passed each other, separated by a curtain of alders and willows. The light breeze that had been in our faces going down, now carried our scent back up the valley to the bear. Round one was over and the bear won.

Several evenings later, while glassing from a high knoll in the same area, we watched as a boar grizzly fed out from cover into the blueberries. Tommy assumed it was the same bear judging by his size and coloration. This time a simple shift in wind direction ended the stalk. The bear obviously winded us and disappeared into an alder thicket. Before losing the bear, and at a point when it looked like we were getting close, Tommy whispered, "Don't think about the bear." Back at camp, as the flames from our fire licked the darkness, I asked Tommy what he meant when he said, "Don't think about the bear." I had an idea what his answer might be, but I wanted to hear it from him. He stared into the fire, as if reflecting on my question. There was a long, silent pause. Then, without raising his eyes, he told me that he believed that some animals, and particularly "the bear," can sense when a man is thinking about them. He thought that if a hunter thought hard enough about an animal he was stalking, that animal would sense those thoughts and be warned. After he had said these things to me, Tommy continued his stare into the fire. Again there was a long pause of silence. I was proud that Tommy had shared this with me. Maybe he did it because he sensed that I would not laugh at him. I did not laugh. Being an avid falconer for some 40 years, I held my own beliefs about what other creatures could sense and feel, especially predators.

The next morning, Tommy and I broke camp and headed back to Big River and the lodge. All along the way I kept taking pictures with my mind's eye. I never wanted to forget this adventure. As we drove along on our ATVs, there was little conversation. I was just very grateful I had this opportunity. I thought of my family back home. I thought of my brand new granddaughter, Bailey Anne. Grandpa could not bring her a grizzly bear, but he could bring her some wonderful stories.

After several hours, Tommy and I arrived back at Big River. We had been 14 nights in the bush. A warm shower and some delicious moose steaks prepared by Ruby, Bob Hannon's sister-in-law and camp cook, set the world right. After a warm meal, I asked Bob if I could pitch in and help around camp, since my plane was not due in until the following morning. I was the last hunter at Big River, and I would fly out with Tommy and another of the guides. My brother, Greg, had flown out a few days earlier. Bob said he appreciated my offer to help, but before I went to do anything, he had something to give me. He opened his notebook and pulled out an envelope with my name on it. He handed it to me, gesturing me to open it up. I took out a note written on Big River Hunting and Trapping stationery and I nearly choked up with gratitude as I read it.

Due to your intense efforts to hunt grizzly, and still no bear, your spring grizzly hunt in 1996 out of Koyuk, Alaska, is paid in full.
  With best regards,
  Bob Hannon

I was overwhelmed. I immediately grabbed Bob's hand and shook it saying, "Thank you." I shook Tommy's hand and watched as he grinned, which we all got a good laugh over after Bob poked fun at him for hardly ever smiling. Bob Hannon was not only an outfitter. He was a hunter's hunter and a gentleman. My spirits were high as I turned in for the night.

The fall and winter months seemed to drag on. Not a day went by that I did not think about springtime in Alaska. I had periodic telephone conversations with Bob. He kindly walked me through the application process for acquiring a grizzly permit for his area. I kept my fingers crossed, and I did manage to draw the required permit.

On April 13, 1996, I was on a flight to the village of Koyuk. It was wonderful to see the gang again. Again, I pinched myself. It was real. A dinner of caribou, potatoes and gravy was shared in the dining hall by Bob, my guide and friend, Tommy, and two younger guides who I met at Big River, Jocko and Jim, and finally another grizzly hunter from Florida named Dick. Everybody was in good form and enthusiasm ran high.

Over dinner, Bob laid out the plans for opening day. Since Dick had already been in camp for a few days, he and Tommy would go out together for opening day, while Jocko, Jim, and I would head in a different direction. Our method of transportation was snowmobile, and we would be going 50 miles out of the village to a spike camp, and then hunt from there. It was plenty cold and I wondered if any bear would be out, but Bob said some had already been seen. That was all I needed to hear. We had plenty of tracking snow and good guides. My hopes were plenty high.

I recall it being very cold on the morning of April 15, the opening day of the spring grizzly season. No time was spent on idle conversation. By the time a cup of hot chocolate had settled, our packs were loaded on the snowmobiles and we struck out from spike camp. We traveled several miles of frozen river looking for tracks. We saw signs of moose and wolverine, but no grizzly. By early afternoon, we left the river and were climbing along high ridges. Sometimes we were in deep snow, while at other times we were sailing over bare rock that had been blown clear of snow.

We stopped on a lofty knoll to glass the surrounding hills and valleys, and grabbed a quick snack. The wind had intensified, pushing the chill factor to way below zero. We moved off the summit and onto the lee side of the hill to escape the bitter, numbing wind. From our new position, we saw a set of big tracks along a distant hillside. Following the tracks through spotting scopes and binoculars, we were led to a large stand of willows at the upper end of the draw. We studied the willows intently, and in a flash we saw him. What at first appeared to be a big mound near the center of the thicket, materialized into a grizzly. He was sitting on his haunches like a giant, shaggy dog. Periodically he would get up, move about for a few minutes and then either sit down again or lie down.

There was little chance to circle up and behind his location to come down on him from above. The ground was wide open from above the thicket, all the way up to the skyline. The wind direction prevented us from going straight in on him, leaving us with only one option. We could possibly go down the open slope. Once at the bottom, we would ascend straight up the adjoining hill, which was heavily timbered and blanketed with hip-deep snow. The plan would then be to side hill up through the timber and try to come out downwind, and slightly above the bear. We selected a large, dead tree as our reference point. The tree appeared to be within 300 yards of the bear.

Jocko and I began our stalk while Jim stayed behind to help guide us with hand signals, and alert us to any changes the bear might make. At first, walking on top of the hard crusted snow enabled good progress. But, when we headed into the timber, we began breaking through the deep, wet snow. To avoid breaking through, we laid on our bellies and crawled. We were both sweating from the exertion, in spite of the intense cold. It took us 2-1/2 hours to cover about 500 yards.

Suddenly Jim was frantically waving at us. Jocko lifted his binoculars and then raised his arms up over his head in a gesture suggesting he didn't understand what Jim was trying to tell us. Jim just continued waving his arms, motioning us to get out of there and come back to where he was. When we began our stalk, we estimated the bear to be 1,000 to 1,200 yards away. When we got back to Jim, he explained that the bear had been laying down for quite some time. Suddenly the bear stood up. He walked to the edge of the thicket, stood there for a brief moment, and then came out and headed into the timber toward us. Jim wasn't sure if that was a coincidence or not; however, he figured that the grizzly could easily come in on us before we even had a clue he was there. The three of us sat down and watched until evening, but did not see the bear again.

The next morning we returned to the area and picked up the grizzly's tracks. They crossed the tracks that Jocko and I had made the previous afternoon. We followed them back up the hill and saw where the bear had come in above our tracks and sat down behind a dead-fall, only yards from where we had been. Seeing the imprint of the bear's big back end, and the heavily clawed footprints in the snow, was a sobering experience. The tracks then filed down through the length of the mountainside and came out onto another high, windswept ridge. We lost his tracks on the open, rocky ground, and decided to head back down toward the river to see if we might pick up the tracks coming off the backside of the mountain.

As we traveled back up the frozen river on our snowmobiles, another snowmobile came into view heading toward us. It was Tommy. His hunter had taken a beautiful blond grizzly and he rode out from Koyuk to join us. After briefly filling him in on the events of the past couple of days, Tommy said to Jocko and Jim, "You go back to Koyuk. Jeff and I will hunt the bear." A round of handshakes and well wishes ensued between the two young guides and myself, and then they left to return to the village.

As we headed back to camp, a snow squall rolled in and turned into a full blown storm. The snow continued falling down in big, billowy flakes as we ate dinner. The next morning, after checking a new area Tommy wanted to see, we returned to spike camp. We had a bite of lunch before starting back downstream. Not long after we passed beneath the high mountain where we had lost the tracks the previous day, we cut a new set of grizzly tracks crossing the frozen river. Our bear had passed in the night or early morning, hours after the snow had quit. The tracks were now several hours old.

After crossing the river, the bear started up another high, rugged mountain. We methodically began tracking him, at times circling way out from where his tracks led into a stand of heavy timber, only to pick them up again when they emerged from cover. It was slow, often difficult going as the afternoon wore on, and the tracks still looked cold.

We moved upward through a stand of dark timber toward the crest of the high hill. Without warning, Tommy came to an abrupt stop. He turned, looked into my eyes and said, "Be ready." Directly in front of us were big grizzly tracks leading over the summit and down into a heavily treed draw. These tracks were red hot.

For a few moments we scoured the forest below. The only movement was the slight swaying of the tree branches in the soft breeze. Tommy looked at me with a "this is it" expression as our eyes met. I chambered a round in my .338 and cranked the scope magnification way down. Tommy nodded, and we started down through the timber.

Tommy stayed right on the big tracks while I moved a little off to his right, and several yards below his position. From that moment forward, I really don't remember looking back at Tommy. The slope angle was fairly steep and dropped over 200 yards before reaching the base of the draw. In spite of the cold, I could feel beads of sweat forming around my neck. My mouth was dry and my eyes strained as they searched through each shred of cover in an effort to detect any movement or anything that appeared out of place. I would take a few steps, moving as quietly as possible, and then pause to scrutinize each tree, deadfall, and contour of the terrain for the twitch of an ear, the raising of a foot, or the moist black of a damp nose.

As I reached the bottom of the draw, I detected motion out of the corner of my eye. Thirty yards from me was the big grizzly. He was silently moving along the slope opposite of the one I had just come down. He was not ascending, but rather walking in a direction almost parallel to me. It looked as though he was attempting to circle in behind me. His head was facing me as he moved, and I had the impression he did not think I had seen him.

Many times I have attempted in vain to recapture in my mind the events of the next few seconds. But try as I will, I always seem to come up empty. It is probably because no thought was given to my next move. It was simply a reaction. I snapped the rifle to my shoulder, found the grizzly in the cross hairs and fired. It was just that quick. I don't recall hearing the rifle shot. In a singular motion, which I vividly recollect as like being in a dream where everything is moving in slow-motion, I ejected the spent cartridge, and replaced it with another, so I would have a full clip.

For what could have been seconds, or possibly even minutes, I stood in the same spot, staring at the place where the grizzly had been standing an instant before. There was no sound, no movement, and no charge. Through the trees and behind a couple of dead limbs that pushed up through the snow, I could make out the top portion of what appeared to be a mound of brownish silver hair.

With great caution I inched my way forward, my rifle raised and ready. I placed each foot carefully in front of the other to maintain my balance. I never took my eyes off the mound of hair, expecting it to erupt into a charging grizzly at any moment. At a distance of maybe 10 yards, I stopped again. Still there was no sound or movement. The 250 grain bullet had done its job. The great bear was dead in his tracks.

I stood there, transfixed by the sight before me. After a time, I noticed movement off to my left and coming toward me. It was Tommy. Quietly, he came up to me wearing a grin as big as the Alaskan sky. After a pause, and in a reflective tone, he simply said two words, "The bear." Again there was a pause as the veteran guide's eyes continued their unflinching stare at the fallen monarch. He then added two more words, "Big bear."

1st Res.

...ING SYSTEM FOR NORTH AMERICAN BIG GAME TROPHIES
...ROCKETT CLUB®

250 Station Drive
Missoula, MT 59801
(406) 542-1888

Kind of Bear: GRIZZLY

H. M.

SEE OTHER SIDE FOR INSTRUCTIONS	Measurements
A. Greatest Length Without Lower Jaw	16 5/16
B. Greatest Width	9 12/16
FINAL SCORE	26 1/16

Exact Locality Where Killed:

Date Killed: 1996   Hunter: JOHN J McPARTLIN

Owner: JOHN McPARTLIN   Telephone #:

Owner's Address:

Guide's Name and Address:

Remarks: (Mention Any Abnormalities or Unique Qualities)

I certify that I have measured this trophy on _____ 19_____

at (address) _____ City _____ State _____

and that these measurements and data are, to the best of my knowledge and belief, made in
accordance with the instructions given.

Witness: _Lay R Cay_ C031   Signature: _Hammer_

Fish C014   B&C Official Measurer   3 8 7 3

                                                    I.D. Number

*Final score chart for McPartlin's grizzly bear, which
scores 26-1/16 Points.*

Grizzly bear, scoring 26–14/16 points,
taken by D. Alan McCaleb near the Teklanika River in Alaska,
in 1989.

Bear Tracks

D. Alan McCaleb

21st Big Game Awards Program

F OR FOUR YEARS MY HUNTING PARTNER, BUTCH KILLIAN, AND I HAD SEEN THOSE BEAR TRACKS, THE LARGEST WE HAD EVER SEEN WHILE WE WERE MOOSE HUNTING IN THE FALL.

In the spring we would go back to that area and look for that large bear, or any large grizzly bear, as we knew that there were some big ones around.

We talked about hoping to get just a glimpse of that big bear or having just one crack at shooting it. We sat for hours and got excited like all hunters do about the prospect of shooting a trophy-size bear.

My partner and I have hunted big game together in Alaska for 10 years, and during that time, we have bagged a number of trophy-size animals. We are both avid hunters and have lived in Alaska most of our lives. In our opinion there is no place on earth that a man who hunts would rather be than here. Every year, we take time off from work to go spring bear hunting, and in the fall, we take off for moose, caribou, sheep, and bear hunting.

The spring of 1989 proved to be different from our other hunts. In the past we had fought crossing the rivers in our Argos. We had been soaked by drenching rains and had literally spent days when we could not get out of our wall tent due to extreme weather conditions.

It was a beautiful day when Butch, his son Ray, and I headed out once again to look for that big bear, or a bear that would at least square 7 feet. We live in Healy, 110 miles south of Fairbanks, and to get to our hunting ground, we traveled all day by Argo (an amphibious, 8-wheeled vehicle), so it was evening by the time we reached our destination and set up our camp.

That first day out, we established camp in our regular spot, overlooking a view of the river drainage and its tributaries. We spent the evening relaxing, checking the river bottom, and spotting the drainage for fresh sign.

Not finding much fresh sign, the next morning we decided to do something we had never done before; we headed farther back to another drainage. The decision proved to be disastrous.

The land had not been touched by many motorized vehicles, largely due to the river that had to be crossed. The river is too swift for a vehicle that will float and too deep for one that will not. An Argos is amphibious, but it is definitely not intended for swift water. We had sunk one in the past and had many other dangerously close calls.

We crossed the river with no problems, but we had virtually no idea of what we were getting into, even though we had looked at maps of the area. There were no trails, so we had to follow game trails where we could. The alders were dense, the ground was swampy, and the mosquitoes numbered in the millions. Since we had not taken on extra fuel for this time-consuming exploration, we headed back to base camp, tired, and disgusted.

Just before reaching camp, I spotted a moose that was acting very peculiar and I drew Butch's attention to that sight. Unknown to us at the time, it is entirely possible that moose was being stalked by my bear.

We went back to camp, set up our spotting scopes and made dinner. After having spent 12 hours in the Argo, it felt good to be able to relax. The coffee was hot and dinner tasted great. We had been spotting for awhile when we noticed the wind was picking up and starting to blow. Butch and Ray decided to go inside the tent to take a nap. I sat out on a point overlooking the drainage, spotting, and then my eyes started growing heavy. I fell asleep too.

Butch was the first to wakeup, and he came out to see if I had seen anything. I woke up and we spotted together for about 10 minutes before Butch said he was going to go back to bed. The wind was blowing pretty hard by then. The time was about 9:30 p.m. We talked it over and decided we would get an early start in the morning.

As Butch got up and started walking back to the tent, he noticed a bear coming out of the brush where we had previously seen the moose. He said, "Is this bear big enough for you? If not, I'll go wake up Ray, so he can shoot it."

You see, since we hunt together all the time, we have worked out a system so that neither one of us would ever have hard feelings about shooting specific animals. From year to year, we have the option to shoot or to pass the shot. If, for example, I shoot the biggest moose one year, Butch gets to decide whether he wants to shoot the first moose we see the next year. If not, I am obligated to shoot that moose for the meat. We use this same system for everything we hunt. Since Butch had already shot a grizzly bear, we were basically hunting for me and it was my option to shoot this bear or pass the chance to Ray. I told Butch, "Go ahead and wake up Ray while I look this bear over."

The wind was blowing in our favor and the bear was heading straight down the drainage toward us. At that point, the bear was probably 400 yards away. While I was looking the bear over, I noticed he was walking pigeon-toed. I had heard that the more pigeon-toed a bear was, the bigger he was. Judging by everything I could see and the numerous bears we had encountered in the past, I knew this bear would square at least 7 feet, and that was big enough for me!

By the time Butch and Ray got back to me I had already headed upstream to get a good broadside shot. The three of us lay down on the bank and waited. Putting the scope of my Winchester Model 70 in .300 Weatherby on the bear while I waited for it to get closer, I realized the bear was magnificent. The bear's dark spring coat shone with the setting sun on its back. It was moving fast toward me and doing very little grubbing.

The excitement of the wait was overwhelming. My heart was pounding with excitement and a bit of nervousness. I had waited four years for that moment.

We had decided while talking among ourselves that as soon as the bear was directly in front of me, I would shoot. If I had any problems knocking it down, I would call for Butch and Ray to shoot. We did not want a wounded bear to get away. We were all in position.

The range was 125 yards when I fired the first shot using a 180-grain bullet. There was no doubt I had hit the bear hard. It went down in a cloud of dust. As soon as it hit the ground, I jacked another cartridge into the chamber. As the bear started to pick itself up, Butch yelled, "Shoot it again."

I shot again. Both bullets hit the bear's spine, paralyzing him behind the shoulders and immobilizing him. The bullets lodged only inches apart. Not wanting to let it linger, I went for a good heart shot. After that third and final shot, the bear did not move.

Butch headed for the bear and I held my shooting position. When Butch reached the bear and was in position, he called for me and Ray.

As I walked out of the brush behind the bear, I thought the animal looked like the pictures I had seen of brown bears. It was definitely the biggest bear I had ever seen. The bear measured 10 feet, claw tip to claw tip, and 8 feet 7 inches from the tip of the nose to the base of the tail; thus, it squared out at 9 feet 3-1/2 inches. It was plenty big enough for me. I had never seen or heard of a grizzly bear being that big before. Ray and I started the job of skinning the monster and Butch went back to camp for the Argo. It was then around 10:00 p.m.

The next morning, we broke camp and headed home. The temperature was in the 70s and we did not want the hide to spoil in the heat.

After returning home, a friend mentioned that I ought to have the bear scored, because it might make the Boone and Crockett records book. Until then, I had never thought about that possibility.

The bear finally scored 26-14/16, which placed it well up in the records book. From the size of the bear, I am sure we bagged the big one that had been making the tracks all those years, for we have never seen them in our hunting area again. 🦌

Grizzly bear, scoring 26-13/16 points,
taken by James C. Blanchard near Otter Creek in Alaska,
in 2001.

A Bear from Above

James C. Blanchard

26th Big Game Awards Program

IT WAS EARLY MARCH 2001 WHEN I RECEIVED AN EMAIL FROM FRIEND AND OUTFITTER JERRY AUSTIN ABOUT AN UNEXPECTED CANCELLATION HE HAD FOR A SPRING GRIZZLY HUNT. HIS OPERATION, AUSTIN'S ALASKAN HUNTING ADVENTURES, WHICH I CAME TO KNOW WHILE ON SEVERAL PRIOR HUNTS OUT OF ST. MICHAEL, HAS HAD GREAT HUNTER SUCCESS ON GRIZZLY BEARS, WITH MANY TROPHY-CLASS ANIMALS TO HIS CREDIT. AS THE SAYING GOES, THIS WAS AN OPPORTUNITY I COULDN'T REFUSE.

Within several days, I had made the necessary arrangements to arrive in St. Michael on April 17 for my third attempt for an elusive griz. While on the plane to Anchorage, I had plenty of time to reflect on past hunts and what this adventure could possibly bring. With the soothing hum of the jet engines and vivid memories of eating berries on a tundra-covered hillside while glassing for bears, there was a thought that I could not get out of my mind.

This day, ironically, marked the one-year anniversary of my wife's passing. With more than 21 days logged to date for grizzly with no success, I had a comforting premonition that my luck was about to change.

St. Michael is a small, native Eskimo community nestled along the shores of Norton Sound in the Bering Sea. As my plane touched down from the short flight from Unalakleet, I could see Jerry and his son Tony awaiting my arrival. After a warm greeting and a few hugs on the airstrip, it was off to the range to check my gun and unpack from what seemed like a never-ending journey from Chicago. Sleep wasn't a problem that night.

The plan was to get up early and leave St. Michael on snow machines to look for a specific bear Jerry had seen several times the previous fall. John Long, who had arrived in camp several days before me, would be the primary hunter. Jerry, Tony, guides John (J.D.) Richardson and Glen (Shears) Shipton, native tracker Mathew Andrews, and I would complete the group.

By early afternoon the next day, we had found a set of fresh tracks; Jerry was convinced this was the big boar we were looking for. Because John had a limited time schedule, Jerry asked that I refrain from shooting if the bear happened to pass within range. I agreed and Jerry quickly headed off with John to follow the tracks.

While waiting with Glen and Tony, it wasn't long before we caught a glimpse of a grizzly moving 300 yards above us through the alder thickets. In what seemed like seconds, the bear suddenly popped out within 50 yards and stood broadside gazing at us, as if he knew I wouldn't shoot. Soon, the bear ambled off in the direction that John and Jerry had taken. In the blink of an eye, an opportunity of a lifetime on a large grizzly had come and gone.

As I stared at where the bear had stood just moments ago, my thoughts of bewilderment were soon interrupted by the report of John's rifle. Several shots later, we could hear the faint shouts of excitement — John had harvested a beautiful 9-foot blonde grizzly. After some high-fives and pictures, Jerry pulled me aside and thanked me for honoring his request. "Just wait, my friend. We'll find you an even bigger bear."

"Bigger bear. Yeah, right," I thought as I went to sleep that night. Sure, I was very happy for John because he truly was one of the nicest people I've ever had the pleasure to share a hunting camp with. Selfishly, though, I knew that my grizzly jinx could have been over. This time, however, it just wasn't meant to be.

The next day was spent back in St. Michael as we prepped John's bear hide and reorganized for our next journey. As with all great bear guides, Jerry had a definite intuition on the area he wanted to hunt next. I was now the only hunter in camp, and the minutes were passing like hours.

Saturday's early-morning departure was marked with frigid cold, yet bright sunshine. As we raced across the ice-covered bay to shorten our ride to Klikitarik, the snow machines left a trail of swirling snow that glistened against the backdrop of the burning sun. Seals were sunning on the ice while various sea birds soared overhead. This barren and unforgiving land was alive and well.

The ride to Klikitarik was uneventful. We would travel a stretch and pull aside to glass for fresh tracks, only to find the landscape void of any sign that the big boars were coming out of hibernation. Once back on land, it seemed like there was a covey of ptarmigan in every opening and snowshoe hares in every thicket we passed. When the day was done, we had covered nearly 100 miles through some of the most beautiful tundra country I had ever seen.

We spent the night at a modest outpost camp near Klikitarik that Jerry keeps stocked with supplies for his hunting clients and emergencies. After a hot meal and a few hands of cards, it was off to sleep. The snowmobile ride was very strenuous, as much of the tundra at sea level had only scattered patches of snow. At times I thought it would have been easier to stay atop a bucking bronco, as snow machines and bumpy, frozen tundra don't go together very well.

Sunday, as we ate a quick breakfast, the enthusiasm in camp was noticeably high. The guides were confident that more bears would be out with each day that passed. Today we would again cover miles and miles of rough country, but our luck was about to change.

As we picked our way through the various creek drainages, each ridgetop would open up to an expansive series of new drainages on the other side. On one particular peak, we finally glassed the unmistakable tracks of a bear on a distant hillside. After a closer look, Tony soon spotted a big grizzly moving in our direction. Unfortunately, it turned out to be a mature sow with two cubs in tow. The bears worked their way into the creek bottom and up the hillside we were glassing from. To avoid a confrontation, we quickly backed off the ridge and worked our way to an adjacent drainage, Otter Creek.

It wasn't long before J.D. motioned to me that he had spotted another bear. By the expression on his face, it was obvious that whatever he was glassing surely had his attention. As soon as I made it over to his vantage point, I only caught a flash of a dark object heading into a large alder thicket. In hindsight, it's probably a good thing I didn't get a good look at this bear.

After discussing possible strategies on how to best approach this animal, we decided to first snowshoe down to a set of tracks we could see below us and check them for size. Since the snow was over five feet deep in spots, walking without snowshoes would have been impossible. Glen, who had the longest legs, made it to the tracks first as the rest of the group anxiously awaited his assessment. Looking at J.D., he calmly said, "Good bear."

However, as I glanced away from Glen to say something to Jerry, I caught Glen out of the corner of my eye with his arms stretched wide, implying to J.D. that it was a "huge" bear instead. For good reason, he probably didn't want to put any extra pressure or fear in me for the inevitable stalk that awaited us.

Jerry, Tony, and Mathew stayed put as Glen, J.D., and I worked our way around the alders. After making a circle around the thicket, it became obvious the bear was still inside and in no hurry to leave his sanctuary.

With less than two hours of good daylight left and a major snowstorm fast approaching, Jerry offered a now-or-never plan that would at least give us a chance at harvesting this incredible animal. "Against my better judgment, I want the three of you to work your way back around to the high side of the alders. When you find a clean entry point, I want you to stay at arm's length and carefully, slowly ease in to see if you can spot where the bear is lying up. If the visibility is too low or something, or anything doesn't feel right, I want you to back out immediately. Mathew will stay here while Tony and I cover your back trail. Don't do anything stupid and get my hunter hurt."

With that said, we were off and running like three kids chasing down the ice cream truck. We found a clearing at the top of the thicket, and slowly eased in for a closer look. Visibility was nearly 80 yards, so we felt comfortable moving in a little deeper. Several steps later I spotted what appeared to be the torso of a massive bear, with its legs obviously buried in the deep snow. I whispered to J.D., "That's him, isn't it?"

"Yes, it is," he calmly replied.

"What do we do now?"

"Just wait," he said.

"With our scent blowing directly at him, he'll probably get up and run the opposite way, don't you think?" I inquired.

J.D. and Glen knew better. When that bear was good and ready, he would get up and investigate the three foreign objects that were pestering him for the last few hours. This was his territory, and I now know that we weren't welcome.

Glen mused, "When that bear gets up and sprints our way, don't turn and run. He'll stop before he reaches us to assess what we are, at which time you need to find an opening and place a good shot."

"Don't worry, Glen, I'm not running anywhere."

With that said, the bear promptly stood up and looked

directly at us. Within seconds, the huge boar was in a full charge directly at our position. Even through the deep snow, the bear plowed his way effortlessly to us in mere seconds and closed the distance to 20 feet. I have never seen an animal cover ground as quickly as this irritated bear did that afternoon.

There is nothing on this earth that can duplicate the feeling of being charged by an angry grizzly. Adrenalin felt like it was pouring out of my skin. The combination of the thick alders and deep snow created an eerily quiet surrounding. I could hear and feel my heartbeat. This silence was shattered as the bear paused to assess its danger. With ear-piercing growls, mouth foaming, and teeth snapping, the bear slowly swung and rolled his enormous head side to side. The problem was his head was so large it covered a majority of his chest.

Finally, the bear moved his head far enough to one side to expose the center of his chest and front shoulder. Without hesitation, I fired my Winchester Model 70 .375 H&H, rolling the bear onto his back. The bear quickly regained his composure and started to angle away from us. My second shot hit true behind the left shoulder, knocking the bear down again in the deep snow. Still moving, I fired a final and fatal shot into the massive grizzly just below the hump.

After thousands of travel miles and endless hours of hiking, riding, glassing, and stalking, my dream of a trophy grizzly had finally come true. As I stood over my bear in absolute awe of its sheer size and beauty, I realized that all things happen for a reason.

I also realized that on this particular trip, I was hunting with my angel.... 🦌

Final score chart for Blanchard's grizzly bear, which scores 26–13/16 Points.

Grizzly bear, scoring 27-3/16 points,
taken by Rodney W. Debias near Unalakleet River in Alaska,
in 2009.

The Unalakleet Experience

Rodney W. Debias

27th Big Game Awards Program

As the midnight sun inches its way along the horizon, a luminous glow engulfs the tundra, more beautiful than any tropical sunset I have ever seen. A shadow appears, which quickly manifests itself in the shape of a gigantic bruin. I whisper to my guide, "Bear! Don, there is a bear!"

As we quickly move into position, Don ranges it at 385 yards. As I'm tightening my release strap, Don softly states, "It's the Big Guy." He's now at 175 yards. We kneel on the soft, dried grass surrounded by driftwood that had washed deep onto the tundra by storm surges, giving us ample cover. I am in front, and Don is so close behind me I can feel his elbow touching my shoulder. With his right hand he continues to range and with his left hand over my left shoulder, we wind-check with a squeeze bottle of white powder. Don mumbles, "Look at that noggin!"

I reply, "Just keep ranging. I'm going to let him walk past us before I draw. If I draw now, he's going to see me."

The moment is drawing near. The culmination of a lifetime of dreaming and after nearly half dozen other grizzly hunts, I ask myself, *Is this finally happening?*

This saga started when I was a very young boy and my dad gave me his Bear Grizzly recurve. I started shooting it seriously when I was 11 years old. After a couple years, the limb split, so I mowed a gentleman's lawn for a full summer and the man paid me with an old fiberglass Ben Pearson bow, both of which I have today. After that bow came a $99 Bear Whitetail. I was 15, and my best friend Lou Mihalko and I painted his grandmother's house for—you guessed it—$100 each. I have since been addicted to archery hunting.

My goal since childhood was to take a grizzly with a bow. I have been fortunate enough to have taken many nice animals, including a very nice brown bear several years ago. The grizzly, however, eluded me almost to the point of conceding.

After months of talking with my booking agent about hunts, the question finally presented itself. Sheep hunt? Moose hunt? Elk hunt?

The consultant said, "How about the grizzly. I have an outfitter, Hunt Alaska, owned by Vergil Umpanour and his son Eric. They will not only take bowhunters for grizzly, but they actually want them."

After booking, the game planning was underway. I started to collect my gear. The weather could be 70° F one day and 0° F the next, so my equipment had to be versatile. I scheduled shoulder surgery in September to fix bone spurs that had developed from sports and drawing heavyweight bows. After Christmas, I would start shooting. The cold and windy days were the ones I would shoot on the most to get used to shooting with heavy clothes under all conditions.

May soon rolled around, and I found myself on a plane landing in Unalakleet. I couldn't figure out why anyone would want to live in this barren, unforgiving land. After a short time, we were on a snowmobile headed for camp. The hunters were Jaun, Bruce, Randy, and me. Vergil, Eric, Don, and Shawn were our guides. Also, we had a 14-year-old camp helper named Shiler who had as many outdoor skills as anyone I have ever met. Shiler's uncle Paul joined us later.

Camp was set up miles short of the area we wanted to hunt, as weather conditions would not allow passage of boats or snow-mobiles. Each of us was assigned a guide and mine was Don Stiles

Day 1: As we left camp and Don and I got to know each other, I informed him that I would be the easiest hunter he ever had.

"I will not question your ability and you will not need to question my heart. I have done my best to get in shape, and I'll hunt 24 hours a day if we can." Believe me when I say that my ability and endurance would both be tested. For two days Don and I pushed further and further from camp.

Day 3: 5:30 a.m. Don spotted a bear as we were glassing on high ground while heading back to camp. The bear was 300 yards away, coming right to us. It was almost too easy. The wind was blowing from the east. The bear was coming north. But as the big bruin closed, the wind started moving southeast. Don ranged him at 69 yards, and the wind was now on the right side of my neck blowing right towards the bear—bad news! He stopped, turned, and ran. We watched him, with the grace of a racehorse, run across the same tundra we could barely walk across.

We shouldered our heavy packs and headed back to camp. When we crossed the track of the running bear, Don noticed the front right paw had blood on the middle toe and remarked that the bear must have cut it on a rock or another bear bit him. This track would identify him in the days ahead.

Upon arriving at camp, we learned the ice blew out and boats were able to make it to the next camp. However, Don and I would stay. We were left a tent, supplies and a Zodiac (a small inflatable boat and motor). After a nap, followed by pancakes and bacon, we inflated the Zodiac and boated up the coast several miles where we eventually beached it on a small stream that emptied into Norton Sound.

Day 4: 1:30 a.m. Don spotted a beautiful blonde bear 600 yards away. I noticed another, this one about 100 yards below

Blondie. Don guessed the blonde to be 7.5 feet, the other one at 7 feet. Either would be a trophy in anybody's book. As we watched them, a huge chocolate bear appeared and ran between them. He dwarfed them as if they were Honda Civics and he was a Mack truck As all three bears ran off, I said to Don, "If they were 7 and 7.5 feet, how big is he?"

Don said, "I don't know what to say—8 feet, maybe more. I don't know what to say. I mean, I just never seen anything like him. At any rate, he's gone now."

Day 5: Brought us to within 100 yards of a huge bear sleeping on the tundra with his squeeze, Blondie. We tried to make a stalk but the wind was not in our favor. At that point, you know how tightly wound your guide is when he doesn't slide his rifle to you and say, "Take him," knowing he would have guided a top 10 Boone and Crockett grizzly. We simply slipped out of there.

Day 6: As morning came, Don said we better check the sea, as the wind changed and ice may be blowing back in. He was right; the ice was half a mile from us and moving fast. We were out of food and would be unable to make it back to camp. Don said, "let's pump up the Zodiac and make a run for town." So, we loaded our gear, pumped, and pushed off into the rough sea. The waves were tossing us left and right, and the crushing icepack was pushing its way closer and closer to the boat. Don said if the ice catches us, it will crush us. But if it doesn't, the sea is calmer near the ice and he could speed up. I decided to get the life vests ready and only saw one. Don said the other was under his backpack. I tried to pull it out as he grinned and said he did not need it. "Up here, we call those body bags. You'll freeze to death long before you make the shore. Vests just make it easier for them to find the bodies."

Thankfully, Don proved to be very skilled in reading the waves, and we eventually made our way to Unalakleet.

Upon arriving, Don used his satellite phone and called his cousin Middy to pick us up. Middy fed us, gave us supplies and drove us to high ground to check the amount of ice that blew into shore. We were iced in as far as the eye could see. Middy suggested taking his and his brother Paul's snow machines along the coast and then packing our way back to the happy hunting grounds. The days ahead would be very cold, with 25 mph winds to the north and not a single bear track

Day 8: 1:00 a.m. Don is so tired, I could have poked him in the eye and he wouldn't have blinked. After a good bit of convincing, he finally said he would take a nap. As Don slept, I glassed several miles of tundra again and again. At 2:50, I noticed something running towards us. I woke Don and we realized it was two wolves hunting. What a sight. They came to within 25 yards and never knew we were there.

After they left, I was thinking, *Three days without cutting a track is just too long. We need a new plan.* So I suggested to Don we move to another area. Just as Don began to nod his head in agreement, I whispered, "Bear! Don, there's a bear!"

I immediately assumed a shooting position. Don ranged him, saying, "He's the Big Guy."

As the giant approached, I whispered to Don to range a small stick in front of me. Don Softly replied "17 yards." I think he's coming to that stick, but there's not enough cover to draw. I made the decision to let him pass me, a tough call, but I felt certain he would spot me if I drew.

He came closer and closer. When he reached the stick, he was 17 yards away and getting closer.

At 10 yards, he suddenly stops. He raises his nose. His nostrils flare, and I can hear him draw a deep breath. He exhales, and I can smell him. He draws another breath, this time curling his lips outward. I'm amazed at his size. He exhales again; I smell him. He knows something is up. With the wind at my nose, I know he cannot smell us. It must be a sixth sense. He takes two steps, stands straight up and looks down on us. With my bow on my knee at rest, I think, *Shoot him with the gun, Don!* Just as quickly as the thought entered my mind, he turns his head and looks the other way. Flabbergasted, relieved, and now determined, I say to myself, *He doesn't know where we are, and I'm going to get him.* He drops down on all fours and begins to walk past us. I watch his eye. When I can no longer see his eye, I know he can't see me.

I draw. He pauses, and then continues to walk. For the third and final time in less than a minute he has abandoned that sixth sense, which served him so well for so many years. He stops, perfectly broadside. I'd really like to watch him more, but I don't know if there's time.

Don whispers, "29 yards." I center the peep on my outer sight ring and place my 30-yard pin just behind the shadow of his right shoulder. I squeeze my release trigger. The arrow flies true and the arrow penetrates his chest. He growls, bites at the wound, turns and runs. He only makes it a short distance before falling hard. I nock another arrow and ask Don to range him. "Sixty yards."

I adjust my sight and say "Don, brace our binoculars on my shoulder. If he's breathing, I'm going to shoot again." Don replied, "He's already dead Rod, you did it!" While photographing the bear, we noticed a cut on his right paw. Turns out, he was the bear that had busted us on day three.

This would be the pinnacle of any hunter's life. However, it wasn't the trophy that made this hunt so memorable for me. During the fifth day, on what could be considered the low point of the hunt, I decided this was my favorite adventure because of the other hunters, Vergil and Eric Umpenhour, and Don. My appreciation would continue to grow as I would get to know the people of Unalakleet. William'"Middy" Johnson (whose grandfather was one of the original mushers on the serum run to Nome, now known as the Iditarod) who, in his grandfather's memory, was planning to (and did) complete the 2010 Iditarod (He finished 33rd). His entire family: his wife and children, brother Paul, Shawn, John, and so many others. What they have is so special.

When everything has you down, and you think there is no good in the world, buy a plane ticket to Unalakleet and walk down the dirt street lined with humble homes. Strangers will invite you into their homes to enjoy their best fish and share stories of their culture, and expect in return, only that you share stories of your own. The people of Unalakleet are the most wonderful, giving people I have ever met. ❦

Alaska brown bear, scoring 30-4/16 points,
taken by Will Gay on Kodiak Island, Alaska,
in 1997.

Big Bore, Big Bear

Will Gay

23rd Big Game Awards Program

THIS IS THE STORY OF A 20-YEAR QUEST FOR A TROPHY BROWN BEAR. THE CHAIN OF EVENTS INVOLVES THE PARTICIPATION OF MANY FRIENDS, TO WHOM I AM GRATEFUL.

My friend, Walter Earl of the Gun Room here in Anchorage, Alaska, brought an Army Navy .450 No. 2 home from one of his many gun show, road trips, in 1985. It had seen a lot of wear, but had character. A sidelock, underlever hammer gun in this nitro caliber is a rare find. When I expressed interest, Walter told me to take it out and shoot it. My hunting and reloading friend, Hank Wilson, assisted with reloading a few rounds and we took it to his cabin on the Deshka River that weekend. I liked the rifle, and although it had the Army Navy name, I was sure Westley Richards built the rifle. It matches Hank's .500 Westley Richards in almost every detail, except his rifle has the perfect original finish. Walter and I made a deal for the gun the following Monday.

In 1994, I called Hank's friend and business associate on Kodiak Island, Mike Anderson, to ask his opinion about the best area to apply in the annual brown bear permit drawing. Each year thereafter, I applied until 1996, when I drew a permit for the spring of 1997.

I called Mike again in February to ask about the best location to be dropped off for my April hunt. Mike had drawn a permit for the adjacent area and suggested we hunt together. He spoke with his friend, Jack King, and called me back the next day with exciting news. Jack would take us on his fishing vessel, the King David. Having hunted on drop hunts before, the mobility offered by this arrangement was very appealing.

Good intentions were overcome by an intense schedule to complete a new house for my lovely wife, Patricia. I made it to the rifle range only once with my .375 Winchester before leaving for Kodiak. The night before, Hank called and asked, "When are you going on your bear hunt?" "My flight leaves at 6 a.m.," I replied. He informed me that he had reloaded 20 rounds for my rifle and waited for me to call to go shooting. I was ashamed for not having practiced. The idea of taking a Kodiak bear with my double rifle had been discussed back in February. Hank's loads used 83 grains of 3031 powder and a 400-grain Kodiak bullet. The idea was too exciting, and although embarrassed, I picked the shells up late that evening before my departure the following morning.

When I arrived in Kodiak, Mike suggested we shoot our rifles, among our many chores to prepare for the trip. The .450 No. 2 grouped two inches high. Mike's .375 Winchester grouped one inch high. He handled his rifle like an experienced hunter and proved to be an excellent shot.

We left the following day for the hunt area, on the King David. Jack King is an excellent seaman, outdoorsman, hunter, commercial fisherman and a storyteller without peer. Jack's positive attitude has given him one of the most interesting lives a person could lead. His friend, Harry Haney, also came along. Harry has never met a stranger or a person who could refuse his cooking. Jack's son, Marcus, provided us with fresh fish and subsequently spotted the bear that is the subject of this story. Also along on the trip was Erik Lockman, Mike's brother-in-law. Erik is strong, bright and also an accomplished outdoorsman.

He would later pack my bear hide, with skull and paws intact. A broken rib 10 days before the hunt made me especially appreciative that Erik was along.

We traveled all day and arrived at a safe anchorage in my hunt area at 11 p.m. The following morning we began to glass and spotted a number of smaller bear we couldn't get to because of the surf. We spotted an excellent boar around noon, and watched him as he bedded down. Mike and I were put ashore in the skiff and stalked to within 60 yards, undetected. The bear was keeping a steady eye on the King David and the sound of its engine. We suspected he was not the bear we were looking for, so Mike whistled to get the bear to stand up for a better look. He began to run away and although his hide was beautiful, we estimated he would only square eight feet. He stopped, stood up, woofed and clacked his teeth, after which he ambled away.

Back on the King David, we spotted a sow and her cub, sleeping on the beach. They were beautiful. Almost immediately, Marcus spotted a large dark bruin on the same beach, three-quarters-of-a-mile further down. The bear was up and moving, not running, just moving deliberately uphill, occasionally looking back. The way he moved, and his relative size said, "BIG."

Mike and I were promptly in the skiff. Once ashore, as we reached the cliff 200 feet above the beach, I caught a glimpse of the bear going over another hill. He was a quarter mile away, moving with the same deliberate gait. Mike and I took off after him. When we reached the knoll where he was last seen, we carefully approached the crest and saw him in a small alpine pond. His head was huge! He raised his massive body and shook himself. It was 200 yards and no cover. I didn't feel comfortable shooting and Mike agreed.

The bear moved along checking his back trail, but never running, and disappeared into a swale. We followed cautiously and spotted him lying down, again at 200 yards. We crouch-walked to a hummock 150 yards from where he laid in the sun, drying from his recent bath. He would lay his head down briefly and raise it again to get a look, covering all quadrants. He was relaxed, but alert. There was grass in front of us and when his head was down, I could only see the top half of his head in the open sights of the .450. Mike and I discussed the situation calmly. The fact that we were both calm raised my confidence. Mike is a good companion to be with hunting a dangerous animal. We decided I would crawl downhill to the left to get a better shot. Mike would stay where he was, which would be an excellent spot once the bear was up.

I crawled on my belly, watching Mike's hand signals, and getting very wet from the tundra, but not caring. I never looked at the bear while stalking. Mike would give me a stiff outstretched hand, whereupon I would lay face down, not moving. When his finger wiggled, I would crawl slowly toward my goal, which was a small hummock, 30 yards away. I remember thinking that we did not verbalize much of our strategy, it just started happening. When I got to the hummock, Mike gave me the wiggle and I raised my rifle from the prone position. It didn't feel good. Maybe the recovering rib played a part, I'm not sure. I looked at Mike again and got the wiggle. I gave him a short thumbs-up, rotated around and sat upright. The bear also began sitting up. I cocked the right barrel and fired into his chest. The bear slumped. I rolled over and fired the fourth and final shot to finish him. He was big, but laying in a swale, making it hard to judge his size.

I went to motion to the skiff, while Mike stayed with the bear. While I was gone, Mike stepped off the distance at 130 yards.

Jack and Erik came quickly, and it took all four of us to roll the bear out of the swale. His hide was magnificent. Jack estimated his weight to be 1,200 to 1,400 pounds. We discovered he had a brown leather collar which was almost completely camouflaged by his long hair. The tattoo on his lip read #230. We later discovered that the bear was 13 years old and had the unusual trait of not denning. This explained why he was so fat early in the spring season. Jack was ecstatic about the size of the bear, the excellent hide and his large skull. When we returned to the boat and spread the hide on the flat deck, our delight was confirmed. The bear squared 10 feet and scores 30-4/16. The pleasure of harvesting such an animal was all the more important to me because of the firearm used, and the participation of my friends. Certainly the enjoyment of this experience would not have been possible without their contribution. 🐾

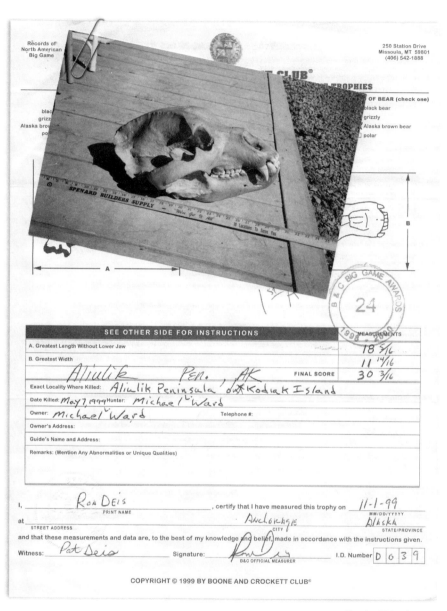

Original score chart for Michael L. Ward's Alaska brown bear,
scoring 30-3/16 points, taken on Alaska's Aliulik Peninsula, in 1999.

Fierce Winds

Michael L. Ward

24th Big Game Awards Program

I COULD NOT BELIEVE MY EYES. I DOUBLE-CHECKED AND IT REALLY WAS MY NAME, AND THE ADDRESS WAS CORRECT. I WAS READING AN ANCHORAGE NEWSPAPER LISTING RESULTS OF THE RECENT DRAWING FOR ALASKA PERMIT HUNTS. I HAD JUST WON A HIGHLY COVETED KODIAK BROWN BEAR PERMIT IN THE BEST AREA FOR TROPHY BEARS, THE SOUTHERN END OF KODIAK ISLAND. THIS WAS JULY OF 1998 AND THE HUNT WAS FOR THE FOLLOWING SPRING, OVER NINE MONTHS AWAY. I FELT LIKE A KID AGAIN WAITING FOR THE OPENING DAY OF DUCK SEASON.

Another fortunate event occurred shortly thereafter when Dr. George Pappas from Denver called me. His son, a former co-worker with me as a biologist with the Alaska Department of Fish and Game in Dutch Harbor, told him about my bear permit. George loves bear hunting, particularly Kodiak Island. He asked me about my plans and who would accompany me. I told him my plans were not set but if he was interested in going, he was welcome to come along. Having hunted the same area six years previously, he was a wealth of information. He killed a huge bear with a 29-inch skull. His hunting story was published in the *Boone and Crockett Club's 22nd Big Game Awards* book. Additionally, his picture is included in the eleventh edition of *Records of North American Big Game*. Yes, George was interested in accompanying me. Over the months we made many phone calls formulating our plans. My permit allowed 15 continuous days of hunting between April 1 and May 15. We would arrive in Kodiak on Sunday evening April 25, then check in with Fish and Game and fly out to camp on Monday morning.

This was not going to be a backpack hunt. George and I planned to stay at least 17 days. Consequently, we wanted a comfortable camp. Instead of my usual Super Cub flight, I chartered Peninsula Airlines Grumman Goose to fly us to camp. This is a large amphibious plane that can carry nearly a ton of gear. We would be fully loaded when we took off.

After an interminable wait, April 24 arrived. I left my homestead near Tok, Alaska, early for the five-hour drive to Anchorage where I would pick up George at the airport. We visited some friends and did some packing in preparation for our flight to Kodiak the next evening.

Winter ran late on Kodiak in 1999. Lakes remained frozen with lots of snow on the ground, not typical for late April. Advice to leave snowshoes behind proved a big mistake. I was unable to borrow a pair but did manage to purchase emergency shoes that pilots carry as part of their survival gear.

Monday morning dawned clear and calm. At 8 a.m. we checked into Fish and Game and then proceeded to the airport for our flight to camp. At 11:00 we took off on the hour flight south to a small bay. The day was gorgeous. Clear blue skies with snowy mountains of Kodiak Island and the Alaska Peninsula to the north and west, and calm blue waters of the North Pacific Ocean to the south and east. Rugged Kodiak Island was spectacular! There is nowhere as pretty as coastal Alaska on a clear day. We unloaded our gear and the plane was off. The rest of the day was spent setting up camp. Kodiak winds are notorious for shredding tents. We used George's eight-man dome tent, double or triple guying each of the numerous tie-off points.

Toward evening we spotted two people walking along the beach. As they neared our camp we greeted them. It was the guide who operates out of that area and a client. They were packing a bear hide taken the previous day. It was a large well-furred male that green scored just short of the Boone and Crockett minimum. They had hunted hard for 13 days seeing few bear.

Sleep came hard to me that night; I was too excited. Red foxes were breeding and their screams could be heard throughout the night. Toward dawn the wind came up and by 8 a.m. it was blowing a gale. It was to be our constant companion for the rest of the hunt. Southern Kodiak Island is wide open, with treeless wind-swept rolling hills and a spine of mountains. We ate a good breakfast and were out early. A long day of hunting produced a sighting of one bear at long range. The wind was fierce, at least 70 knots. We hid from it most of the day, spending long hours glassing.

The second day was pretty much a repeat of the first, very strong winds making hunting difficult. A sow and two cubs were spotted at long range. The snow line was at about 900 feet and very few tracks were visible. It appeared few bears were out of their dens yet. This would correspond to what the previous hunters had seen.

We decided to change tactics the next day. We would hunt up in the mountains in the area George had taken his bear. The wind had switched directions and was now out of the west, again at a fierce 70 knots. We followed an old bear trail used for many years and by noon we arrived at a good vantage point just below snow line to glass for the rest of the day. We hid behind car size boulders daring to stick our head up into the raging wind to glass as long as we could stand it. I cannot overstate how fierce the winds were. After about three hours George looked up, and on the mountain right above us about 1,000 feet was a bear digging roots. We sized him up and decided he was very large and unrubbed with long hair blowing in the wind. I decided to circle back downwind and climb up to him. A large boulder was my goal. It would shelter me from his view during the half hour stalk and allow me a good rest for a shot at about 100 yards. The harsh wind was now my ally. It remained constantly in my face.

The bear was intent on digging out something and he was not looking around. Climbing the steep mountain was fatiguing. As I closed to within ten feet of the boulder I felt the wind on the back of my neck for just an instant. I ran to the boulder, peeked around, and was horrified to see the bear, with his nose up, moving away. After over three hours of constant wind I had been betrayed. He was speeding up as I chambered a round and I quickly threw a shot at him as he disappeared around the mountain. It was a foolish off-hand shot. I was tired and unsteady. After over an hour of searching his tracks in the snow I was relieved to find no blood. A fortunate miss, as a wounded bear traveling long distance would have been the most likely result if I hit him with a bad shot. I was also very sad. It was a very large bear with a beautiful hide. I was afraid it would be my only chance at a great bear.

We glassed a few more hours before returning to camp. A delicious lamb chop dinner livened my spirits. Hunting conditions may be harsh, but at least we were eating well — no freeze-dried food on this trip.

The next morning we arose early and headed north to hunt a large valley that looked like good bear habitat. The valley was ringed by steep snow covered mountains that would provide good denning areas. Very few bear trails could be seen in the snow, however. A creek meandered through the valley floor, terminating in an estuary at salt water. This would provide good early season food in the form of grass and roots. Winter-killed deer could be found on the flats. We glassed from a knob most of the day. The west wind was still howling. I literally threw myself to the ground to keep from being blown down the hill. A young bear that spent about an hour roaming the flats was spotted early. It was fun to watch, and encouraged us. Spring bear hunting on Kodiak Island involves long hours of patient glassing. This is the breeding season. Large males roam widely in their search for a mate. Winter snow has knocked down the luxuriant summer vegetation allowing excellent glassing over expansive terrain. We did spot another medium-sized bear before returning to camp for dinner, after which I climbed into the hills behind camp and glassed the flats to the south. The hills trailed off to the ocean about two miles away. A few deer, survivors of the hard winter, and a fox kept me entertained until dark.

We were on the same knob enduring the same raging west wind on the fifth day. George quickly spotted two bears, one chasing another, far to the south near the ocean. This is the area where the previous hunter took his bear. These bears appeared to be a large male chasing a female. They soon moved out of sight heading up into the foothills. Shortly I spotted another bear, nose down like a bird dog, following their trail. This bear also quickly moved out of sight. This was very encouraging. Bear were becoming more abundant as the hunt progressed. After a few more hours of glassing we returned to camp for lunch. I decided to hunt up in the hills where the bears headed while George remained to work around camp. Toward evening I spotted two bears, presumably the same courting couple, near where we had last seen them. The third bear was not seen. Possibly there was a fight and one was run off. They were moving slowly, allowing me to approach to about 500 yards. The larger bear appeared to be a medium-size male that was rubbed. They slowly moved out of sight over about an hour while I enjoyed watching them. The smaller, presumably female, bear would not allow the larger bear to get close to her. Returning to camp at dark I was again treated to one of George's lamb dinners. We discussed the next day's hunt and decided on the area where the previous hunter made his kill.

There was a diminishment in the wind that evening, still a gale from the west but only about 40 knots. We hiked south about two miles to a small range of hills where we spent much of the day glassing from the highest point. Remains of the previous kill could be seen. Eagles and a fox took turns feeding on the meager remnants of what a week previously must have been close to half a ton of brown bear carcass. The gray whale migration was now in full swing around Kodiak Island. From our vantage point we would see three or four whales an hour swimming past on their way north to summer in the Bering Sea and Arctic Ocean. I was getting drowsy in the mid-day sun when all of a sudden George said, "There's a bear." About 400 yards away stood an enormous bear. He was absolutely huge, with a belly to match. He was pestering a female that would not let him get near her. She was much more aggressive toward him than the female I observed the previous day. He cornered her at the edge of a 100-foot cliff with jagged rocks below where she whirled on him, snapping at his face, and then agilely eluded him. He stood over twice her height and was also completely rubbed; no trophy here, except for the potential World's Record skull. I decided not to take him. This hurt George. He really wanted me to get this bear. The two quickly moved off. We attempted to follow, but never did see them again.

We returned to camp for an early dinner and then hunted behind camp until dark. No more bears were seen that day. We discussed the next day's hunt and decided to climb into the mountains again.

The next day the wind conditions kept us from going to the mountains we planned to hunt and ended up not seeing a bear the entire day. We were starting to feel a little discouraged.

A big break came during the night when the wind switched around to a west wind. This allowed us to hunt the area we considered most productive, the mountain where George killed his bear and I missed a bear. A big breakfast of bacon and eggs started our day. We were then off on the three-hour climb into the mountains. A comparatively calm 50-knot wind blew into our faces. We posted ourselves on a rock affording the best visibility and settled in for a long day of glassing. In early afternoon George spotted a good-sized bear below us, probably about a nine-footer, moving along slowly at 300 yards. George strongly recommended I quickly go down and kill it. I looked it over. He was obviously rubbed. George reminded me we were running out of time and not seeing many bears. "I'd rather go home without a bear than kill one I would not be proud of," was my reply. "That may well be the case," was his.

The next morning we rode out a biting sleet storm and stayed in camp to set up another dome tent. We did hunt close to camp in the afternoon, but no bears were spotted.

The wind gradually switched around to a north wind during the night. We decided another try in the mountains was in order. We took our customary promontory to glass from throughout the day. In early afternoon I decided to take a hike and look over some country to the south. After a couple hours I returned and continued to glass with George. All of a sudden he spotted a bear. It was on the mountain across a narrow pass from us. I looked up in time to see it stand, stretch, yawn, and then lay back down. I got a good look at the hair on its back and side blowing in the wind. He was not rubbed, and a good-sized bear. He was lying on a bench high up on a steep mountainside above us about 250 yards away. It seemed tired and we felt it had just emerged from its den. We wanted to get closer but to do so meant dropping down off our mountain into the pass. My only shot was to shoot from where we were. He was lying lengthwise to us with only his head and shoulder tops visible. He looked small through my scope. The wind was also roaring out of the north crosswise to us at about 50 knots, a very difficult shot. I set up a padded rest and waited, planning to shoot when he stood.

After about 45 minutes I was getting cold. Temperatures were in the high 30s and I was exposed to the wind. I was afraid I would start shivering and miss my shot. About every five minutes the wind would stop for 5 or 10 seconds. I told George my predicament and that I planned to shoot during the next lull. We got ready. Sure enough the wind stopped a couple of minutes later, at which point I said, "Here we go, George" and fired. It was a hit. Just when I thought he was finished he arose and staggered off behind a rock, apparently dying. I now had the formidable task of climbing up a snow chute and skinning out the bear. This would obviously be an individual effort as I would not ask George to attempt the climb. I was crossing the pass to assess the situation when all of a sudden the bear appeared, staggering through the snow, obviously hit hard. He was crossing in front of me at about 50 yards as I fired twice more at his lungs. Down he went for the final time. As I approached I had the feeling that he looked rather small. I poked his rump repeatedly with the muzzle of my rifle, then in the eye. There was no movement. Still, I was afraid to touch him. He wasn't small anymore, but I finally mustered up the courage to touch him. His hide was the most luxurious I had ever seen. His claws were white and his head was massive. He was flawless, a perfect bear. I said a prayer of thanks to God for allowing me to kill such a magnificent animal.

George waded across the thigh deep snow and after a few minutes of admiring the bear we decided pictures were in order. It was now 6 o'clock, not enough time for us to skin out the bear and return to camp. We rolled it onto its back. I worried the thick hide and huge body would insulate it from the snow and keep it from cooling down. I decided to skin open the belly and down the sides to allow it to cool as best it could. I left some stinky socks near the bear and relieved myself around it in the hope of discouraging any scavengers.

I awoke the next morning to beautiful, calm blue skies. It is as if killing the bear also killed the wind. For the first time in 12 days it was pleasant to be out. I left camp with my pack and skinning gear. George loaned me his .44 magnum revolver to carry in place of my rifle. The farther I walked into the hills the more I regretted that decision. I felt nervous walking those hills in the presence of large bears without a rifle, especially as I neared the kill, which a bear may have been claiming.

Once I finally had the hide off I was then even more in awe of the bear. What a physical specimen. Not fat as you think of a large bear. It was all massive muscle. There were some puncture wounds in one leg that were festering, probably from a fight the previous fall. The neck was nearly three feet in circumference. It took me seven hours to finish the skinning chores and I was tuckered out. I tried to load the hide and head back to camp, but kept bogged down in the deep snow. I would have to return the next day with more cord and my snowshoes. I returned to camp with only the head. George was amazed when he saw it. His bear scored high in the Boone and Crockett book and he said this one was bigger. We did a very rough measurement without calipers of about 12 inches by 19 inches or 31 inches, which was larger than the current number one bear. I was excited but worried as I still had an unprotected bear hide in the hills to pack out. I gathered up my snowshoes and the cord I needed to attach it to my pack the next day.

After a long struggle I finally got the hide back to camp. The stretched measurement was 11 feet claw to claw and 9 feet nose-to-tail for a squared size of 10 feet. I added 50 pounds of salt to the hide, and covered it with a tarp to keep off the light rain while we waited the last two days for our trip back to Anchorage.

After our plane ride back we checked into a hotel and cleaned up before heading to Fish and Game for the mandatory check out. When John Crye at Fish and Game saw my bear he said, "This may be the one we've been looking for." A few years previously, a very large bear was tranquilized, sampled, measured, and a number tattooed in its lips. A very rough measurement of the skull with, of course, the hide still attached indicated that it was larger than the current number one bear. John proceeded to measure my bear. While not the big one, it still was the fifth largest bear sealed by Fish and Game since they started record keeping in 1954. John also discovered that my bear had been sampled, as he found a number tattooed in the lips. A year later I received a letter from him telling me that the premolar tooth he extracted was sectioned and found to be 12 years old.

I will always wonder if the huge bear we saw was the big one, a new World's Record. Body wise, he was substantially bigger than my bear. Still, I would not trade my bear with its flawless hide for the World's Record skull. 🦌

Alaska brown bear, scoring 29-9/16 points,
taken by Robert J. Castle near Uganik Lake, Alaska,
in 2006.

Thirty-Three Days

Robert J. Castle

27th Big Game Awards Program

IN 2005 I DID A SPRING AND FALL BEAR HUNT ON CHICHAGOF ISLAND IN SOUTHEAST ALASKA, AND BETWEEN THE TWO HUNTS WE SPOTTED OVER 150 BEARS. THOUGH SOME LOOKED PRETTY BIG, NONE WERE AS BIG AS THE BEAR I WAS LOOKING FOR. IT WAS VERY HARD TO KEEP PASSING UP BEARS MOST HUNTERS WOULD HAVE TAKEN, AND WHILE I WAS GETTING TIRED AND DEJECTED, I HAD PROMISED MYSELF IF I WAS GOING TO SHOOT A BROWN BEAR, IT HAD TO BE AT LEAST A 9-FOOTER. I DIDN'T WANT TO SHOOT AN ANIMAL AS SPECIAL AS A BROWN BEAR AND COME AWAY WITH SOMETHING THAT WASN'T WHAT YOU ENVISION WHEN YOU THINK OF A BIG BROWN BEAR. WITH THIS GOAL IN MIND, MY ATTITUDE WAS SUCH THAT IF IT WASN'T TO BE, THEN SO BE IT.

When I first returned home from the Chichagof Island hunts, I was tired of Alaska and wanted no part of returning. But as most hunters know, once you get rested, the itch starts to come back. I figured if I get an opportunity to hunt the right place, I might give it one more swing of the bat.

After finally settling on hunting Kodiak Island where the majority of the top-ranking Boone and Crockett Alaska brown bears have been taken over the years, I did some research for the best brown bear guides on Kodiak and found that nearly all of them were booked out three to four years in advance. I decided I was not going to wait that long. As far as I was concerned, it was now or never.

When I found out that Rohrer Bear Camp Outfitters annually donate a brown bear hunt to the Wild Sheep Foundation, formerly called the Foundation for North American Wild Sheep, I got set up to bid by telephone. I was lucky enough to win the hunt through the auction, which enabled me to be hunting brown bear on Kodiak Island on May 4, 2006.

Upon arriving at Rohrer Bear Camp, there were five hunters in camp, and Kodiak Island was everything you would expect it to be. On the first day of my hunt, we settled down on a good spotting point, and it didn't take long before we were seeing big bears. The biggest difference on this hunt was that if you decided to go on a stalk, you could easily lose a half day with the amount of ground you had to cover, so you wanted to really make sure the bear was big enough and that you could get to him in time for a good shot before the day ended.

On the second day we spotted a bear that my guide Sam said was well over 9 feet. The bear had a rub spot on his back that I didn't like, but he looked huge. After too much thinking, I said, let's go, but our stalk came up empty because we had waited too long. It was late in the day when we decided the stalk was fruitless, so we returned to camp. When we arrived back at camp, we found out one hunter had shot a really nice bear that went about 9 feet 5 inches, which got me pumped up.

The next day we made another stalk and were just getting in range when the bear busted us and took off. Again it was late in the day, so we went back to camp and heard that another hunter had shot a big bear that went 9 feet 8 inches. At this point I had just a little doubt starting to creep into the back of my mind.

On day five we made a third stalk that failed once again. The next day, the hunter with whom I shared a cabin shot a monster bear that went 10 feet 3 inches. As we sat around the dinner table the next day, our outfitter, Dick Rohrer called in the floatplane for the following day. One hunter who had not shot a bear had to leave, and the other three who all had nice bears jumped on the plane with him and took off, leaving me at camp alone with all the guides. We all began to wonder what was up with my luck. With 22 days at Chichagof, plus 8 days at Kodiak and nothing to show for all this effort, I was at the point of mental exhaustion and was pretty tired physically, to say the least. My outfitter was a great guy and on days 9 and 10, he kept me going, plus he had three of the other guides in addition to Sam coming along with us each day so we had five sets of eyes glassing.

On day 11, my second-to-last day, it seemed as if I was just going through the motions at times and was getting discouraged. It was about 8:30 p.m. when we caught just a glimpse of a bear near the top of a mountain. Dick had us move about 400 yards to get a different angle. We looked for a while and got another glimpse of the same bear. After we discussed it, Dick suddenly said, "You have to get up there to take a look."

I said to myself, "Wait a minute! It's 9 p.m., we don't have a very good idea how big the bear is, and it's way up there on the mountain." Then with one look from Dick and a few words, I knew that there was one more day of hunting left and we needed to take a gamble. I called it a "Hail Mary" effort. So up we went as fast as we could.

There was a lot of huffing and sweating, but as we neared the top of the ridge we slowed down and finally reached the exact spot Sam had in mind where he thought the bear was located. We sat for just about three or four minutes before we could hear a bear walking. I immediately started to get pumped.

Out came a bear and the first thing I could see was a face and body of a very ugly …sow! I took one look at my guide, Sam, and we both were thinking, "You have to be kidding. We came all the way up here for that?" That sow walked about 50 yards in front of us and kept on going right out of sight.

At this point I had the mindset that I was jinxed and was not going to kill a brown bear. Then, after another minute or two, I heard a noise and looked back to where the sow had emerged from the brush and I saw this big fat head of a bear. I elbowed my guide, Sam, and when he looked over I saw the look in his eyes and immediately knew it was something big. I said, "What do you think?"

Without hesitation he said, "Shoot him!"

He said it in such a way that I knew to just shut up and shoot. The bear was following the sow, so when he was about 50 yards away and broadside, I fired a round right behind the shoulder. He roared and took off into the brush. We knew he wasn't going to go very far.

After we all went crazy for a minute, I asked Sam, "Well, how big do you think he is?"

All he said was, "Real big!"

We found the bear only about 70 yards from where I shot him. Sam measured his front pad at 8¼ inches.

It was late in the day, so after we skinned him, we went back the next day to get him out. He ended up squaring a little smaller than we thought at 9 feet 5 inches. But I was thrilled to death. Then came the bonus. We talked a bunch about how huge his head was, but for some reason the thought of this being a records book bear never came into my mind until we got back to camp. The first thing Dick did back at camp was to grab the skull to measure it. Then it hit me, and I was like a little kid. I kept asking, "Well? Well? Well?"

Dick looked at me and said the bear's skull was over 29-4/8 inches, which just floored me. When I got back home, and after the 60-day drying period, the bear measured 29-9/16. It took

33 days of hunting (which my guides kept reminding me of throughout this hunt) and a "Hail Mary" stalk at the end, but wow, was it ever worth it. 🦌

Alaska brown bear, scoring 29-7/16 points,
taken by Scott Weisenburger near Alaska's Meshik River,
in 2004.

98% Boredom, 2% Adrenaline

Scott Weisenburger

26th Big Game Awards Program

IN JANUARY 2004 I MET JOE KLUTCH OF KATMAI GUIDE SERVICE AT THE SCI SHOW IN RENO. BEFORE I KNEW IT, I WAS SIGNED UP AND ON MY WAY TO ALASKA FOR A BROWN BEAR HUNT.

I flew from Phoenix to Seattle and on to Anchorage the first day, and on the following day flew from Anchorage to King Salmon. Joe and one of his guides met me at the airport, after which we did a little bit of final shopping and off we went to the other side of the airport where Joe kept his Cessna 185.

His pilot, Dale, flew me and a plane loaded full of gear about an hour and ten minutes farther out on the Alaska Peninsula to base camp on an old abandoned runway used during World War II. Here I met up with several other hunters that were all getting ready for opening day of spring bear season. The cook shack and dining room was a metal building that had been pulled in on a sled 60 years ago to facilitate the workers who were building this and many other runways strung along the Alaska Peninsula. Although it was cold and windy outside, it was cozy warm inside.

Somehow, Joe had talked a former chef from a five-star restaurant to come out to this desolate place; therefore, the food was top notch. By the end of the day, all of the hunters had arrived. Over dinner, Joe began pairing up hunters, guides, and spike camps. His pilot would fly each group out to their spike camps in a Husky with big tundra tires.

After he had gone all the way around the table, he came back to me and said that I would be with a guide named Lance Kronberger, but he didn't mention what camp we were going to. After a little bit, I asked Lance where we were headed. He asked me if I was up for an adventure. With a little bit of trepidation, I asked what he had in mind. He said he knew a great place to go but we would have to backpack. I couldn't say no, so our plan was set.

The next day, I picked through all of my gear for just the essentials and loaded my rifle and pack in the Husky for another 40-minute flight to another abandoned runway where we would begin our adventure. We had about six miles to go from the valley floor along the base of the mountains. We had hip waders on and occasionally would sink almost to the top of them as we slipped into the marshy muskeg. The further we got back into where Lance wanted to go, the more bear tracks we began to see. I was becoming really excited.

We finally got to where we were going to camp but we had to cross a stream that was deeper than the last time Lance had been here. The stream was really moving, and the water was just inches from filling up my waders. I wasn't very excited about beginning my hunt with all wet gear, but luckily we made it across without mishap.

We set up our tent and made some dinner. Spring had arrived in this area and the mosquitoes were so thick that we had to walk fast with our food to keep from being attacked. Even while walking, we had a cloud of mosquitoes swarming around us all the time. We finished eating, cleaned things up, and crawled into our little backpack tent to get ready for tomorrow — opening day!

The next morning we were up and on our way. Lance led me several miles up and over two ridges. We finally climbed on top of a knob were we could watch 270 degrees. Lance said this would be our spot for several days watching for bears traversing the mountains. We would watch for them in the snow on the ridges to the left and right and on the ridge that our knob was part of. He said to look for their tracks that he called "zippers" and follow them from each end to find a small spot. We would then get our scopes out and determine if the bear would be worth stalking and if we felt we could get to it.

We saw about half a dozen bears that first day, but all were either not the size that we were looking for, or they were headed in a direction so that we would never be able to get to them. You could tell how powerful they were as they climbed straight up, over and back down the other side of these rugged mountains. They didn't miss a beat no matter what the terrain. With the beginning of long days of summer, it was late when we began back to camp to start all over again tomorrow.

The next day we were back in the same spot on our knob glassing and glassing. Lance had told me to be prepared that bear hunting was 98% boredom and 2% sheer adrenalin rush. By the end of this day, I was beginning to understand what he was saying. Even though we were still seeing bears, I was starting to get tired of sitting in the same spot. Lance said that we would try our spot one more day and then maybe think about moving to a different knob.

Day three was to be a day to remember. After a couple of hours on our knob, Lance spotted a bear that he thought we should watch for a while. It came over the ridge to our left and began strolling down the mountain to the valley floor. Once it reached the valley floor, it appeared to be a nice-sized bear. Lance thought that this might be the bear for us.

Amazingly, it turned and began across the valley toward us. When it got to our side of the valley, it began up our ridge in the cut that our knob was next to. The intensity was growing. About halfway up the ridge, Lance unfortunately said this was not the bear that we were looking for. If it had been closer to the last day of the hunt, maybe, but not on the third day. I have to admit I was a little disappointed. This bear kept coming right toward us. It was almost as if it smelled us.

When it got to about 75 yards, out popped a little bear cub from the bushes. This little bear must have been there all day. The big bear began chasing this little bear. They got to about 60 yards and then the little bear took off down the ridge to the valley floor. We never really saw them come out on the valley floor. I was looking over my shoulder for hours after that, wondering what happened to that big bear.

After a while, we went back to glassing for bears. From my spot, I could see different ground than what Lance could see. At about 5 p.m., I saw a dark spot in the snow on the second knob along our ridge. I watched it for a long time and it finally moved a little. Sure enough it was a bear.

I called over to Lance to take a look and he thought that it might be a nice one. It was too far away to see very well and, because of its location on that knob, there was no way to get any closer. We were going to have to wait and see which way it went down that knob. We figured it was unlikely that it would come toward us on the ridge and if it went to the left or away from us, we would never be able to catch up with it. We would have to hope that it went down the ridge to the right.

We watched this bear for hours. It never looked up or cared about its surroundings. It just lay in its little patch of snow and occasionally rolled from side to side. At about 10 p.m., it got up and began to walk down the knob out of sight to the left. We thought that we were done, but a couple of minutes later it popped out of the brush on the right. The bear had gone down to the left and circled around the knob just below the top and come out on the side we needed.

Lance and I couldn't believe it! We packed up our gear and raced down the ridge toward the valley floor. It was more like a controlled slide because it was so steep where we had to go down. About halfway to the bottom, we saw the bear come out on a rock outcropping and survey the valley floor. We only got a brief look, but he looked big. We estimated where we thought he would enter the valley floor and continued our slide to the floor.

When we got to the bottom, we began making our way up the valley floor along the side of the ridge toward the spot we had identified. We came around a little protrusion in the ridge and there was a perfect bump in the valley that would make a great rest and keep us above the grass. We got everything ready and waited.

Lance said to let the bear come out in the opening about 25 yards or more so that he could get a good look and confirm that this was the bear for us. He said that if it was the bear, Lance wanted me to hit it in the hip, then the shoulder, and then a couple in the chest. Lance said if the bear turned in our direction, I had better shoot fast or he was going to send some lead over as well. We were too far out in the middle of nowhere to have issues.

A couple minutes later he came out of the brush and Lance started checking him out. I had him in the sights of my .375 H&H Magnum that my father had given me for this hunt. When Lance said shoot, the lead started flying. Within minutes, I had my first bear — and a big brown bear at that! We walked toward him but stopped about 10 yards short until we knew he was done. We could tell that he was a giant. What an unbelievable day! Lance guessed he was more than 9 feet and maybe 10 feet!

We took a bunch of pictures and then began the daunting task of skinning a huge bear. It took us until about 3:30 a.m. to finish. I packed all of Lance's optics and gear in my bag along with the skull and then we stuffed the hide in Lance's pack. It was so heavy that we couldn't pick it up to get it on his back. We set it on a high spot and got Lance sitting on the ground in the pack. It took both of us to get him up off the ground.

Finally, we were headed back to camp with our trophy. My flashlight had died at the end of the skinning process and somehow my headlamp had gotten left behind at base camp when I was lightening my load. I followed Lance pretty close to avoid sinking in to my waist on the way back. With the smell of blood all over me, every time I heard a twig snap, my head turned expecting something to come out of the darkness looking for an easy dinner.

We got about two miles back toward camp when Lance said he couldn't go any farther. We still had a pretty large hill to go up and the other side was straight down. Even if I got it up the hill, going down the other side in the brush at night wasn't going to be any fun. We decided to leave it on a gravel bar along the stream in the middle of the valley and come back in the morning. Hopefully then we could get it over the ridge, or possibly find or make a landing strip long enough that Dale could fly in and get it. I hated leaving it behind but Lance didn't think anything would mess with it. This guy was clearly the king of the hill. He figured it would be left alone until the other animals knew it was dead. I reluctantly agreed and we went back to camp for a little rest and a quick bite to eat.

First thing in the morning, we were back at it. We decided that we could make the gravel bar just long enough for the plane. Lance called him in on the radio that he carried and we waited for his arrival. He made two passes over the strip to see if it was long enough and finally gave it a try. To give himself all that he could, he actually skimmed the water when he landed. We repositioned the plane, loaded him up, and off he went back to base camp. He would be back to get us that afternoon at our original drop point. We again had some work in front of us.

When we arrived at our pickup point and Dale flew in to get us, the first thing that he asked was if we had any idea how large the bear was? We knew that it was large but we had lost our tape measure somewhere along the way. Lance guessed that it would square 10 feet and that the skull would score 28 inches. Dale wouldn't tell us the actual size. He just grinned. He was going to make us wait.

He ferried us both back to base camp. I went first, and when I arrived some other hunters were out looking at three bear hides spread out on the ground. They said that mine was the largest and I couldn't believe it. When Lance got back we laid a tape across the hide. We didn't even bother to pull it tight. It was an unbelievable 10'8". I had never put any thought into the size of a bear hide, but a 10'8" bear has almost 40 percent more surface area then a 9' bear. We did the best we could to measure the skull but the calipers they had weren't large enough. We estimated it at 29 inches!

After the mandatory drying period, an official measurer in Phoenix scored it at 29-7/16 inches — just amazing. Thanks Joe and Lance for the hunt of a lifetime! 🦌

*Cougar, scoring 15-6/16 points,
taken by Dick Ray (right) in Archuleta County, Colorado,
in 2004.*

A Big Lion, Like Gold, Is Where You Find It

Dick Ray

26th Big Game Awards Program

HE GLARED AT US WITH GOLDEN GREEN EYES THAT DANCED WITH CONTEMPT. HE HAD NO USE FOR THOSE OF US BENEATH HIS TREE, AND WE KNEW IT. HE WAS HUGE BY ANY STANDARD, BUT I HAD NO NEED, NO WISH, NO DESIRE TO TAKE HIS LIFE. THE DAY HAD BEGUN WITH ONLY THE HOPE TO FIND A LION TRACK THAT THE HOUNDS COULD TRAIL, AND PERHAPS, CATCH AND RELEASE.

The day prior, an outfitter friend, Mark Davies, of Grand Junction, Colorado, had arrived at our place near Pagosa Springs, Colorado. Mark had wanted to take a pair of our hounds that might replace a couple of dogs in his pack of lion dogs. Well, a little snow was predicted to fall that night, so my son Mike and I encouraged Mark to stay over and hunt with us the next day. More than half the time, predicted snow fails to materialize, but when we looked out at 4 a.m., sure enough, about one and a half inches had fallen.

It was February 25th, and that late in winter, such a small amount of snow usually melts by 9 or 10 a.m. But if you can find a track early, sometimes you can get a lion treed before the track and scent vanishes.

We left with high hopes, invigorated by the cold, crisp, clear morning and knowing that we had as good a chance as anyone to find a lion track that day. We knew that some of the numerous other hunters in the area were sure to be out and about as well. The quota for this area was almost full, with only one lion left to be harvested. With so many hunters out, that would almost surely happen, closing the season by sundown.

Mike and I chose to try Devil Mountain because we had seen sign of a big lion there about ten days earlier. Mike made his way up a drainage, while I went up another a few miles west. I found the track of a female lion right away and released my three dogs on it. The snow was already melting, for the steep slopes were composed of black shale that held warmth from the day before. The dogs were able to trail up and onto a ridge for nearly a mile before the sun took the track and its scent away from them. They weren't going to make any progress and didn't, as I climbed up to them. Catching and leashing them, I headed back.

I went to see if I could find Mike, knowing that our trailing conditions and time were passing fast. Mike had come back down his mountain, and we got together. He had a story. He had found a big lion's track up higher, where there was a little more snow. If we hurried, and were lucky, the dogs might still be able to work it.

It took us about an hour to get up to the track. That which had been a big, beautiful fresh track at daylight was now a pathetic half-melted, barely recognizable line threading under old-growth Ponderosa pines.

Mark took a long look and said, "It's big, but most hunters would say that it's too melted out to work."

I said, "Mark, we would agree, but let's see what the hounds say."

We released all six dogs, and they took the track onward. And on they went, over a ridge and out of hearing. Now you always hope that a lion has a fresh kill just over the next ridge and that the dogs will tree him not far from the kill. It happens sometimes, but not that day. As we climbed and crested the ridge, we could again hear them in the distance, trailing; then, out of hearing again. A few steep, slick shale slopes more, and then we could hear the dogs bark treed.

As we walked up to the tree, he appeared the same as every lion I had ever seen — splendid, noble, and a word that is overused but should be reserved for the truly special — awesome. We gazed up at him, and he glared back. Both Mark and Mike urged me to take the lion. I had never killed a lion in Colorado, and had never planned to. In 1985, Mike and I treed a lion in New Mexico, which I took with my Bear take-down bow. I had wanted to take that lion. It scored 15-8/16 and was the New Mexico state record for eleven years. I didn't need another lion.

Mike and I have enjoyed our years of work guiding lion hunters. The first Boone and Crockett lion that I ever saw was the one Father Anderson Bakewell, a Catholic priest, took with me in 1978. Mike's first lion was a Boone and Crockett that he took alone in 1982, just out of high school. How could I justify taking another lion of this class?

Suddenly, it became very personal to me. To be sure, the novice may kill without question, having not done it before — he has not experienced the pondering and twinge of remorse that accompanies the still, lifeless form that the act of killing produces. Why we kill is a mystery, outranked only by the mystery of death itself.

Once again, Mike said, "You may as well take him. If the quota doesn't fill today, someone else will kill him on the next snow. Besides, at your age, this might be the last really huge lion that you ever see."

"True," I thought. "I don't have a gun," I said.

Mike handed me his .44 from his backpack. I questioned my conscience and wondered if it would be enough to immortalize this creature with humble respect and a life-size mount? And then, at the shot, he fell from the tree, dead.

As I looked at his splendid form, I wondered, "What stories could this lion have told?" He was about seven years old. Being an obligate carnivore, he had to kill to survive, and at a rate of about a deer or an elk a week, he would have made several hundred kills.

We packed out his hide and his meat in our backpacks and led the dogs back across the canyons and down the mountain. As we walked, I remembered Ray Bailey's Boone and Crockett lion taken with us in 1986. It wore a collar that had been placed on it five years earlier west of Grand Junction, Colorado. We took the lion about 300 miles south of there in northern New Mexico. It made me wonder, who is this lion? Where did he come from? Has anyone ever laid eyes on him before? Does he have a brother out there? And then I thought, a lion is what we would all like to be — a true free spirit. He goes where he wants, kills when he's hungry, and doesn't pay taxes.

My last thought before I came to peace with myself was that I hoped that he had left many sons behind, for all living things will die, and be replaced by their own kind. It is the nature of things. 🦌

Records of
North American
Big Game

Dick Ray   15 6/16
Pagosa Springs, CO   ID: 29995
cougar   26th
Date of Kill:
Kill Location:

OFFICIAL ... CKETT CLU ... ...MERICAN BI... ...

	MINIMUM SCORES		KIND OF CAT (check one)
	AWARDS	ALL-TIME	☒ cougar
cougar	14 - 8/16	15	☐ jaguar
jaguar	14 - 8/16	14 - 8/1	

BOONE & ...ETT CLUB   7/17/04

SEE OTHER SIDE FOR INSTRUCTIONS	MEASUREMENTS
A. Greatest Length Without Lower Jaw	9 0/16
B. Greatest Width	6 6/16
26	FINAL SCORE 15 6/16

Exact Locality Where Killed: Devil Mountain, Archuleta County, Colorado

Date Killed: 2-25-04   Hunter: Dick Ray

Owner: Same   Telephone #:

Owner's Address:

Guide's Name and Address: Mike Ray,

Remarks: (Mention Any Abnormalities or Unique Qualities)

I, Tom Watts , certify that I have measured this trophy on 5-11-04
PRINT NAME   MM/DD/YYYY

at Jicarilla Game & Fish Department   Dulce   NM
STREET ADDRESS   CITY   STATE/PROVINCE

and that these measurements and data are, to the best of my knowledge and belief, made in accordance with the instructions given.

Witness: Tom Watts   Signature: Tom Watts   I.D. Number W 0 7 3
                                          B&C OFFICIAL MEASURER

COPYRIGHT © 2000 BY BOONE AND CROCKETT CLUB®

*Final score chart for Ray's cougar, which
scores 15-6/16 Points.*

*Cougar, scoring 15-8/16 points,
taken by Brice D. Folden near Trout Creek, Alberta,
in 2008.*

Fat Elvis

Brice D. Folden

27th Big Game Awards Program

MY LEGS WERE RUBBERY, MY LUNGS WERE BURNING AND THE SOUND OF BLOOD WAS RUSHING IN MY EARS. IN ORDER TO LOCATE WHERE MY TREED COUGAR WAS, I HAD TO HOLD MY BREATH FOR A FEW MOMENTS TO HEAR THE HAUNTING SOUNDS OF THE BAYING HOUNDS ECHOING ACROSS THE MOUNTAINSIDES.

"Ok, there they are, and I'm getting much closer. They sound like they must be just ahead in that patch of heavy spruce," I panted out loud in the thin mountain air.

A heavy shot of adrenaline pushed me onward and upwards, with heavy emphasis on the upwards. Wearily I climbed towards where my friend and outfitter Paul Pierunek of Timberline Guiding was impatiently waiting for me — the client he jokingly refers to as "Fat Elvis."

Before I continue, however, allow me a moment to describe the events leading up to this hunt and to explain my dubious new nickname. I did not receive this wonderful handle as a result of being overweight, nor for my prowess on stage. It was earned the previous year on my first cougar hunt with Timberline Guiding. Climbing steep foothills in insulated hunting clothing made me sweat as much as the King himself did while performing in concert.

I had first inquired about a mountain lion hunt 13 years earlier while still in college. The price of a hunt represented a fortune for a 23-year-old student saddled with rent, tuition, and a vehicle payment. However, the conversations I had with the outfitter only deepened my resolve to collect a big cougar.

Fast forward 13 years. The college student gets a little older and more financially secure. Despite dwindling wall space, there was still space for a life-size cougar mount in my trophy room, plus the desire to collect one still burning deep within me. Apparently, however, the mountains got a little steeper during the last 13 years.

I did my research and kept hearing about Paul at Timberline Guiding and his reputation for results. I spoke with Paul numerous times, and the hunt was booked for 2008. I can attest to the fact that you will not find a more honest or harder working guy to book a hunt with. Paul conducts traditional-style hound hunts. He runs experienced and highly trained hounds and possesses a high success rate for big cats.

Our first hunt had originally been planned as a horseback hunt deep in Alberta's Rocky Mountains. We intended to camp in wall tents for a week, while bowhunting for an elusive mountain lion. Plans changed when Paul phoned me one evening three weeks before our scheduled hunt. I could tell by the excitement in his voice that he had found an exceptionally nice track.

"Brice, can you come tomorrow?" he asked. "This tom has a 23-inch stride and toes bigger than a loonie." A loonie is the nickname for the Canadian one dollar coin.

"So does this mean he's a nice cat, Paul?" I inquired, as the dimensions he provided really meant nothing to me.

"He's an absolute Boone and Crockett mountain lion, Brice," he replied.

And just like that our mountain lion horseback hunt was scrapped. I jumped from behind my desk and immediately left my office for home to pack my bow and hunting gear and head for Sundre, Alberta, that very night.

Take my advice, don't go straight from a desk job to trying to climb mountains with your hunting guide, as you will discover in short order how good of shape you ARE NOT in. Invest some time improving your cardio or you may well end up with a dubious nickname like the one I received.

We hunted hard for five thoroughly enjoyable days. The scenery was breathtaking, and the hunt was highly informative. I learned to tell the difference between male and female cougars by the shape of their toes, as well as other traits concerning mountain lion behavior. It was exciting to watch the hounds work and to listen to them bay as they trailed the cougar.

We chased the big tom daily for several miles, but he just kept running and refused to tree. My guide and his excellent hounds did their best for me, and in all fairness to Paul and the dogs, we did pass on lesser cats. Prior work and family commitments put an end to our initial attempt for my trophy. I immediately booked a hunt for the following year.

I do not measure the success of a hunt with a tape measure. The memories and experience of that hunt are priceless to me. One long year and several hours on a treadmill later, I finally received that greatly anticipated phone call.

"Fat Elvis, drop everything and get in your truck and leave NOW! We've cut a huge track, another giant of a cat. Can you get here tonight? He is huge with toes like 'toonies,'" which is a reference to the Canadian two dollar coin. "This may be the biggest cat I've ever found; it's certainly in the top three!"

Paul sounded quite excited about this cat, but I felt he might have been pulling my leg a bit, as we've become good friends and we enjoy giving each other the gears.

"C'mon Paul, don't kid me. How big is be really? Is he about the size of the big one we hunted last year?"

"I'm telling you Brice, if you don't get here tonight, I intend to shoot this cat myself tomorrow. It's huge. Last year's cat was likely a 'Booner' as well, but this one is a truly exceptional cat. He doesn't even walk properly. His body sways like a big old bear waddles, and he smears his tracks. It's a giant, so get your bow and get down here!"

Paul has helped put several cats in the record book and into people's trophy rooms. He has treed well over a hundred mountain lions and has yet to harvest one for himself. I knew this had to be a particularly special cougar to have him excited enough for him to want to harvest it himself. To say that I was now truly pumped would have been a dreadful understatement.

It is still a family joke and the topic of great amusement about how I sped around the house like a madman finding my hunting gear and leaving my supper un-eaten at the table. It felt like the longest hour of my life, but my family is certain I was packed and gone in about 10 minutes. They also assure me I went a little crazy while doing so.

The following morning, Paul, Tyson, and I were on the big cat's track in the snow at first light. Glancing at the tracks, I knew what all the fuss was about. This track was clearly larger than the tom we chased the previous year, and it was very apparent that this was an enormous mountain lion.

Words cannot describe my anticipation, the beauty of the surrounding mountains, or how grateful I was for the opportunity to be there. It is something that is only understood by other hunters who have experienced the grandeur of Alberta's Rockies while pursuing the noble cougars that dwell there.

I also can't describe how hard Paul and his fellow outfitter Tyson Mackin worked for me that day. We followed the cougar's huge tracks over one ridge after another. The chase went on for several miles. The wily tom would climb a tree, and then jump several feet through the air to the ground in an effort to shake the dogs off his scent.

In desperation the big tom wound his way around the

mountainside, hooked up with a female and treed with her. When the hounds arrived at the tree, the crafty tom would bail out, leaving the female treed in an effort to ditch the hounds. Paul's experienced dogs would have none of it. They quickly sorted out his track and continued pursuit of the tom we were now referring to as "toonie-toes."

Repeatedly the old tom would circle, re-tree with the female, and then bailout trying to escape Paul's determined hounds. The day waned, and I began to think we would never tree the tom before dark. Then suddenly disaster struck.

We were out of hearing range of the hounds, so Paul suggested that Tyson and I return to the Ski-Doos and circle well ahead to see if we could hear them.

Meanwhile, Paul remained on foot trailing his hounds and our elusive quarry.

We were dropping down a steep slope into a gorge when Tyson's Ski-Doo slid out of control and rolled. I was following behind him and upon hitting the brakes my Ski-Doo also began a sideway's slide down the mountain. I was picking up speed and hurtling towards him. We can laugh about it now, but the look of concern on Tyson's face clearly indicated he thought he was about to meet his untimely demise by being run over by "Fat Elvis. I gunned the engine, roared off the trail into the trees and wrecked myself.

Our sleds damaged and pride bruised, we picked up gear strewn about the mountainside. Unfortunately, my Mathews bow had been heavily damaged in the wreck and was unusable. There is a lesson to be learned here about having your bow in a hard case for a hunt of this nature.

The hounds had treed the cat further up the mountain, meaning a long, hard climb up the steep, timbered slope in deep snow. I approached the large spruce tree where the hounds were baying and looked up at the sight I had anticipated for so long.

The muscular cat was crouched in the thick spruce, glaring disdainfully down at the noisy dogs and two humans that had been pursuing him relentlessly the entire day. Paul tied up the dogs as I prepared to collect my trophy with a .30-30 in lieu of my damaged bow.

At the first shot absolute pandemonium broke loose in the tree above me. Branches began breaking, tree bark rained down, dogs went ballistic and with an angry snarl the big tom began descending backwards down the tree.

I certainly do not feel the big cat intended to attack us. He was badly hurt and was simply trying to escape. Nevertheless, the moment was quite intense as he locked his unwavering gaze on us and did not so much as blink as he rapidly descended the tree.

I was standing only eight feet or so from the tree, trying to thread my next shot through the thick branches into his vitals. A split second later, I had an angry mountain lion at eye level with me. My final shot at uncomfortably close range left the mighty cougar in a heap.

Following some hearty handshaking we excitedly relived the hunt. Next Mick and Ginger we allowed to worry the tom's hide as a reward for their day-long chase and outstanding trailing job. Paul informed me that the stocky cat should exceed 180 pounds and was definitely a Boone and Crockett contender. He also declared it was quite likely the second largest cat he had ever taken.

It was then that we realized that in my haste I had left my camera and skinning knives in my hunting pack back at the Ski-Doo. Imagine my sheer delight at having to scorch my legs and sear my lungs on another trip down to the snowmobiles for my gear, and then back up the mountain. The picture taking session took place in near darkness. My long -awaited trophy far exceeded my expectations. The cougar ended up weighing in at 192 pounds and placed well into Boone and Crockett Club's record book with an official entry score of 15-9/16 points after the mandatory 60-day drying period. The score was later verified at 15-8/16 when it was re-scored by the 27th Awards Program Judges Panel in Reno, Nevada.

Incidentally, the big tom actually edged out Paul's previous largest cat to date. That monster scored 15-7/16 points

In closing I'd like to thank Paul and his talented hounds Mick and Ginger for all their hard work that resulted in our trophy of a lifetime. The entire experience is one I highly recommend to others.

Each time I look at the huge cougar on my wall, I recall the planning, the effort, the sights and sounds of that hunt. I still chuckle when I remember the look of concern on Tyson's face as I bore down on him with the Ski-Doo. The memories and friendships created on my quest for my cougar mean as much to me as the mountain lion itself and will be treasured for the rest of my life. 🐾

Elk & Deer

American Elk

Mule Deer

Columbia Blacktail

Sitka Blacktail

Whitetail

Coues' Whitetail

*Typical American elk, scoring 412-7/8 points,
taken by Doug Degelbeck in Utah County, Utah,
in 2006`.*

The Experience

Doug Degelbeck

26th Big Game Awards Program

My story began in the summer of 2006 when my wife, two boys, and I stopped by the Mule Deer Foundation banquet held in Midway, Utah. I had heard that they were auctioning off a muzzleloader Wasatch bull elk tag, and it piqued my interest. I purchased a dinner-for-four package, which included $100 worth of raffle tickets. Call me lucky, but I walked out with three guns, a bow, and the coveted Wasatch tag!

I was stoked about the upcoming hunt and couldn't wait to start scouting. I have to give credit to my wife and family because I dragged them up to the mountains every weekend we could manage from July to the week before the hunt to see if I could find the bull I wanted. Each week we went, I would video 10 to 15 bulls and go home and try to score them from the video.

The muzzleloader hunt was to open after the rifle hunt, and my dad, brothers, and sons wanted to be up there to see what was going on in my area. Opening morning of the rifle hunt seemed to be slow for those with permits, but we still saw 15 mature bulls and very few hunters, which made me all the more excited.

My dad and two brothers, Mike and Greg, wanted to be there to support me and help if I were to get one. The day before the opening, we set out with food, supplies and hopes for the big bull. I was planning on hunting the entire season, if necessary. On the other hand, I wanted to get a big one quickly because my wife was expecting our third son any day.

Opening morning came and my older brother Mike and I headed up a ridge where we had seen a lot of big bulls. We were able to get right where we wanted to be as the sun broke over the mountain.

At first light, we had a five-point bull within shooting distance. I passed it up because I knew there were bigger bulls in the area. We then spotted a big six-point bull with his harem of cows in the head of a canyon. We took off hiking but never saw this herd again, or anything else for that matter.

We hiked out in the dark, getting back to our trailer about 9 p.m. In the meantime, my dad had gone home to take care of his mink ranch and returned with my other son Easton, who is six. He was promised he could come the second day to hunt. My brothers went home because they had to work.

I was very discouraged. We watched a couple of hunting videos in the trailer that night and commented on how they made it look so easy. We talked about our strategy for the next day and decided my dad, Easton, and I would try a new area.

The next morning we hopped in the truck to go around the backside of the spot we had hunting the day before. From the road we spotted a nice 6x6 with 10 cows and two or three smaller bulls. We knew we needed to get closer. We started driving up a small side road to get closer, but it soon dead-ended. We decided to hike across several ravines to get to the elk.

At this point we split up. My dad went high, and Easton and I went low and moved slowly toward the elk. We had gone a short distance when several bulls started bugling back and forth. The brush was thick, and we were having a hard time staying quiet as we moved. Easton was full of quirky smiles as the elk bugled back and forth. We kept moving slowly toward the bugling when

I heard a branch break on the hillside above me. I knew my dad was in the area, so Easton and I stopped to see what was breaking the branches.

All of the sudden, I saw this huge rack coming through the quaking aspen and I told Easton not to move or even breathe loudly. The monster bull came running down the hill about 220 yards from us and then stopped to look back up the hill. I thought perhaps my dad had scared it down.

His pause gave me five seconds to take the freehand shot, which connected perfectly on this majestic animal. After the smoke cleared and I reloaded, I looked and the bull was gone. We had just stepped forward when the bull turned and came back down the hill. I could see from his reaction that I had hit him well. Within seconds, he put his head down and was on the ground. My boy and I gave each other big hugs.

Easton said, "Nice shot, Dad!" He was my good luck that day.

We sat down for a minute to regain our composure and then tromped through the brush to this amazing animal. I could not believe how big he was. I yelled out for my dad to come see. As he approached us and saw the huge rack on this six-point bull, the look on his face said it all. He gave me a big hug and said, "Good job! That's a monster, bud. What now?"

It was all the two of us could do to turn the elk over so we could field-dress the bull. We then headed down to get some help. I knew he was a big one. I also knew my wife would be happy that I was done in only two days!

I had no idea the attention this bull would get. A good friend of our family, John Gray, came over to score him for me. As he told me what he thought, I could not believe that I had killed an animal of that size. After the official 60-day drying period, the actual score was 412-7/8, which is the new World's Record muzzleloader typical American elk. In retrospect, I know I was just in the right place at the right time. 🦌

Typical American elk, scoring 404-1/8 points,
taken by Duane Chapman in Graham County, Arizona,
in 2007.

Brothers

Duane Chapman

27th Big Game Awards Program

To anyone familiar with the pursuit of big bull elk, the San Carlos Apache Reservation is a very familiar location. I am very fortunate in the fact that I reside on San Carlos Apache Reservation in San Carlos, Arizona. I have been hunting for several years and most of my hunting experience is on San Carlos. For local residences, we must qualify to get drawn on a lottery basis. I have been applying for several years in both hunting units of Dry Lake and Hilltop, the two top-producing units for world-class bulls. I was finally drawn for a trophy bull elk tag in the Dry Lake unit in December 2007. I never dreamed that I would have the opportunity to kill a 400-plus bull elk, especially in December.

After I purchased my tag, I was excited and could not wait for December to come. I was thinking of what type of rifle, ammunition, and other types of equipment I should be preparing for the hunt. I had started a daily exercise regiment because I knew how tough the rough country is around the Dry Lake unit. I also called my brothers, Commander Chapman Jr. and Danny

Chapman, to see what days they could get off work to assist me on this once-in-a-lifetime hunt. I wanted to have everything lined up and ready prior to opening day.

Once December 2, 2007, the first day of my hunt, arrived, I was so excited. I was up and out of bed at 2:45 a.m. I ensured that all of my equipment was loaded in the truck, then had a huge breakfast. After breakfast, I headed off to pick up my brother. The drive from home to Dry Lake was a good two and a half hours.

When my brother and I hunt together, we try to get onto a ridge top to look down into the canyons where we have had our best success finding the big bulls. The two of us prefer this type of hunting since we can cover more ground just by spotting and glassing for hours than just walking. Over the next couple days we spotted several bulls but none of them were the caliber of bull I was looking for.

My brother was still sure we could find something over 400 inches but my hope was starting to fade as the hunt continued. As a late season hunt, the biggest issue we faced was that many of the bulls had already broken off tines, and with points missing, it is nearly impossible to attain the 400-inch mark. I could feel the pressure mounting since my window of opportunity was closing and the odds of getting drawn for a bull elk again were slim to none.

We had spotted one bull that my brother estimated would reach 400 inches, but dense brush prevented us from closing the distance to where I felt confident taking the shot.

The two of us were hunting everyday, getting up at 2:45 a.m. and coming home at 8:30 every evening. Commander Jr. was the brother that I had been hunting with until that point, but work commitments required him to return home. I called my other brother Danny, and asked if he could come with me to hunt and he agreed. When Danny arrived, we continued with the same regiment, getting up early in the morning and coming off the mountain late. I was getting exhausted but the motivation to take a world-class bull kept me going. Tuesday evening, Danny and I saw a nice bull down in a canyon. After looking him over, I decided that he was a good bull worth some effort but I was just so exhausted, I couldn't make the two- hour hike into the canyon to try for a better look or shot. I took the next day off since my brother had to return to work and I needed some rest.

I slept in late that day and took my time getting ready to head into town. I couldn't get the thought of that big bull we had seen the night before out of my mind. I knew Commander Jr. would have the day off so I called him and he agreed to go with me for an afternoon hunt.

On the 90-minute drive up there, I told him about the bull Danny and I had seen the day before. We parked the truck where the road ended, got our gear ready, and checked our batteries in the GPS and flashlight. We started working up the trail, slowly and carefully glassing into the canyons on both sides of us. After about a half mile, we spotted the bull we thought we had seen the night before. He was on the upper third of the ridge and had seen us before we had gotten onto him. The bull started walking up and over the ridge but Commander Jr. calmed me by saying it was out of range and didn't even appear to be that good of a bull.

This slowed our pace considerably. The sun was dropping quickly and there was a storm forecast for the next two days. We continued on to a little over a mile from the truck. There was about an hour and a half of daylight left and we stopped to take a break for a minute. While standing there, we heard the distinctive sound of an elk hoof breaking a twig. We began carefully scanning the surrounding area and quickly picked up a good bull on the top portion of a close ridge. Commander Jr. pulled out the spotting scope just to verify that the bull would break 400 as he had predicted. After judging the bull through the scope, Commander Jr. told me it was near the 420 mark. I was so excited, but I knew it wasn't an ethical shot due to the fading light and distance. We sat and watched as the bull calmly fed across the ridge. We discussed a plan for the next morning and how I will have to hike up an extremely steep slope to get into position. We hiked out of the canyon at dark and went home.

I called Danny that night and asked him if he was ready to pack a 400-plus bull elk for me. He laughed and thought I was joking, but said ok. That night I couldn't sleep; I kept thinking this was a once-in-a-life opportunity. I just could not wait until morning. I only slept for three and a half hours that night and was up early for my huge breakfast. My brothers and I met at my dad's house and hooked up the Rhino (UTV). After arriving at the end of the road, I turned on my GPS and set it to lead me back to where I had left the bull the night before. We had left some of our gear there to make sure we could locate the spot in the morning, and after finding the stashed equipment, we knew we were in the correct spot. Commander Jr. and Danny set up there to watch as I hiked up the ridge to try and get into position. Darkness prevented me from being able to see anything other than my GPS unit that I could illuminate with my flashlight

As I climbed and fought my way through the brush, I was trying my best not to make a lot of noise. My heart was pounding and chest was heaving both from the strenuous climb and excitement as I neared the spot where I thought I needed to be. I found a nice rock to place my bag on and loaded my 7mm Remington Magnum. The sun was slowly rising over the next ridge across from me when the bull stepped out into a little opening where I could identify him. I put down my binoculars and picked up my rangefinder and ranged it at 230 yards. I found the bull's shoulder in the crosshairs of the scope on the 7mm Mag. and slowly squeezed the trigger. As the bull expired I couldn't help but think, Please don't fall and break any points. The bull was down with one shot. I was so happy, I was yelling to my brothers,

"I got it! I got it!" Commander Jr. asked if I was sure. I told him I definitely had the bull elk down.

I made my way over to the bull, not sure if he was as big as we had thought. When Commander Jr. got over to it, he confirmed that his original guess of a 420 bull was correct. After all the pictures were taken, we caped and quartered the elk. I'm glad Commander Jr. and Danny were there helping me pack the elk out. It took six trips down to the rhino and back up the hill.

After we returned home I called a friend of mine, Julius Hostetler, to come over and give me a rough score of the bull. He came up with 413, it was definitely the class of bull I wanted.

I took the bull over to a taxidermist in Payson, Arizona, and it was officially scored at 404 1/8, the score that was verified by the 27th Awards Judges Panel in Reno, Nevada. I received the bronze award from the Arizona Wildlife Federation.

I would like to give a huge thank-you to my hunting partners, Commander Chapman Jr. and Danny Chapman. They were both a great help during the whole hunt, especially helping me pack the bull elk out. Also, thanks to Mogollon Taxidermy who completed the measurements and did a great job with the shoulder mount. 🦌

*Non-typical mule deer, scoring 269 points,
taken by Lavonne M. Bucey-Bredehoeft in Weston County, Wyoming,
in 1961.*

Is She the One?

Lavonne M. Bucey-Bredehoeft

25th Big Game Awards Program

NEARLY 43 YEARS AGO, DAD TOOK OUR FAMILY ON WHAT BECAME THE HUNT-OF-MY-LIFE. I WAS 12 AT THE TIME AND THERE WAS NOT A SINGLE MOMENT THAT WAS NOT AN ADVENTURE.

You might say the "hunt" began when I was born. My dad, George R. Bucey, was sure that he was going to have all sons, so along with my brother, Erich, I received knives, rifles, and gear for all of the special occasions. I learned to hunt small game at an early age and was ready for deer in the fall of 1961.

Loaded in the pickup, with a homemade camper that Dad had made in about two days, we were off for Newcastle, Wyoming, and the 30,000-acre ranch of Vic Lesselo. We were prepared to rough it in the teepee that would sleep 12, with a fire in the center. My mom, Marie, had spent weeks sewing it on her Singer Sewing Machine and we all took turns holding the canvas to keep it straight as she sewed. Even though my sister, Marcie, did not hunt, she was involved. All we would need were the 24 lodge poles that we would cut when we got to the ranch. The drive out was non-stop; it was the only way Dad ever took a trip. The sooner we got there, the more time we had to hunt.

The first day was spent catching up on what everyone in camp had done the past year, setting up our teepee, and planning strategies for the next day's hunt. The result of the pow-wow around the fire was that Joe, a family friend who drove out with us, and his son would go together, Dad would take my brother, and I would go with Bob, Vic's son-in-law. He lived on the ranch and knew where the best hunting was. That was my advantage.

At first light, we drove a long distance from the ranch house. We parked the truck and each set of hunters went in a different direction, with a designated time to meet. It was a cold, sunny day in October. Bob and I walked for awhile and then paused by some trees. The noises of nature were all around, but no deer. It was nearing 10 a.m., and finally we spotted three. They winded us in time to run directly away from us, giving me nothing good at which to aim. We slowly and quietly followed.

We were at the edge of a wooded area when we spotted my deer. It seemed too far away. I looked at Bob; he nodded and mouthed, "Shoot."

I aimed, exhaled half of my breath, and fired. The deer stumbled and then bolted. We ran after it. The buck moved down a slope and dropped behind a log. All we could see was the rack. It got bigger the closer we got to it. Bob patted me on the shoulder and said, "You got it!"

Bob and I studied the buck for a long time. It was huge. All the way back to the truck we talked about what Dad would say and decided to cook up a story that I had shot a little spike buck.

It was late afternoon when we retrieved my deer. I will never forget Dad's face when he actually saw it. Expecting a spike, the closer he got, the slower he walked. He turned and said, "Are you sure you didn't shoot a small elk?"

Excitement erupted. Dad crushed me with hugs, as did my brother, who had taken a very respectable buck with a typical 5x5 rack.

Word spread quickly. Bob said that hunters had known of this buck for many years, so when Dad took me (with the guys) to the local coffee shop, I was the center of attention. I remember when we walked in, a gruff voice from the back said, "Is she the one?"

Since I was the only female in the place, I knew that meant me. I took two steps behind Dad, hoping to disappear. Dad then proceeded to tell everyone about teaching me to shoot the Rock Island .30-06 with peep sights (the same rifle with which he took his first deer). "I took her to the targets beside the barn and told her the rifle would kick. I pushed her shoulder hard with the heel of my hand to simulate the kick. She took the shot, hit dead on, and was nearly knocked off her feet. Her eyes got big and before she could react, I asked her if she was hurt. She said, 'no' and I told her to do it again. She did. Each time she was kicked and each time she went back and did it again. After she shot the buck, she was anxious to tell me that the rifle didn't kick anymore. I was afraid she would get buck fever and that she was just dreading the kick from the rifle."

For 41 years, the "39-point buck" (points we could hang a ring on) hung majestically on the wall overseeing the active life of my family. The buck became the silent member who was introduced to guests and silently acknowledged by friends who would come and go. It was never officially scored.

Just as Dad had introduced me to hunting, he introduced me to woodcarving. I took a class with Kirt Curtis, well known for his animal carvings. The project was to carve two mule deer heads and capes. I asked if I could carve the non-typical rack from the deer I shot when I was 12. He agreed. As the carving progressed, everyone wanted to know what it had scored. I decided that I would have it done so I no longer had to say, "It has never been scored."

It was officially scored at 269 points. The actual number of points is 27 and the greatest spread is 33 inches. And so, the hunt continues. Thanks, Dad! 🦌

Non-typical mule deer, scoring 306-3/8 points,
taken by Kyle Lopez in Douglas County, Colorado,
in 2007.

Gut Feeling

Kyle Lopez

27th Big Game Awards Program

BEEP, BEEP, BEEP! THE ALARM WENT OFF, SIGNALING THAT MY HUNTING SEASON HAD FINALLY ARRIVED. I ROLLED OVER TO MY NIGHTSTAND AND SILENCED THE ALARM, THEN JUMPED OUT OF BED. TO NO SURPRISE, MY DAD WAS ALREADY UP AND READY, ALONG WITH MY UNCLE. I GRABBED SOME BREAKFAST AND BEGAN TO GET READY. I HAD TO MAKE SURE I HAD ALL MY GEAR—RIFLE, KNIFE, CAMO CLOTHING, AND, OF COURSE, MY ORANGE. WHEN WE WERE READY, I RAN OUT TO THE TRUCK AND WE WERE OFF. IT TOOK ABOUT 35 MINUTES, IN THE DARK, TO GET TO OUR HUNTING AREA.

On the first day we chose to go to a more popular area to see how many hunters were out in the unit. After a long and hard day of hunting, I came home empty-handed. However my uncle harvested a great buck, which Dad green scored at 194. We hunted hard the next day, including a trip into the area where I would eventually take my trophy. On this first trip into the area I missed a great buck and once again came home empty-handed.

The next morning I had to go to school. I was still feeling frustrated and thinking about the buck I had missed. I was not able to hunt the next evening because of an after-school appointment to turn in football gear. That turned out to be an even more frustrating day; all I could think about was the buck that I had missed. We were not able to hunt for the next two days, but finally on November 7, 2007, Dad and I were both able to take off early one day. Dad said he had a gut feeling that it would be our lucky hunt. We decided to make a trip back into the area where I had missed; however, we had a different plan of attack this time. We quickly and quietly maneuvered our way up a deep creek bottom surrounded by steep hillsides on both sides, weaving in and out through the tangled maze of burned timber to the base of the mountain. It was a good three-mile hike. As we started to top out at the head of the creek, the hillsides became more visible. Dad paused for a moment and pulled up his glasses to look ahead while we still had the cover of the creek. He quietly whispered that there were two young does up ahead. I looked at them through my binoculars to make sure they were does as well. I just couldn't draw antlers on either of them. So we snuck around to their left. As we did, the does spotted us. We paused for a moment to see what they were going to do. The excitement was starting to build. Just the sight of those deer and how close we were to them made it feel as if we had stepped into their bedroom.

In that moment we were struck with luck. The does curiously started walking toward us. As we held our position, I could only wonder what was going to happen next. *Would the does finally realize what we were and blow out of the country, taking the rest of the forest life with them? Or would we be able to trick them and slip past to continue our quest for a buck?* They paused about 50 yards from us, discovered that we weren't deer and quietly trotted off. They left in the direction from where they had come, which worked in our favor. Dad's plan was to move away from them and toward a steep hillside that had lush, green vegetation on it.

As we turned toward the hillside, Dad stopped and looked ahead again. He said, "Kyle, there is a buck looking right at us." As Dad was looking through his glasses he told me it was definitely a mature buck worth shooting. Dad was standing next to a burned tree, and as he stepped around it, he told me to rest my rifle against the side of the tree to take the shot. As I got my first look at the buck through the scope, it appeared to be just what Dad had said. He was facing us, looking in our direction with an intense stare.

I steadied my breathing, let out my breath, held it, and squeezed the trigger—Pow! The buck jumped a mile high as the shot went off. As he turned in mid-air, his head immediately hit the ground, and like a bulldozer, he plowed his way over a small bluff. He collapsed out of sight. Dad exclaimed, "You got him Kyle, good job!"

We hugged as Dad's gut feeling about me getting a deer that evening came true. We gave the buck a little time (what seemed like hours) before we went to find him. The adrenaline was definitely flowing and the excitement welled inside me. Dad told me to get another round ready as we took off to go track him. When we arrived at the spot where we last saw the buck standing, we immediately found blood and tracked him about 50 feet. He was in a small ditch. As we were approaching him, it looked like he had fallen into an old dead bush. My dad told me to get my gun ready. My heart was pumping; I could see the grey color of his body as Dad picked up a rock and tossed it toward the buck's belly. As the rock hit and bounced off the buck's body, Dad said, "He's done, Kyle."

That is when our luck took an enormous turn for the better. As I was securing my rifle, I heard my dad say, "Oh my God." He just kept saying, "Oh my God, Oh my God," over and over. Neither one of us was prepared for what we found lying at our feet. We assumed I had shot a good buck, but never in our wildest dreams thought it was that tremendous. As I stood next to my dad, looking at the buck, there were so many points coming off his antlers, it looked as if the bush that he had fallen into had overtaken him. His antlers were heavy; it seemed as if there were hundreds of points going in all different directions. From that point on, there would be no words to describe the buck—at least not that anyone would believe without seeing it with their own eyes.

Dad gave me a big hug. We had several high-fives before we dressed out my deer and got him ready for the journey back to the truck. Dad had decided to drag the buck out; we were losing light, making it too difficult to quarter the deer. What should have been an hour-long pack-out turned into a four-hour ordeal through a creek bed knotted with twisted, fallen, burned timber. It seemed as if we would drag for a hundred yards then clear debris for a hundred yards. Finally, we made it to the truck and loaded up my deer. We had done it, and now everything was over—so I thought.

Not too long after killing my deer, the phone calls, emails, and many other things began pouring in. It first started with offers to write magazine articles for such publications as *Eastman's*, *Hunting Illustrated* (then-owned by King's Outdoor World), *Muley Crazy*, and *Trophy Hunter*. (Many articles were written by Greg Merriam.) Then it escalated into offers to attend and present my deer at the various hunting shows. That's when I got a phone call from the man who made most of this possible, Roger Selner. He was the one who escalated my fame for me.

There is just no way to explain the excitement and emotion over what we were looking at that day. I am very proud of myself and what I accomplished. I would like to thank the entire Eastman family for all the work they have put into my deer, King's Outdoor World for its article and calendars, Mel Siefke at Wildlife Recapture Taxidermy, and Greg Merriam for the articles he has written. However the two most important people I would like to thank are Roger Selner and my dad. 🦌

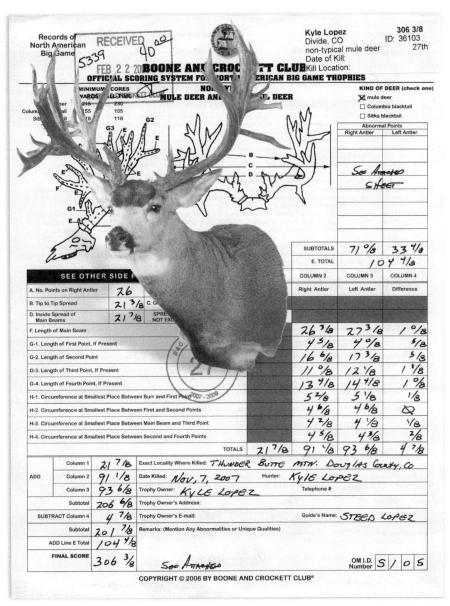

Final score chart for Lopez's non-typical mule deer, which scores 306-3/8 Points.

Typical mule deer, scoring 205-2/8 points,
taken by Jason Gisi in Sonora, Mexico,
in 2005.

Perfect Luck

Jason Gisi

27th Big Game Awards Program

WE ALL LIVE FOR THE ANTICIPATION OF THE HUNT. THE PROMISE OF A NEW ADVENTURE MAKES THE REST OF THE YEAR BEARABLE. AS I BOARDED THE FLIGHT TO HERMOSILLO, MEXICO, FOR MY ANNUAL DEER HUNT, I SMILED AT THE THOUGHT OF SEEING MY OUTFITTER AND FRIEND AGUSTIN HURTADO. I KNEW THAT HE WAS DRIVING AROUND HERMOSILLO, WOUND TIGHTER THAN A CLOCK, MAKING LAST-MINUTE PREPARATIONS TO ENSURE A SMOOTH AND SUCCESSFUL TRIP FOR ME AND MY FATHER.

Chad Smith, our guide, was probably down to the cuticle of his last fingernail worried to death about either: A) the big buck he had seen prior to our arrival, or B) the lack of a big buck to hunt the next morning. Chad takes enormous pride in doing his job well and as a result, he heaps tremendous pressure on himself to perform at the highest level possible. As a client, this is exactly what I want in a guide. As a friend, I sometimes wonder if his head is going to explode! His mind is not calm.

I had the pleasure of sitting next to a young endodontist from California who was headed south to hunt Coues' deer. He clearly had a passion for hunting and was quite knowledgeable about the overall trophy-hunting scene. As our conversation turned from elk to deer hunting, he made the comment that he was still searching for an opportunity to harvest a trophy mule deer. He asked my opinion after mentioning that he was on the waiting list of a high-profile ranch specializing in trophy mule deer. As I knew the property and those surrounding it, I commented that the chance to kill a big buck certainly exists and thought he would do just fine once his number came up. He then asked if my father and I hunted there anymore. I grinned and laid my standard reply on him, "Brian, I would mow lawns and walk to Hermosillo, if that is what it took to hunt deer in Sonora ever year!"

Admittedly, I have far more experience hunting Coues' deer in Sonora than mule deer. In fact, this was the first time I ponied up for the cost of a mule deer hunt in the last five years. All informed hunters recognize that the opportunity to harvest a super buck in Sonora still exists. However, it exists at a hefty price. In years past, I could never get comfortable with the price of the hunt versus the opportunity I perceived to bag a big buck. I hoped that this hunt would be the pay-off for all the research I had conducted in years past. Chad played a vital roll as well. He understood my concerns and worked diligently at seeking an opportunity that would fit my desires and those of my father.

As I disembarked from the plane, my predatory juices started flowing. The smell of Hermosillo's air always reminds me of hunting seasons past and the promise of adventure to come. After a quick lunch at the finest Mexican seafood restaurant on the planet, Marco's Los Arbolitos, it was off to Agustin's father's ranch to hunt mule deer.

At the ranch house, I got a look at shed antlers from a giant typical buck. What is it about sun-bleached white bone that can set a hunter's imagination on fire? If you love big deer, you love their sheds as much or more than the bucks themselves. I think it is the mystery that every large shed holds—so many questions that can normally never be answered. How big? How old? What would he look like today? Where the heck could he be? We caress and rub them while asking these questions. It's almost like we think that if we hold them long enough and rub them just right, a genie will pop out and answer our questions. It hasn't happened for me yet but I'm sure I'll keep trying until I die!

Cochillo, the foreman of the ranch, is the one who found the big sheds. And of course, the buck had not been seen in the previous three days that Chad and Matt had scouted the ranch. The fact that the buck had not been seen was no surprise. Chad's gut instinct told him to keep looking. With sheds from the two previous years found on the ranch, he felt that the buck had to still be there.

As Chad and I glassed that evening, we discussed the odds of the buck being around. Our friends, all more knowledgeable than us about mule-deer hunting in Mexico, had informed us on multiple occasions that the bucks tend to travel far due to the wide open spaces and low deer densities. Oftentimes, it is a waiting game as a hunter persistently checks the same groups of does for days on end during the rut in hopes of catching a big buck in their vicinity. This could mean that the "shed ghost" could be on our ranch or rutting a hot doe five miles in any direction. I glassed the same six does Chad had told me about. The only buck around them was a small 3 x 3. The does were near the highest glassing point on the property where we planned to start in the morning.

Gray light found Chad and me high above the desert floor, waiting on enough light to begin glassing. As I puttered around getting set up to glass, I heard Chad snapping his fingers behind me. As I turned and looked at him, I knew in an instant that he had found the buck that had produced the huge sheds. Chad's eyes looked the size of saucers as he exclaimed, "I found the typical!"

I couldn't help but laugh out loud. I was still hacking from the exertion of the early morning hike. The day was five minutes old. I had been hunting mule deer in Sonora for just over 12 hours after five years of researching the right opportunity. The giant buck we had hoped to find was incredibly 550 yards below us and Chad was up my nose for laughing when it was time to get down to business! Sometimes things just come together.

The pre-game pep talk from my new drill instructor went something like this, "What's so funny? I don't want you looking at the buck! Get your stuff packed up quick. We're going right at him before he slips out onto the flats! Keep up with me and don't make any noise!"

I told Chad to head down the hill and I would catch up with him. I thought he needed a little time alone to decompress. Hiking down the hill was more like a controlled slide. It was steep and covered with basketball-sized, loose, mini-boulders. I did my best to cover ground with a minimum of noise but it was impossible. I rushed a bit in a slide area and dislodged a 100-pound rock. As I lay still on my back, I prayed to the hunting gods that I hadn't just ruined my opportunity. I looked down past my toes and could see no running deer. Chad wasn't yelling, so I figured I was okay to proceed.

When I caught up with Chad, he instructed me to range the buck. I picked up the buck in an arroyo with my new Leica Geovid 10x42 BRF-Y binoculars and pressed the button. Just as the LCD read 318 yards, the buck turned and fed straight away from me. His rack extended well past both sides of his body and I let out an audible gasp. I was quickly reprimanded for not following instructions, as usual. We decided that if we had made it this far undetected, we could make the next rim rock below, putting us as close as we were going to get.

At the rim rock, the rangefinder read 247 yards to the tree we expected him to pass by. Two rocks were hurriedly stacked on top of each other and my backpack was balanced on top. The makeshift rest on the steep slope was complete. In the meantime, the buck had moved into a brush-choked arroyo. We had to wait. In hindsight, this was the best thing that could have happened. It allowed time to get my breathing and emotions under control prior to taking a shot that I knew might only present itself once in my lifetime. I tried not to think about the fact that I had never dared to dream of seeing a trophy of this size, let alone be minutes from squeezing off a shot at such a specimen.

I let Chad know that I was ready but was not going to look at the buck in order to relax. I told him to let me know when the buck was clear. I looked away and he narrated as the buck came out of the wash, walked behind a tree, and stepped broadside in the open. It was time! The crosshairs settled on his shoulder and we both saw a doe directly behind him so I couldn't shoot. I mumbled some choice words but stayed off of the trigger. The buck walked on, then moved from behind another tree and stopped broadside, clear of all obstructions.

I remember reminding myself that the downward angle was steep and I needed to hold low. At the shot, my high quality rest shifted, and I couldn't see the buck. Frantically, I tried to cycle the bolt while searching for the buck. I was thinking there was no way he could've gotten out of there that fast. I couldn't cycle the bolt because my right arm was pinned to my ribcage. Chad was hugging me yelling, "He's down! You hammered him!"

During the walk down to the buck I wondered if what had just happened was real or just another hunting addict's daydream. When we got close, I snapped back to reality. The buck was enormous! Chad asked how big I thought the buck was and I stammered incoherently that I didn't have a clue and it didn't matter. I was completely humbled by this magnificent buck, knowing full well that I could hunt a thousand lifetimes and never have this experience again. It was way too much to absorb at the time. His antlers were massive, long-tined, and tapped 35 inches wide. Later, the rest of our party arrived on the scene. The whooping and hollering started immediately and then quickly subsided, as we all stood there in awe of the magnificent buck.

For the rest of my life, my friends and acquaintances will ask me about the events of January 8, 2005. I will never have a story heroic enough to match the size of the buck. I had done more homework than the average guy in hopes that it would increase the odds of replacing my daydreams with reality. My greatest contribution on that fateful day was making the shot and not folding under pressure like I have done in the past. The simple fact will always remain that I was in the right place at the right time. As in life, we are all only as good as the ponies in our stable. Without my father's guidance, the hard work of Chad and Agustin, the understanding of my wife Tammi, and the friendship of all, my experiences, could not have been possible. 🦌

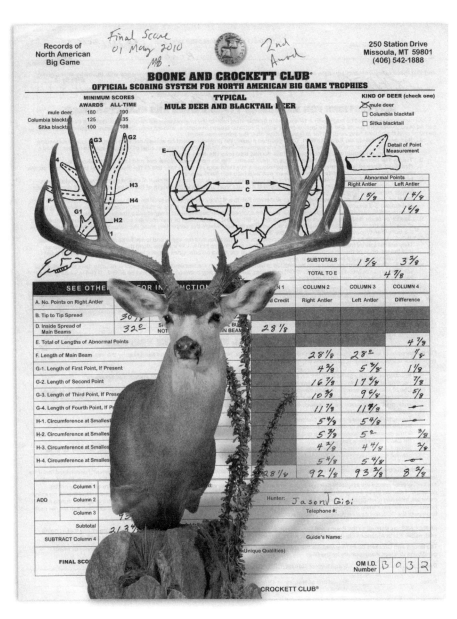

Final score chart for Gisi's typical mule deer, which scores 205–2/8 points.

Typical Columbia blacktail, scoring 155-7/8 points,
taken by J.L. Bennett & F. Duell in Pierce County, Washington,
in 1983.

Hunting Partners

Jim Bennett and Floyd Duell

19th Big Game Awards Program

IT WAS THE OPENING DAY OF THE OCTOBER 1983 DEER HUNT-
ING SEASON. WE HAD STAYED UP LATE THE NIGHT BEFORE
PREPARING FOR A TRIP INTO AN AREA WE HAD EXPLORED THE
PREVIOUS SUMMER THAT WE HOPED WOULD PRODUCE SOME BIG
BUCKS. IT WAS OUR THIRD YEAR OF HUNTING TOGETHER, AND
WE HAD BEEN VERY SUCCESSFUL AT TAKING BOTH DEER AND
ELK WITH BOWS AND RIFLES. THIS WAS A RIFLE HUNT, AND WE
WERE BOTH LOOKING FORWARD TO HUNTING AND LEARNING A
NEW AREA.

It was an area about two hours drive from where we live
in Olympia, Washington. More precisely, it is southeast of the
small town of Buckley, Washington, located in Pierce County. It
is an area of steep terrain, mostly covered with second growth fir
and alder, with some brushy draws we felt would be productive.

Legal time to shoot wasn't until 7 a.m., but as is our custom,
we like to arrive and be in place well before daybreak. So, Jim
picked me up that morning at 4 a.m., after only a few hours of
shut-eye for each of us. With a couple cups of coffee in us, and
a lot of good-natured razzing, we were raring to go when we arrived right on schedule about a half-hour before sunup. We had
driven to a high ridge with the intention to hunt down it into

some good-looking patches of timber. When we arrived, the wind was blowing straight across the ridge at better than 20 miles per hour and raining about as hard as it can rain here in Washington (which is one helluva lot). Both of us dislike wearing all that noisy raingear, but this certainly was going to be an exception. We compromised and decided to wear only rain jackets, leaving the noisy rainpants in the truck.

As we set in the truck sipping coffee, we listened to the rain beat sideways against the truck and we could feel the truck move as it was buffeted by strong gusts of wind. We both looked at each other. Someone made the comment that the only other person crazy enough to leave a warm bed, with little sleep, drive for two hours to the top of a ridge to go walking around in a driving rain is a duck hunter, and as everyone knows, they are totally crazy!

We had driven to the end of a road. As we anxiously waited for daybreak, we both hoped other hunters wouldn't show up at the last minute and cause us to get started before we could see in the timber. We were also somewhat concerned that the timber may not be the best place to be with the high winds. However, it was second growth and a pretty thick stand, so we figured it would be all right. Our luck held good; no other hunters showed up. I guess the sensible hunters were down low, out of the storm.

As soon as it was light enough to see antlers, we flipped a coin, with Jim winning the toss. He elected to go down the ridge and hunt parallel with me, while I stayed nearer the top of the ridge. We hunted this way for several hours, meeting up with each other at pre-determined places to compare notes. We hunt well together and pretty well know each others pace and habits. With the use of hand signals, we can do a lot of "communicating" several hundred yards apart.

We had both jumped several does, and another hunter had downed a small buck, but we had yet to see a deer with antlers. We weren't discouraged though; the storm had broken and the sun was out, and neither one of us was "back at the office" doing paperwork.

It was close to 11 a.m. when I spotted Jim and made my way over to the edge of the timber to plan our next move. Since the weather had been so poor the night before, we figured a nearby draw might still be holding a few late-feeding deer and we walked over together to have a look.

When we got to the draw, I sat down to get out my binoculars while Jim gave the draw the once over. I had just bent over, when Jim exclaimed, "There's a buck!" Even though he had said it in hushed tones, I knew Jim had seen a "keeper." I looked where Jim pointed, about 175 yards away, and I could see a very nice buck looking straight at us at the top of a hill. You didn't need binoculars to see those antlers. They were silhouetted against a blue sky and were quite large.

I raised my .30-06 and turned the variable scope up to eight power to get a good look at the buck. I watched the buck as Jim quickly looked for a rest. The walk had been up hill, we were both a little winded, and the front of a deer isn't the largest target if you want a clean kill. As I watched the buck through my scope, I could tell he was getting very nervous and I hoped Jim would shoot quickly. I didn't shoot, as Jim had seen the buck first and by rights should have first crack at it. I told Jim the buck was going to go and he had better shoot or get off the pot! He raised his .270 Ruger, which was enough for the buck. As he started to go, I fired, at the same time as Jim. The buck went down hard and I knew we had us a fine animal. But, before we could catch our breath, that buck was up and running. I could tell he wouldn't go far, but sometimes they can fool you, so we each fired one more round, putting the buck down for good.

The shots had startled a couple of deer below us, so Jim took a stand while I made my way over to the buck. We jumped two more does but no bucks. Our buck had gone over the crest of the hill and died very quickly. It was the biggest buck either of us had ever seen on this side of the mountains.

The easy part was over. We were at least a three-mile walk, uphill, to the truck, with about four hours of daylight left. While we didn't weigh the buck, we estimated the weight to be in the neighborhood of 250 pounds. The pack boards were back at the truck, and we figured it would be past dark by the time we got them and came back to the buck. So, we caped and quartered the buck and left it hanging in a tree, not sure when we would make it back. After a tough three hour-climb, we were back at the truck. We decided to return home to pick up our Honda Trail 90's which would allow us to use a ridge trail to cut our packing distance in half.

By the time we got to Olympia, loaded the bikes and grabbed a sandwich, and made the return trip, it was close to 9 p.m. I had talked my wife Pam into coming with us to see the big buck. I assured her this wouldn't be one of our "wild-hair" trips, it would only take a couple of hours and she wouldn't get cold, as she could wait at the truck. Jim's wife, Laura, couldn't go as she had to take the car and their daughter Anya. (Or, maybe she just knew us too well.)

We unloaded the Hondas and headed down a ridge trail into a fog shrouded patch of old-growth timber. Several times we missed the trail in the fog, ending up down the side of the ridge. We would then have to "muscle" the bikes back up to the trail. About the fifth time this happened, we weren't so sure how much of an energy saving device these bikes really were.

After a couple of hours of these fun-and-games, we decided we were a little lost and had missed the ridge we wanted. We decided to turn around and very, carefully look for the other ridge. We had only gone about 50 yards when my trailbike quit. Being a patient man (and having left my rifle at home), I couldn't shoot the damn thing, so I began checking the spark, etc. Well, as it turned out, I had to take the entire carburetor apart and clean the jets with only the aid of one of those "disposable" flashlights. Our other light had been lost when we went on one of our off-trail excursions earlier.

I was rewarded though, as it fired right up when I got it back together. It ran fine for a whole hundred yards before it quit again! I had just bought the bike from a guy who had stored it in his garage for five years without draining the gas tank. I unscrewed the gas cap and looked inside; I've seen frog ponds that were cleaner!

We shoved and pulled my bike until we found the ridge we were looking for. We left my trail bike there and headed out on Jim's, when Jim remarked that we had forgotten to put gas in his bike. Upon checking his tank, we found it was almost empty and would never get us back to the truck. We also found the key to Jim's truck and realized there would be no way for Pam (remember Pam, my long-suffering wife) to keep warm in the truck.

We went back to my bike with the intention of straining the gas from it into a container to then put into Jim's bike. That was a fine idea until we discovered that we had no container. Jim did manage to find a used plastic sandwich bag, with holes in both corners. (Have you ever tried to pour gas out of a baggie with holes in it, into a little round hole in a gas tank? In the dark?) Well, we managed to soak our pants and the ground, and we even got about a quart of gas into Jim's bike.

Off we went, down the ridge riding double on Jim's bike. After our third spill, we decided to walk. We finally found our marker, don't ask me how, and by another stroke of luck walked right down to the deer. By this time it was almost 4 a.m. and we had been up some 24 hours on very little sleep. In our shape, there was too much deer to pack in one trip, and not enough to pack in two trips. Know what I mean? So we each made one trip back to Jim's bike, then he made trips back to my disabled bike while I made the last trip.

Finally, a little past daybreak, we had the deer mostly loaded on the disabled bike, with part of it on the back of Jim's. With a lot of pulling, shoving, cursing, and muscle, we got back to the truck at approximately 9:30 a.m. We found Pam huddled on the floor of the truck, covered only by our unused rain pants, and very cold. My, "Hello honey, look at the nice buck," wasn't met with the greatest of interest. All in all, she was a pretty good sport; it was several months later that she divorced me.

Thirty-six hours after our little adventure began, we had the deer hanging in Jim's garage, clean as a whistle, and we were headed for the sack and some much needed rest.

We were both so sore the next few days that we could hardly walk, but we were laughing and looking forward to our next adventure together. Neither of us knew we had a buck that would make the records books, and I was surprised when Jim told me how high it had scored. We split the cost of having the cape mount done, and now we each take turns displaying the rack in our living rooms.

While neither of us will ever know which bullet did the old buck in, I don't think either of us really cares. We shared the work, we shared the costs, we shared the fun, and we'll share the credit. After all, that's what having a hunting partner is all about. 🦌

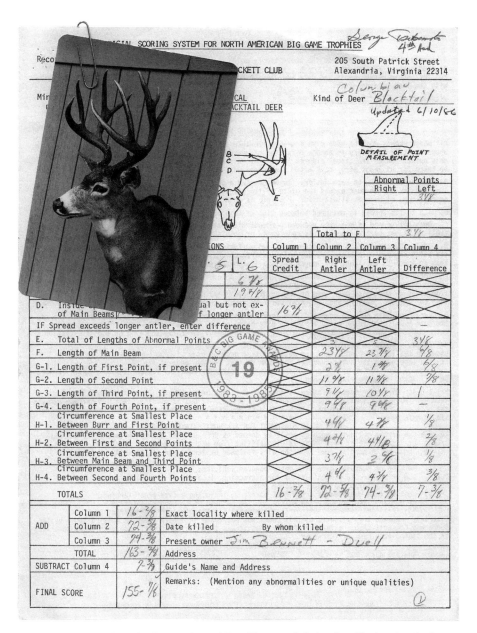

Final score chart for Bennett's and Duell's typical Columbia blacktail, which scores 155-7/8 Points.

Non-typical Columbia blacktail, scoring 185-1/8 points,
taken by J. Peter Morish in Trinity County, California,
in 2005.

Trinity Alps

J. Peter Morish

26th Big Game Awards Program

THE VIEWS ARE BREATHTAKING, THE AIR IS CLEAN, AND THE HUNTING IS EXCEPTIONAL. FOR TWENTY-SEVEN HUNTING SEASONS, I HAVE EXPERIENCED ALL THAT THE TRINITY ALPS HAD TO OFFER. FOR ANYONE WHO DESIRES TO HUNT PUBLIC LAND AND WANTS A MEMORABLE HUNTING EXPERIENCE, THE TRINITY ALPS MAY BE THEIR DREAM AREA; IT HAS BEEN FOR ME.

I have taken many deer in the Trinity Alps, both small and big. As the years passed, I became more specific on what size of deer I wanted to harvest. I found that passing up a legal buck was just as rewarding as taking a deer. When I got to the point of passing up a decent four-point buck to try for a larger one, then I knew that my perspective on hunting had changed. Most hunters in the United States don't associate good hunting with California, especially trophy deer hunting; however, I do.

The name Alps speaks for itself. Though the height of the Trinity Alps does not come near to the elevations found elsewhere, the steepness and ruggedness of the back country rivals the most well known of tough hunting areas. Add to this the thick underbrush and you have a challenge for even the most seasoned hunter. The blacktail is certainly not as well known, or even hunted as much as the mule deer or the whitetail deer. However, it is every bit as much of a challenge and worthy adversary as any other species of deer. For many, the blacktail is one of the most difficult deer to hunt. To find a nice buck is a difficult and oftentimes daunting and consuming task. A trophy buck can require a lifetime of hunting. If you are able to hunt hard and choose to do so, then a trophy can be found in the coastal mountains of northern California.

As I have done for twenty-six prior seasons, I headed for my favorite hunting grounds in mid-September of the 2005 season. I often choose to not hunt the opening weekend because of the increased hunting pressure. After the opening weekend, the number of hunters in the backcountry drops significantly. Usually, the only hunters you see, if any, are those like yourself who have also hunted the area for years.

On this particular weekend, I planned on going with a hunting buddy but, at the last moment, he cancelled. Hunting in the wilderness is certainly not something I would recommend someone doing on his or her own. However, being that I had been planning this hunt since the end of the prior season, I decided to go anyway.

The first leg of my hunting trip was to drive to the trailhead. I arrived early on a Friday morning. It was mid-September, which is often just an extension of summer. This day was clear, with temperatures in the low 90s. Though this area is known for hunters who horse pack into the wilderness area of the Trinity Alps, I had chosen to backpack. I did this because I have been able to do so physically and because I just didn't want those who would pack me in to know just how well I did hunting. It takes about seven hours of hard hiking to reach my camp. It is only about four or five miles, but the terrain is either up or down.

By the time I got to camp, I was extremely tired and sore. I was reminded of earlier hunts when it was difficult but not so consuming, and I wondered how much longer I would be able to do this kind of hunting. But, I was here now and tomorrow would begin another hunting season.

First, I needed to set up camp. When backpacking, you learn to pack in only the essentials. If you do get a deer, then you will be packing out both the deer and all your gear. This can be a very heavy pack if you do not wisely choose what you bring. If I did get a deer, I would bone out the deer, cut the antlers off the head, and take the cape if the deer is a trophy animal. One of the positives of hunting the blacktail deer when backpacking is its size. It is smaller than mule deer or whitetail, so packing out the meat isn't too bad.

My camp was relatively simple. Over the years, I had cut out a level pad in a timber stand on the side of a mountain. This time of year the weather is often very nice, so a tent is not needed. I will lie out under the trees and peer through the tops to watch the stars. This is when I think about what tomorrow may hold and where I would hunt. The air was still and the skies were clear. Not the best conditions for hunting, but I was in the backcountry of the Trinity Alps and anything was possible.

The hunting area is so steep, rugged and dense with brush that you just don't do any walking or stalking for deer. The area I wanted to hunt overlooks two ravines and a sidehill. It usually takes me about 30 minutes in the dark to find the rock outcropping where I would sit for the next three or so hours. From this place I would setup and spot for any deer that might be around.

I awoke well before dawn. I took my pack, which has an external frame. It comes in handy should I need to pack out a buck. I left for one of my favorite hunting sites.

I hiked out of the timber from camp and into a manzanita patch on the south side of the mountain. I snaked my way through brush and finally came to my rock. It was still dark and I had made little noise. I had made this trek from camp many times and I can do it in the dark with the help of a small flashlight, which I keep pointed on the path in front of me and toward the ground. I didn't want to alert the deer or other hunters that may be across the canyon. As I quietly set up on the rock, I began to see the faint light of the sunrise to the east. I could see the outline of part of the Alps. It was very quiet and still.

I use a lightweight eight power pair of binoculars and find

that binoculars are the most important item in harvesting the deer other than my weapon. I began this morning by slowly working my binoculars across the hillside just adjacent and below me. With the binoculars, I continued to follow two ravines below the rock I was sitting on. I began to glass a second time, starting with an area directly across from me. I looked intently into an opening in the brush patch. The rays of sun were beginning to show over the mountains, but it was still relatively dark in the lower parts of the canyon.

I saw something across from me that looked out of place, but I couldn't see if it was a deer or just a shadow. I looked away and began to look lower on the hillside. It was still quiet and I hadn't heard or seen anything. I looked back at that spot adjacent to me and felt that something just wasn't right. I again looked intently, but I wasn't convinced that there was anything there. It was less than 100 yards away and I figured that I should be able to see a deer if it was there.

I looked downhill and then felt I needed to look back to that partial opening again. As I studied the area with my binoculars and as the light was getting better, I thought I saw what looked like a fork to a set of antlers. I just wasn't sure because there was so much brush in the area and things were not clear. As I was straining to see what was in the brush, I saw the entire top of the brush patch move slightly! I realized immediately that I had spotted a buck and the brush that moved was the deer's rack! I couldn't tell how many points it had but, as it moved, the rack looked to be the extensions of the brush patch that it was standing in front of!

I had seen and shot many big blacktails but rarely had my heart begun to race at the sight of a deer. This was certainly the exception and my heart was pumping fast. It was now getting light enough that I could make out the outline of the deer's body. The deer was facing uphill and the front half of the body was behind a brush patch. Only his antlers from the middle of the ears up were visible above the brush. In the opening of the brush I could see from the middle of the deer's body to its back end. I immediately thought that all the buck had to do was take one step forward and he would be safe. From where he was standing, there was a steady and thick patch of brush running up the mountainside. If I was to get this deer, I was going to need some luck.

My gun was already positioned on the rock on top of my pack. I quietly slid down onto my stomach and positioned the gun toward the deer. I located the deer in my scope, which I later determined to be 65 yards away, and to my surprise it was still standing in the same position. I could see him from midway back and felt this was going to be my only chance. Because of the size and number of points to the antlers, I was going to have to give it a try. I decided I had a pretty good chance of getting this buck if he would just stay still for another few seconds. If I could get a spine shot midway on the deer, it would be fatal. Being that the deer was as close as he was, I decided to take the shot. I lined up on the deer, held steady and shot!

Through the scope, I saw the buck flinch and take a step backward. As I pulled away from the scope, I looked up to see the buck take another backward step and fall to the ground. He fell partially in the open in the brush, but only enough to see part of the body. He was down on his side and wasn't getting up.

It took a couple of minutes to compose myself and realize what had just happened. I knew I had just harvested a deer and he was huge, possibly the largest deer I had yet taken. It was still very early, so I decided to sit on the rock outcropping and relish the moment. I sat on that rock for an hour watching the sunrise and taking in the beauty that was revealed before me. The morning colors seemed brighter and the view even more majestic. I thought then that I probably had shot the deer of a lifetime. It had taken 27 years for my dream of a trophy to come true, but it happened and it occurred in the most beautiful area I have been fortunate enough to hunt — the Trinity Alps. 🦌

Typical Sitka blacktail, scoring 114-7/8 points,
taken by Darin L. Crayne on Alaska's Revillagigedo Island,
in 2007.

Three Dollars

Darin L. Crayne

As told by Jack Reneau

27th Big Game Awards Program

D ARIN L. CRAYNE WAS FIVE YEARS OLD WHEN HIS FAMILY MOVED TO ALASKA IN 1971. HIS FATHER, A COMMERCIAL FISHERMAN, PREFERRED TO HUNT ROCKY MOUNTAIN GOATS AND MOOSE, BUT INTRODUCED HIS SON AT AGE 14 TO SITKA BLACKTAIL DEER HUNTING ON ADMIRALTY ISLAND. BECAUSE HIS FATHER HAD SERIOUS CONCERNS ABOUT THAT ISLAND'S HUGE BROWN BEARS THAT CAME RUNNING AT THE SOUND OF GUN-SHOTS, HE HUNTED SITKA DEER ALONE DURING HIS JUNIOR AND SENIOR YEARS IN HIGH SCHOOL ON WOEWODSKI ISLAND, WHICH IS LOCATED 75 MILES SOUTH OF THEIR HOME IN WRANGELL.

After spending three years at Fort Bragg in the 118th Air-borne Corps, Darin returned to Wrangell and spent three more years hunting Sitkas on Woewodski Island. Eventually, he moved to Ketchikan, Alaska, where there are countless opportunities to hunt Sitkas on nearby Prince of Wales Island and numerous other neighboring islands.

During this time, Darin did a lot of trapping and com-mercial fishing. He also worked on a tug boat that set up and dismantled remote logging camps. Four years prior to taking his trophy buck, he helped set up a logging camp in Lucky Cove on Revillagigedo Island. When he helped take the camp out a year later, he noticed lots of does and immature bucks along the shoreline. He took a short hike inland and found some great rubs (blazes) that had to have been made by some huge bucks. All of these experiences gave him a good, basic knowledge of what Sitkas are all about, and he began formulating plans to return to Lucky Cove in three years for a Sitka deer hunt. He knew the buck that had made those blazes wouldn't be there, but he figured the immature bucks he saw would be "booners" by then.

The actual hunt for Darin's trophy Sitka started in Ketchikan where he hired Carson Lindli, the owner of the yacht Capella (formerly owned by heavyweight fighter Jack Dempsey) to take him and one friend to a remote location. Darin was very secretive about where he was going. Not only didn't he tell his friends were he was going, but he didn't even tell Carson where he was taking them until they dropped anchor in Lucky Cove. The only thing he told Carson was, "This is my Boone and Crockett hunt." Darin knew this was going to be his last Sitka deer hunt before his upcoming move to the lower 48 states, and he wanted to get his trophy-of-a-lifetime.

On the first day of his hunt, he lowered the Capella's skiff into the water and headed for shore. He first looked for big rubs where the logging camp had been, but didn't find any. It was the rut, and if there were any big bucks in the area, there would be big blaze marks on the trees where they rubbed.

Darin hunted until about two hours before dark, when the weather turned nasty. The wind was blowing 50 mph, and the rain was coming down in horizontal sheets. He hadn't seen anything all day and was getting discouraged when he came upon a small muskeg opening with a pond in it. No deer were present, so he noted it and moved on with plans to check it out on the way back to the boat.

When Darin returned to the muskeg, he blew his deer call and brought in a three-pointer he promptly dropped with one shot. While traversing the muskeg to retrieve his buck, he spotted three does, two spikes, and a forked-horn buck off to his left. The bucks bolted, but the forked-horn returned after Darin grunted on his call. Darin dropped that buck, then field dressed and boned out both deer and was back on the boat at 6 p.m., which is about two hours after dark that time of year.

The bad weather continued through the night. In fact, it was so bad that the yacht was blown off anchor twice, and they had to reset it closer to shore. It was still miserable when he headed out in the morning.

As the next day wore on, Darin became more discouraged. It was near dark when he was about to turn around and head back to the boat when a forked-horn ran down the ridge to his left. He paused at 150 yards, and Darin dropped him with one shot. As he approached this buck, he looked off into the logged-over basin below him, and to his surprise, he could see buck blazes, huge buck blazes, and lots of them from the top of the basin to the bottom. There were so many, he quit counting at 32. After three days of hunting, he had finally found the hunting area he was looking for, but it was too late to hunt any more that day, so he dragged the forked-horn out and took the skiff back to the Capella.

That evening he made himself a doe deer call from two bamboo stirring sticks and a rubber band that came off a broccoli bunch in their refrigerator. He also started teasing his hunting companion who still hadn't even seen a deer saying, "I have found my boonie."

The weather that night was more of the same as the previous night. The wind would blow the yacht off anchor and the captain would have to move it closer to shore and reset the anchor. However, the morning was different than any other. When Darin scraped the frost off the cabin windows, it was a clear, sunny day. He told his partner, "It is a Boone and Crockett morning!"

Once he was back on the mainland that morning, he jogged all the way back to where he had seen the blazes the night before. As he drew nearer, he slowed down to a walk so that his heart could slow down, and he could make a steady shot if the opportunity presented itself.

He tucked himself between a log and a stump about 50 feet up in the basin. There was about 10 years of second-growth in the basin with only one opening and a beaver pond off to his right. He blew his new call the first time and waited. Nothing happened so he blew it two more times at 10-minute intervals. He knew that if he didn't have any action after three tries, it was counterproductive to try a fourth time. In fact, more than three calls tend to spook deer.

After the third call he turned his head slightly to the left and spotted a buck standing broadside on top of a rocky knob facing to the right just below him. He pulled the covers off his scope and slowly laid his .270 Remington across the log in front of him. He sighted right behind the armpit, flipped the safety off, squeezed the trigger, and heard the most deafening "click" he had ever heard. He slowly eased his rifle back over the log, chambered a round, and again laid the rifle across the log. To his great surprise, the buck was still standing there. He sighted again on the armpit and squeezed the trigger.

This time, there was no loud "click." At the sound of the shot, the buck turned and made two hops into the brush like he wasn't even hit. Darin's mouth was dry, his heart was racing, and he was mad at himself. He couldn't believe he missed.

A half-hour later, Darin walked down to the rocky knob where he found a piece of lung tissue the size of his thumb. There was no blood or any other evidence of a hit. However, he knew the buck was his. Now he just had to find him in the dense underbrush. The ferns and underbrush were all red because it was November, so he couldn't see any blood even if there was some. He started searching in the direction the deer had run, but the brush was so thick that he had to plow his way through it backwards.

For the better part of two hours, he was down on his hands and knees unsuccessfully crawling through the brush knowing that he was going to spend the rest of his life looking for his deer, if necessary. He knew it was there, and he wasn't coming out without it.

When he was about 200 yards from the rocky knob he decided to head back up to it. He was 20 yards from the knob when he stepped on the white belly of his buck lying totally concealed in the brush. He reached down, grabbed him by the nose, and pulled him up to get a good look at the antlers. It was the prettiest thing he had ever seen, and the rack had all the features he expected and wanted in a big rack.

It was a struggle to get his buck up the hill out of that basin, but it was all worth it. On the way back to the boat, he ran into his hunting companion who hadn't even seen a deer and promptly reached into his wallet and settled their bet by handing Darin three dollars for getting the first buck, the heaviest buck, and the largest antlers. As he handed him the money, he told Darin, "You got your boonie!" 🦌

Typical whitetail deer, scoring 201-1/8 points,
taken by Bradley S. Jerman in Warren County, Ohio,
in 2004.

Determination

Bradley S. Jerman

26th Big Game Awards Program

THE FIRST TIME I SAW THE BUCK WAS AT LAST LIGHT THE NIGHT BEFORE TAKING HIM. I'D TAKEN MY VIDEO CAMERA WITH ME FOR THE AFTERNOON HUNT TO FILM SOME DOES AND A SMALL BUCK I'D SEEN THAT MORNING. THE VIEW WAS POOR BECAUSE THEY WERE 150 YARDS AWAY IN SOME TREES, AND IT WAS GETTING DARK QUICKLY. NOISE TO MY RIGHT MADE ME TURN THE CAMERA JUST IN TIME TO SEE THE MONSTER EMERGE FROM A THICKET ABOUT 125 YARDS AWAY. I DID MY BEST TO KEEP MY HANDS STEADY AS I CAPTURED 45 SECONDS OF VIDEO BEFORE HE ANGLED AWAY AND DISAPPEARED INTO THE DARKNESS.

Even though I could no longer see him or the other deer, I knew they were less than 200 yards away, and there was only some light timber and a few thickets between us. It was at this point that my brain stopped working. I believe it short-circuited due to overload. I called my wife on my cell phone and told her I planned to spend the night in my stand. I thought this would be the best way to keep from alerting the deer to my presence. I was in a comfortable tripod on private property and thought I could make it.

Surprisingly, she didn't offer any protest. She knows I'm a nut when it comes to hunting, so she simply accepted the call as standard strangeness. She wished me well after mentioning that I was missing one of my favorite Mexican dinners.

Reality set in a few hours later. I was dressed for an afternoon hunt and missing several layers of clothes that would've made the stay possible. I just couldn't take the cold. So, with my crossbow perched on the shooting rail of the tripod, I removed the arrow and placed it on the platform and slowly descended the ladder. I wanted to stay as unhampered as I could, knowing I would be back well before light.

I crawled from the thicket where my stand was, staying on my knees for another 100 yards across a mowed field opposite of where the deer were. With the camera tucked in my jacket, the exit seemed to go well.

Once home, I headed straight for the TV to play the tape. My wife, surprised to see me, quickly gathered my three children. We watched the video in amazement. The video was dark, but his antlers were bright white. He was magnificent.

I began preparing for the next day's hunt. I laid out some extra layers and covered my camo with scent-free spray. I readied a daypack in preparation for an all-day hunt if needed, remembering to include some heat packs, which I was so desperately missing earlier that evening.

After tinkering with everything, I lay down and tried to get some rest, but my mind was still buzzing. I found myself nervously looking at the clock every few minutes. I was not going to sleep, even though I tried for a couple more hours.

At 2 a.m., I decided that if I was going to be that wide awake, I might as well be in my stand. I raided the fruit bowl and headed for the shower. At that time, I had no idea how important being scent free was going to be.

By 3 a.m. I was back at the edge of the field and decided that I should crawl back in. It took me 45 minutes to cross the 100 yards back to the thicket. While still on my knees, I hung a scent bomb on a limb just behind my stand.

I was proud to have gotten there without making a sound, but that arrogance was quickly dashed. As I stood, a briar that had latched on to one of my pant legs made a loud popping sound that tore through the silence. Just then, a deer that I believe was the monster buck blew loudly and took off. In a panic, I blew back and followed with a few short grunts. The deer stopped after three bounds and was quiet.

It was very dark. I was in full camo and the deer was on the other side of the thicket; I don't think he could see me. I heard the deer move away slowly, so I slid up the ladder and sat down dejected.

I put my pack down and started praying for all I was worth. Hunters know that when a deer blows at you, it is usually the kiss of death. My spirits were lifted, though, when about 20 minutes later the deer snorted/wheezed at me from some distance away. I believe that having the deer blow actually helped me be bolder; I felt there was nothing to lose. So I tried to mimic what I had just heard as loudly as I could.

All was quiet for an hour, then I heard crunching leaves from the direction I had seen the buck the night before. Afraid that he might lose interest, I used a can doe-bleat call and added a few tending grunts. I did this two more times before daylight whenever I heard noise from that area. It was a miracle that he didn't respond any of those times and bust me before shooting light.

As the first glimmers of daybreak arrived, I was able to make out a couple of does browsing near my stand. Shortly after, as if they were glow-in-the-dark, a huge set of white antlers appeared. I could tell immediately that this was the same deer I'd seen the night before. I then tried to ignore the antlers and began focusing on the task at hand.

Now within range, he was moving between the does, causing them to jump away. I readied for the shot as he once again made a doe jump. This time she lunged right at my stand and continued to walk right up one of my shooting lanes. To my surprise, he followed her until they were both right underneath me. I remained frozen!

He was only a foot from one of the legs when he pointed his nose up and sniffed at the estrous scent I had put out. Letting the doe walk, he huffed at the scent and moved into the thicket without offering me a shot. With a couple of head-bobs, he disappeared completely into the brush and stopped just out of sight.

This gave me a chance to breathe again. I scanned all sides of the thicket as I waited. It was almost 15 minutes before a doe appeared in the closest shooting lane to the thicket. This caused him to respond by lowering his head and pushing through the thicket, bending several small trees over as he muscled his way out.

The buck was angling away sharply when he began to give chase. As soon as there was a shot I took it, hitting him just behind the ribs on the right side. The dart from my crossbow went through the diaphragm, right lung, and the arteries above the heart. He picked up speed as he hooked left behind the thicket, but I could see his head drop. When that happened, he snagged on some ground vines, flipped over and was not able to get back up. His last breath was less than 10 seconds later.

I remember telling one of my friends that day that I had just killed a "Booner." I had no idea that I had just taken what would become the 11th-largest typical whitetail ever recorded by Boone and Crockett at that time. He was also the largest typical entered in B&C's 26th Awards Program, as well as the new Ohio State Record. I feel blessed beyond measure, and am having a great time with the deer. 🦌

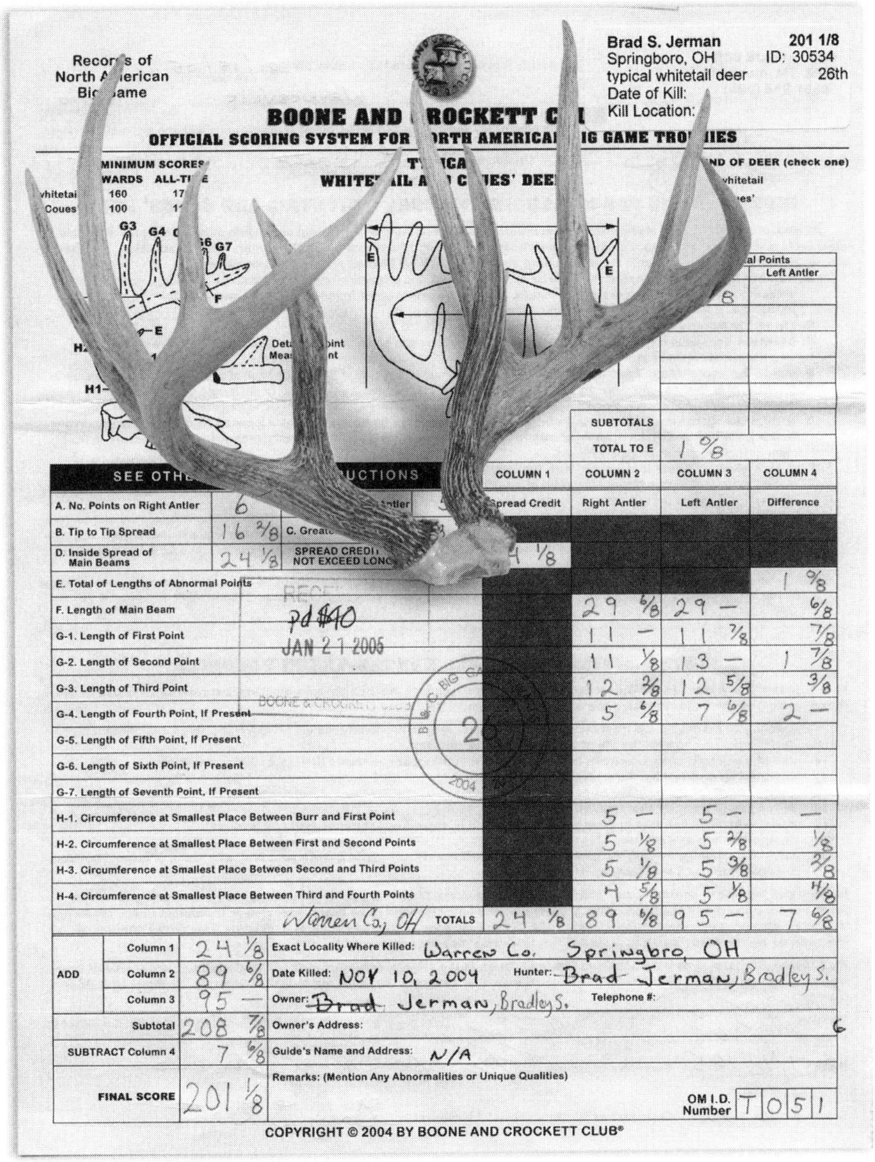

Records of
North American
Big Game

BOONE AND CROCKETT C[ ]
OFFICIAL SCORING SYSTEM FOR [ ]RTH AMERICA[ ] IG GAME TRO[ ]IES

Brad S. Jerman — 201 1/8
Springboro, OH — ID: 30534
typical whitetail deer — 26th
Date of Kill:
Kill Location:

T[ ]ICA[ ]
WHITE[ ]IL A[ ] C[ ]IES' DEE[ ]

MINIMUM SCORES
WARDS ALL-TIME
Whitetail 160 17[ ]
Coues 100 1[ ]

[ ]ND OF DEER (check one)
whitetail
[ ]es'

	COLUMN 1	COLUMN 2	COLUMN 3	COLUMN 4
	Spread Credit	Right Antler	Left Antler	Difference
SUBTOTALS				
TOTAL TO E	1 ⁶/₈			
A. No. Points on Right Antler	6			
B. Tip to Tip Spread	16 ³/₈			
D. Inside Spread of Main Beams	24 ⅛	4 ⅛		
E. Total of Lengths of Abnormal Points				1 ⁶/₈
F. Length of Main Beam		29 ⁶/₈	29 —	⁶/₈
G-1. Length of First Point		11 —	11 ⁷/₈	⁷/₈
G-2. Length of Second Point		11 ⅛	13 —	1 ⁷/₈
G-3. Length of Third Point		12 ⅜	12 ⁵/₈	³/₈
G-4. Length of Fourth Point, If Present		5 ⁶/₈	7 ⁶/₈	2 —
G-5. Length of Fifth Point, If Present				
G-6. Length of Sixth Point, If Present				
G-7. Length of Seventh Point, If Present				
H-1. Circumference at Smallest Place Between Burr and First Point		5 —	5 —	—
H-2. Circumference at Smallest Place Between First and Second Points		5 ⅛	5 ³/₈	⅛
H-3. Circumference at Smallest Place Between Second and Third Points		5 ⅛	5 ⅝	⅜
H-4. Circumference at Smallest Place Between Third and Fourth Points		4 ⅝	5 ⅛	⁴/₈
TOTALS	24 ⅛	89 ⁶/₈	95 —	7 ⁶/₈

pd $40
JAN 21 2005

ADD	Column 1	24 ⅛
	Column 2	89 ⁶/₈
	Column 3	95 —
	Subtotal	208 ⁷/₈
SUBTRACT Column 4		7 ⁶/₈
FINAL SCORE		201 ⅛

Exact Locality Where Killed: Warren Co. Springbro, OH
Date Killed: NOV 10, 2004   Hunter: Brad Jerman, Bradley S.
Owner: Brad Jerman, Bradley S.   Telephone #:
Owner's Address:
Guide's Name and Address: N/A
Remarks: (Mention Any Abnormalities or Unique Qualities)

OM I.D. Number: T 0 5 1

COPYRIGHT © 2004 BY BOONE AND CROCKETT CLUB®

*Final score chart for Jerman's typical whitetail, which
scores 201–1/8 Points.*

*Non-typical Coues' whitetail, scoring 134-2/8 points,
taken by William B. Bullock in Yavapai County, Arizona,
in 1986.*

Persistence and Patience

William B. Bullock

20th Big Game Awards Program

I'M NO DIFFERENT FROM ANY OTHER TROPHY HUNTER. I HUNT TO SEE GAME AND ENJOY IT, NOT TO JUST FILL A TAG AND GO HOME. I ENJOY THE COUNTRY AND THE ASPECTS OF HUNTING: GLASSING, STALKING TO GET A CLOSER LOOK, STUDYING THE PREY, ENJOYING THE INCIDENTAL WILDLIFE, AND SIMPLY EXPERIENCING NATURAL TREATS THAT MOST NON-HUNTERS NEVER EVEN KNOW EXIST. I'M USUALLY SUCCESSFUL AT EVENTUALLY FILLING MY TAG, BUT I ALMOST ALWAYS KNOW THAT I COULD HAVE FILLED IT SOONER, HAD I WANTED TO DO ONLY THAT. HOWEVER, I MUST HONESTLY ADMIT THAT I'M USUALLY JUST A TOUCH DISAPPOINTED WHEN I APPROACH MY FRESHLY DOWNED QUARRY; MAYBE I SHOULD HAVE TAKEN THE ONE YESTERDAY, OR HELD OUT A LITTLE LONGER. SURE HE'S A NICE ONE, BUT MAYBE, JUST MAYBE, THERE'S A B&C TROPHY WAS OUT THERE SOMEWHERE.

In the late 1970s, my dad and I began to hunt Coues' whitetails, before they became popular. It seemed that every time we went hunting javelina, quail, mountain lion, or whatever, we found whitetails. Not lots of whitetails, just enough to make us think about a new hunting spot come fall.

Dad had taken a dandy buck in 1973. At 107-1/8, it made the Arizona Records Book, just missing the B&C minimum of 110. Every time I looked at that buck, I began to dream. There had to be bigger ones out there, and most people didn't really care about them.

We found a spot just north of Roosevelt Lake that had a fairly good Coues' deer population. While Arizona hunters must wade through a drawing process to hunt deer in the fall, this particular area was a cinch to get a permit for whitetails only. We had to pack in about three miles, carrying our own water and food. After the first year or two, we had our packing down to a science. While we saw bucks every year, and only one or two other hunters, we actually took only four deer in six years. None scored above the 90s. In the meantime, new hunts were being opened up during the late December rut in north-central Arizona, closer to home. A few bigger bucks were being taken, some approaching, and a few even making, the "book."

In 1985, we both drew permits and decided to give it a try. Dad took a buck midway through the season that was respectable, although still in the 90-point range. I passed up about a dozen decent bucks, looking for that rare exception. I finally took a smaller one to fill my tag on the season's final day. The sound of my rifle had just completed its final echo when I heard rocks roll and then watched a real nice Coues' buck trot off. Of course, he had to stop and look back at 80 yards. I think he even smiled. His beautiful rack would have crowded the "book." If a lion didn't get him, he would probably be there next year. But, would I?

Permits were getting tough to come by. Coues' whitetails had become popular, and not just to trophy hunters. Someone decided that those cute little deer were good eating. I eat wild game year round, and the fact is that they're really not all that good. They're usually tough and dry, and they're strong from being in the rut. But, Lady Luck again gave me a permit in 1986. Maybe this year would be different.

By opening day my hunting partner Steve and I were excited. We still remembered the buck that trotted off on the last day of the year before. We turned on the last two-track road that would lead to "our" favorite country. As we topped the last ridge, we counted three sets of taillights a half-mile or so ahead. Two more vehicles were leaving camps not far ahead of us and heading in the same direction. Since I didn't feel properly invited to that party, I spun the Bronco around and we headed for some "new" country that we had casually looked at while scouting.

An hour later we were looking at a series of rolling pinon pine and juniper ridges that we had never been on before, Glassing looked to be much more difficult than where we had hunted the year before, and we now had a very late start. But something about new country and opening day really gets the juices flowing. It felt good to be hunting whitetails again. It turned into quite a day. As well as seeing several bull elk, we saw over 20 Coues' deer, far more than I normally see in my style of hunting. We saw no respectable bucks, but we did see several smaller ones. We got a "feel" for the country that turned out to be valuable.

The next day, we had a plan of attack. We climbed to a fairly high vantage point that gave us about a 200 degree view, including the heads of two juniper-covered basins. Glassing was tedious. Steve and I would spot a deer. That same deer would vanish in the thick trees in seconds, leaving us with strained vision while trying to detect even parts of other deer in that area. I studied likely looking places for as much as 30 minutes, only to see a deer that had been there all along step into view and then disappear again in seconds, leaving me to wonder if I had really seen him at all. Meanwhile, Steve had spotted three does in the open, feeding near a rocky outcropping some distance away.

While Steve is a good hunter, he chose to stay with hunting mule deer for meat. Blessed with an exceptional set of eyes, and being a good friend, I have found him to be very helpful in looking for that special buck and in keeping the hunt lively. I'm sure that many times he has asked himself what in the world I'm waiting for. Moments later, he knew.

It was Steve who spotted the buck. I quickly set up the spotting scope. The eyepiece showed a mass of antlers. I didn't know how many points. I simply stated, "That's him." My next move is normally a stalk.

Steve and I discussed it. We could get to the rocky out-cropping, but we would take a chance of spooking the three does and probably never see the buck. The other direction was out of the question, too low. Due to the lay of the land, a move in any direction to shorten the distance would cut off our view. We had to try it from there.

I knew that the Remington 7 mm Mag could do the job, I just didn't know if I could. I have to admit I was nervous. I found a rest, and Steve set up to call the location of my shots, should I miss. I settled the cross hairs until they lay right on the buck's back. My instincts told me to hold higher, but I have always believed that I should never hold off an animal on the first shot. I squeezed. The buck jumped forward, toward us by about five yards, and stood dead-still. I thought I had hit him. Steve had flinched at the blast and wasn't sure what had happened. As I chambered another shell, the buck disappeared. Seconds later, Steve spotted him again, slowly moving uphill.

When the buck stopped again, I raised my hold slightly and fired. "You're low! Below his feet," Steve said. Again the buck was on the move. When he finally stopped, I held four feet above him and fired again, and again. "You're still low," was, all I heard. The buck topped the ridge and disappeared over it, pausing just long enough for Steve to gasp at the antler structure. Meanwhile, I desperately tried to reload.

We spent the next two hours trying to find blood, tracks, or any sign of the deer, but to no avail. On the ride home, we tried to assess the situation. We decided that my first shot must have been barely low; it probably sprayed the deer's back with rocks or brush on impact. My last shot was longer than my first shot. But, the season was young and there were plenty of does around. We hoped we could find the buck again. I was definitely after only one deer.

We had planned to skip the next day, but the thought of that buck was more than I could take. I called Steve that night and he was ready to go. My 12-year-old son went along the next day. He watched with his mouth open as a high-90 to low-100 point buck lay down about 500 yards away. He was a nice 3-point (actually an 8-point by eastern count). Arizonans have a funny habit of ignoring the first point on any deer, calling it an "eye guard." In many cases, that's the biggest point on a Coues' deer. At any rate, my buck was not to be seen on that day, or on the next three hunting days I had over the next week-and-a-half. With each day, I learned more about the country. Occasionally I spotted some large tracks that I hoped were his, but I really believed that they were made by a passing mulie.

In the meantime, word had gotten out that I had missed a huge, non-typical whitetail. Luckily, no one else was hunting the area, since the country really doesn't look like typical white-tail country. My dad had gotten a nice buck that scored about 97. He had over-estimated it in the field, mostly due to foggy conditions. But that had me convinced that "my" buck wasn't as big as I had first thought.

By 7:15 Christmas Eve morning, Steve and I were heading back to our vantage point. Two deer were working the hillside to the right of the rocky outcropping. I set up the spotting scope and looked. It was him! In our earlier confrontation he had been to the left of the outcrop. The previous outings had served as an education. I felt that I could make a stalk this time.

We dropped down to our left and, in minutes, we were completely out of any sightline to the deer, that were about 500 yards away. The doe was feeding, and the rut had begun. The buck couldn't take his eyes off the doe. We moved along quickly and quietly, Steve staying about 30 yards behind. If anyone was going to blow it, Steve was making sure it would be me. As I approached the outcrop, I eased up behind a small cedar tree. I couldn't see the deer or find the right spot. I backed off and moved further up the ridge. As I moved to the edge again, I reached down for my field glasses and eased them up to my eyes. They came to focus right on the buck. He was about 200 yards out, still watching the doe. I put my hand down and Steve stopped, recognizing my signal.

I had nowhere to take a rest. I couldn't risk another move until both deer were out of sight again in the brush. Finally, they moved and so did I. I found an open spot behind a huge juniper tree and sat down, exposing just enough of myself so that I could see clearly. Another doe appeared from above, walking downhill toward the other two. I breathed a sigh of relief that she had not seen me, even though I never knew she was there.

When the doe disappeared, I stood and positioned myself behind a chest-high rock. I decided to start glassing with my scope instead of my binoculars. As I patiently watched, the first doe moved from behind a giant patch of prickly pear. As she did, the buck stepped into view, slightly quartering away from me. I positioned the cross hairs right behind his right shoulder and squeezed.

This time, there was no doubt. I recovered from the recoil in time to see the buck somersault down the hill and land under a big cedar tree. Steve was at my side in seconds. I held the gun, with the scope fixed on the tree where I'd last seen the buck. I had been shooting across a shallow ravine. As we moved toward the deer, I could see the spot clearly until we bottomed-out. From then on we hurried until we came to the big patch of prickly pear. From there, we circled around for what seemed like minutes, although I'm sure it was only seconds until I spotted the back of one huge antler in the brush beneath the cedar tree.

As Steve and I hauled the buck from beneath the tree, I was completely amazed. I had never dared to imagine that the buck was actually that big. The big tracks we had seen were his. His front feet were as big as a good mule deer. I guessed his score to be about 135, non-typical. He weighed 117 pounds. By Boone and Crockett standards, he had nine measurable points on his right antler and seven on his left. He was very heavily palmated and webbed, unlike any pictures I had ever seen. A 2-3/4 inch drop point was on his right antler, and his left antler sported a forked point that stuck straight out to the side.

I thoroughly enjoyed the next few hours. Dressing the buck and dragging him out was a pleasure. The following morning (Christmas), we green scored him at 137-7/8 points. Two-and-a half months later, Mike Cupell officially scored him for entry at 138-7/8. Steve wrote an article capturing his views of the hunt titled "Trophy Buck For Christmas" that was later published in the Christmas edition of the *Arizona Hunter and Angler Magazine*. The Arizona Republic newspaper made mention of the buck the following spring. That beautiful buck was definitely a trophy hunter's dream, not taken strictly by chance, but with a measure of persistence and patience. He was my buck-of-a-lifetime. 🦌

Moose & Caribou

CANADA MOOSE

ALASKA-YUKON MOOSE

SHIRAS' MOOSE

MOUNTAIN CARIBOU

WOODLAND CARIBOU

BARREN GROUND CARIBOU

CENTRAL CANADA
BARREN GROUND CARIBOU

QUEBEC-LABRADOR CARIBOU

Canada moose, scoring 227-6/8 points,
taken by Frank A. Hanks near Kawdy Mountain, British Columbia,
in 2004 (pictured with his son, Wade).

Dad's Moose

Frank A. Hanks

As told by Wade Hanks

26th Big Game Awards Program

On Christmas of 2003, mom and I decided to do something special for Dad. We arranged for him to go on a Canada moose hunt. He had already taken an Alaska-Yukon moose, but had been talking more and more about wanting to get his Shiras' moose in Idaho. That, of course, is through a draw, so I thought it might be fun to get him one step closer to an all three categories "moose slam" by taking him on a moose hunt in Canada.

I had some good friends who had gone to Northern British Columbia the previous year and had what I felt was an exceptional hunt on Canada moose. I contacted him and he helped me set up our 2004 hunt with Fletcher and Sherry Day, owners and operators of Tahltan Outfitters out of Dease Lake.

Dad and I have both been to Alaska numerous times and so the only preparation we made for the trip was to sight in our guns. We both took our tried and true .338 Winchester Magnums. I also took my bow, in hopes of finding an opportunity favorable for a good stalk.

We drove the 24-hour scenic trek straight through from northern Idaho and arrived in time to catch our float plane into Fletcher's camp. Bruce, of Dease Lake Air Charters, flew us into camp in a prehistoric DeHaviland Beaver on floats. Sherry Day was accompanying us on the flight. She spends most of her time at home coordinating hunters and arranging hunts for upcoming years.

Fletcher met us at the lake with an Argo on a clear sunny day. There was snow on all of the peaks around us, and it just felt like a good time and place to hunt moose. Once the two-hour Argo ride was over I really felt ready to hunt. Little did I know that tomorrow we would again travel all day to our spike camp. This time it wasn't in a comfortable Chevy half-ton, or a float plane, or an Argo; it was on horseback.

Vernon Marion and Chuck were to be our guides. They were cowboys in every sense. They were trained in moose hunting with horses; I had always hunted moose from a spike camp with a pack frame. The only thing we had in common was the fact that we had both glassed up a lot of moose in our lives, and had spent our fair share of time butchering and caping these enormous animals. I could tell that everything I thought I knew about moose hunting would be worthless to me in this new environment.

Though sore, I survived the 20-mile horseback ride. We awoke the next morning from a great night's sleep only to find fog and rain. We thought it would be fruitless but still trudged up to our knob (a hill providing the only vantage point in the area). After a couple of hours of unrelenting wind, rain, and fog, I suggested we return tomorrow. Relieved, Vernon and Chuck gave in and we called it a day. This choice turned out to be the right one as the fog and rain continued all day and night.

Day two was a little bit better than day one, but there was still some snow in the air. We got to the top of the knob and the moose hunting started slow. Chuck was the first to spot a bull. It was a good one, just not a great one. Before long, we were spotting moose all over. Chuck saw another bull that appeared huge but was into the trees before we could get a better look. In the valley below us, we had spotted 13 different bull moose, including a bull with two cows that had potential, but he was staying in the trees as well. Thanks to his cows he was in and out of the trees and gave us enough of a look at him to decide to take him.

He was over a mile away, so we had to ride the horses closer to start the stalk. Vernon led us across the tundra and through the spruce thickets to an opening where we parked the horses. I wanted Dad to take this one, as he appeared to be around 60 inches wide with good palms and points. Since he would be shooting, I left my bow and only took my rifle as back up.

We began sneaking through the willow brush with a good wind in our face. The rain had momentarily stopped, and conditions were perfect. I was getting the feeling that this moose was in the bag. If he were still in the same place he had bedded 1-1/2 hours ago, it would be a cakewalk.

Just when we thought we should be able to see the moose with his cows, we were surprised by a spooked pair of moose. A different bull and cow had gotten between us and our target. It didn't take but a second to realize that this moose was bigger and better than our target bull. Both Vernon and I were telling Dad to shoot. He was struggling to find a rest and was going to miss out on the bull of a lifetime if he didn't hurry.

I tried handing him my tripod, but it wasn't tall enough; he tried a willow bush or two but they were too short as well. Finally, after what seemed like forever to me, dad fired an offhand shot at the still curious moose.

The bull was hit and turned back to the safety of a small grove of spruce. The cow ran forward and out of sight into the thick black forest. Dad rushed to the partially hidden moose and prepared for another shot. The big bull, still unsure of what had just transpired, stepped back out of the trees to see what the commotion was all about. Dad fired again and the disoriented bull began running for safety in our direction.

I don't think he was charging us, but we were right in the middle of his exit strategy. Dad fired a couple more times before the giant came to a stop and finally collapsed 60 yards from us.

What a celebration we had when we realized just how big this trophy was! Dad was pleasantly surprised. During all the excitement he hadn't even looked at the rack. He simply had trusted his guide and his son. The bull was about 60 inches wide, with incredible palms, and had 33 points. We couldn't believe it.

As we were soaking up the moment, two cows appeared on the edge of the trees near where the original bull had been. Chuck and I decided it was worth a look, and took off in that direction. I knew at that moment I should have had my bow.

We jockeyed into position downwind and behind the two alert cows. We looked and looked for the bull. As we moved around seeking different angles, I finally spotted him. He was looking straight away and was directly upwind. There was a clear opening through the 150 yards of brush between us and the bull. I was sick that my bow was in the scabbard on the horse. I am not sure if I could have drawn a more perfect scenario for an archery stalk.

Chuck asked if I had a clear shot. I had found a scrubby spruce tree for a rest and felt comfortable with the shot. We knew there was only enough opening for one shot, so I caught my breath and calmly took the shot. At the crack of the rifle, the bull lunged forward. We watched the few openings in the direction they went but did not see the cows or the bull. Chuck questioned the shot, but it felt good to me. I was fairly confident the bull would be lying just out of sight.

We approached the fallen giant and realized that he had only traveled far enough to stumble once and go down. What a day — two trophy bull moose within 500 yards of each other, and within 30 minutes! My bull was also about 60 inches wide. It had good palms and a total of 23 points. I knew instantly that

I had been outdone by my father, but I suppose I wouldn't have wanted it any other way.

After the bulls were down, the real work began. Daylight was fading and we were still over an hour's ride from our camp. We prepared the bulls for their last evening in the wild and hoped no visitors would show up by morning. We had a couple of good campfire stories that night while dining on some fine stew.

Morning came with a rainstorm. We spent a miserable day in the field butchering and loading the horses. We did see a couple more bulls during the day, a big black grizzly bear, and a lot of wolf tracks, but nothing that compared with our two trophies.

With the two moose out of the way, we were ready to look for our mountain caribou. We made the journey back to main camp with 24 horses laden with spike camp and moose. The long ride home was hard but pleasant as I followed the two horses carrying the antlers and floated on cloud nine. It was definitely the agony of victory.

Days later, from the comforts of the main camp, dad was able to harvest a respectable caribou. It was the biggest one we had seen the entire week. The weather had been cold but cooperative. I was being quite selective and did not take a caribou. As it turned out it was probably a good thing. We could not have fit one more pound of meat or another antler into the truck for the journey home.

Fletcher and the crew were happy for us and welcomed us back anytime. The camp and experience were spectacular. The two bulls both ended up qualifying for Boone and Crockett. My moose officially scored 203-2/8 points. Dad's bull, however, scored 227-6/8, placing it seventh all-time. Congratulations, Dad! 🦌

Alaska-Yukon moose, scoring 247-7/8 Points,
taken by Mark S. Rose near Rapid Creek, Alaska,
in 2003.

The Next Level

Mark S. Rose

25th Big Game Awards Program

"Mark, you need to take your hunting to the next level," urged my big brother, Gary. I knew I should listen to him. I have hunted whitetails in my home state of Texas all my life and have shot a pronghorn in New Mexico; my brother, however, has hunted all over the world. I finally agreed, and Gary made all the arrangements for my moose hunt on the Alaska Peninsula. Even after all the preparations had been made, I had a difficult time being comfortable with the trip, which would be a big deal for me, and also being away from my business for two weeks.

I arrived at Wildman Lake Lodge with several other hunters in early September, the day before moose season opened. The following day, my guide, Bill Burwell, and I waited our turn for the bush plane to take us to a spike camp. We were the last group to go. By afternoon, the weather had turned for the worse and we had to stay at the lodge another day. This seemed to be a bad break. I had really wanted to be in the field for opening day.

The next day we flew out and set up spike camp at the base of a frozen volcano. We had several hours of daylight left after setting up camp, so we decided to glass. We made our way through thick alders to a spot overlooking Rapid Creek Valley. I learned at this point the terrain was terribly rough and the hunt was going to be very physically demanding — much more so than anything I had faced on previous hunts — but I was ready for the challenge.

From our vantage point we could see probably two miles in either direction. As we began glassing the valley, we saw the flash of an antlered palm belonging to a moose that was lying on the edge of the alders. We continued to watch the bull, which was about 800 yards away. When the moose stood up, we almost died. Bill said it was the biggest bull he had ever seen (and he had seen plenty of moose in his long career of guiding) and guessed that the bull's rack had an 80-inch spread. I knew the moose was a monster, but I did not know how good Bill's long range judging was. I couldn't legally shoot the moose on the same day that we arrived in spike camp, so we returned to camp and waited for tomorrow.

The next morning, we went back to the same overlook and were shocked to find the monster moose in the same spot as before. With the help of a spotting scope, we counted 34 points. Bill insisted the moose was 80 inches wide with a bell about 30 inches long. We proceeded down the mountain across the raging stream and battled our way through the woven alders to the grassy area where we had located the bull . . . but it had vanished. It had probably heard us thrashing through the alders. We found a 20-foot circle where the moose had been bedding down, and waited for it to return. We never saw the moose again that day.

The next morning we returned to our overlook and saw a smaller bull with a cow. "He's about 70 inches," Bill said, "You might consider going for it. He's definitely a shooter." I told Bill that I had six more days in the field and we were going for the big one! The next day we saw the huge bull back in the exact spot where we had first spotted it. Bill and I discussed what went wrong with our previous stalk and came up with a plan so the moose would not hear our approach. We hiked about 300 yards downwind before cutting into the alders to work our way back toward the animal along an old game trail.

I was ready! We walked up the trail until the giant moose stood up in front of us. It was looking straight us at about 100 yards. I shot it twice behind the front shoulder. Bill yelled to keep shooting. He was afraid that the moose would run into the alders, making the task of skinning and quartering much more difficult. I took two more shots and then saw the moose collapse in the grass.

Bill field-measured the antlers with a string and told me the rack was close to 81 inches wide. We spent the rest of the day taking photos, skinning and quartering the huge moose. It got late in the day and since we were three hours from spike camp, we pitched a tent right next to the carcass. I will always remember Bill telling me to make sure I had a bullet in the chamber and to turn the scope all the way down. "If we have some action tonight it's going to be really close," he warned me. It rained all night long, but fortunately, the bears stayed away.

With a score of 247-7/8 B&C points, it ranks fourteenth in the all-time records book. The moose rack has a spread of 80-3/8 inches, making it the third largest spread ever recorded. 🦌

Shiras' moose, scoring 177–2/8 points,
taken by April H. Preston in Shoshone County, Idaho,
in 1999.

More Than the Score

April H. Preston

24th Big Game Awards Program

BOTH OF US STOOD STARING IN DISBELIEF AT THE 1999 IDAHO MOOSE PERMIT WITH MY NAME ON IT. "THIS IS A ONCE-IN-A-LIFETIME OPPORTUNITY," MY HUSBAND SAID, "YOU BETTER MAKE THE MOST OF IT." ONCE-IN-A-LIFETIME OPPORTUNITY WAS MEANT LITERALLY! IF A PERSON BEATS THE REMOTE ODDS OF GETTING DRAWN FOR A MOOSE PERMIT IN IDAHO, IT IS THE ONLY ONE YOU GET. IT WAS EARLY JUNE WHEN THE PERMIT ARRIVED IN THE MAIL, SO WE HAD ABOUT THREE MONTHS TO PREPARE.

I began hunting with my husband, Ken, a few years earlier. He started me out shooting grouse while I accompanied him on preseason scouting trips for deer and elk. My husband had once been a professional guide, and had a knack for putting me in the right spot at the right time. I was able to take whitetail deer and elk, despite being a relative newcomer to the wonderful sport of hunting. My permit area for moose was located approximately 50 miles northeast of where we live. Ken knew the area, and suggested that I also purchase a bear tag because he had seen a considerable amount of bear sign in that region. His suggestion would later prove prophetic.

To prepare for this special hunt, Ken, our son Zack age 7, our daughter Hillary age 11, and I, spent every weekend in my permit area. We camped, scouted for sign, and target practiced as a family. Normally, I use a Remington Model 7 in .260 caliber for deer. However, the .260 was too light for me to use responsibly on an animal the size of a moose. So Ken took a Ruger M77UL Ultra-light in .30-06 caliber to a local gunsmith where the stock was cut to fit my length of pull exactly, and a delightfully cushy recoil pad was installed. Ken then put a Nikon Monarch 4X power scope on a .22 magnum, bolt action rifle, which was to serve as practice simulation. The Nikon scope was identical to the one on the Ruger I was to use for moose, and the rifles were nearly identical in weight. This provided me an opportunity to target practice with hundreds of more rounds using identical optics and virtually matching rifle weights. Had I used the .30-06 exclusively, my shoulder would have become bruised and sore even with the special recoil pad. Each day of practice I would use the .22 magnum to shoot 50-100 rounds from a bench rest, another 50-100 rounds off hand, and finally, finish my practice session using the .30-06 until soreness began to set in.

Weeks went by, and despite all of our scouting, we hadn't sighted a single moose! Ken kept saying, "This spot looks good," or, "we'll be back at this spot once the season opens!" I voiced my concern about not seeing any moose, but Ken reassured me they would be there by the time the season arrived. The first part of the season was unusually warm, and Ken advised against getting an animal as big as a moose down in those temperatures. So, I agonized with anticipation, waiting for a cool spell that would allow us the time necessary to pack out and properly care for an animal of such size. At last, the weather forecast was for the first frosts of the season, and we made plans to head into the mountainous region of my permit area.

On our first day out, we set up on the edge of a tree line where we could watch a brushy cut-over area. We nestled behind a blow down which provided good cover and a perfect bench rest.

Ken had called moose many times before, and had a particular sequence of grunts and bawls, which he liked to use. He had barely finished his first sequence, when to our left, a magnificent bull elk stepped out of the timber to investigate the sounds. I got to look at him for nearly two minutes before he jogged away. I had an elk tag, but the season wasn't yet open for them. Nevertheless, the experience was a breathtaking moment I'll never forget! Interestingly, Ken had two more smaller elk come to the moose calls on different occasions. It was their rutting season and they seemed to want to check out the sounds.

A couple of weekends had passed, and the only moose we had seen were one cow and her calf. Ken had seen a small bull while scouting alone one day, but overall, sightings were few and far between. The next weekend we were just getting ready to set up overlooking a steep, brushy draw. Ken was getting things out of the pack, and I was glassing the steep terrain below. As if by Mother Nature's sleight-of-hand, a handsome bear suddenly materialized on the slope below us. He climbed up onto a log jam and stood broadside. His coat looked like wet coal in the early morning sun. His head bobbed gently as he tested the air. I nudged Ken and whispered, "Bear!" Ken said the bear was about 150 yards away, urged me to stay calm, pick a spot on the bear, and shoot just like during target practice. When I fired, the bear flipped end over end down into the brushy ravine. All that happened next is a story in and of itself for another time. I'll just say that what transpired in that brush-choked ravine was an exhilarating encounter that neither I, nor my husband, shall ever forget! Fortunately, neither of us were seriously hurt, and I finally got to finish the bear. He's now a beautiful rug on our wall, and one of our most cherished hunting memories!

The following weekend, we were back to the task of trying to find a big bull moose. On the way to our hunting spot, we stopped the truck and looked at some fresh moose tracks, which had crossed the logging road sometime during the night. Ken asked if I was ready to go get my moose. I told him that after the bear incident of the previous week, I was ready for almost anything! We parked the truck at the head of an old gated logging road. The plan was to hike the trail for about 1.5 miles as it twisted down to a ravine choked with mountain maples and alders. At a spot where we had seen moose sign earlier in the season, we would set up and Ken would try calling in a bull.

The old logging trail was covered with knee-deep grasses and some small trees. The morning sun had melted the night's heavy frost, and our legs were soaked quickly, almost as if we had waded a stream. Barely 200 yards from our truck, we came upon some very fresh moose droppings. We pondered whether or not to call from that location and finally agreed there wasn't a good place to set up, and we should continue farther down the trail. We hadn't gone more than 50 yards when my "guide" grabbed my arm and whispered in my ear, "There's your moose!" All I could see were the huge palmated antlers sliding across the brush about 80 yards away. The moose stopped just before entering the grassy trail. I could see his head and massive rack, but none of his vital shoulder area. My heart was hammering the inside of my rib cage like an angry blacksmith as I waited in the kneeling position with the rifle ready. Ken was crouched just behind me and whispering in my left ear to "relax." I was breathing as heavily as if I had just run a mile! Ken said, "Calm down! You sound like an obscene phone call! Just relax, and when his shoulder comes into view, take him."

The huge animal stood there twisting his big rack from side to side against some maples. He nudged out a bit further and I whispered to Ken, "He's a big one, right?" "He's exceptional," Ken whispered back. I don't know if it was Ken's whispering in my ear, or the cold, wet grasses I was kneeling in, or just the sight of that moose's huge rack, but chills were racing across my whole body like capillary lightning. After what seemed like waiting for geologic time to pass, the massive bull stepped forward, and his shoulder was now squarely centered in my 3-foot wide shooting lane. I was concerned about flinching because I was so overwhelmingly nervous. I squeezed and squeezed on the trigger. I thought the gun would never go off! Finally, the gun fired and the barrel leapt upwards; the stock jumped back against my shoulder as if it were as startled as I was by the gun's report.

I was amazed at the speed and agility with which the moose swapped ends and bulldozed uphill through the tangled brush. Ken said he thought I had made a solid hit, and I, too, believed the shot was good. We gave the big fella some time to himself before trailing after him, (the harrowing experience with the bear the week before was still fresh in our minds).

Remarkably, the bull had run nearly 160 yards despite having the back of both lungs perforated by a .30-06 bullet. He had fallen barely 200 feet from the logging road we had driven in on before parking at the gated road. This proved fortuitous, as it enabled us to winch the big bull up onto a cleared, level log landing, where working on him was much easier than on the steep, heavily brushed hillside where he had dropped.

We took the antlers to Kirk Miller of Kirk's Taxidermy in Moscow, Idaho, to be mounted on a plaque. Kirk immediately called local Boone and Crockett scorer, Randy Byers, and told him there was a moose rack in his shop that Randy would definitely want to see. When Randy walked into the taxidermy shop, he took one quick glance at the rack and stated, "Yep, that one makes the book!"

What began as an "opportunity of a lifetime" in early June of 1999, had ended as the "hunt of a lifetime" on October 17, 1999. What makes this moose so special to me though, is much more than just his final score and ranking. It's all the memories that surround him that matter most to me. I'll always remember the family outings to target practice and scouting for moose sign, the huge bull elk that came to investigate the moose calls, the pulse-pounding thrill of tracking a wounded bear in thick brush, the fun of having a great guide (who just happens to be my husband), and the ultimate culmination to it all — a Boone and Crockett Club Shiras' moose.

In closing, I would like to say thank you to the following folks: first, to everyone associated with Boone and Crockett, they've all been so friendly, thoughtful, and helpful; second, to the Idaho Fish and Game Department for their guardianship and stewardship of our wildlife resources; third, thank you to the logging companies who so graciously allowed us access to their landholdings; and finally, thank you to my guide and husband, Ken, for sharing the sport of hunting with me. 🦌

*Final score chart for Preston's Shiras' moose, which
scores 177-2/8 Points.*

*Shiras' moose, scoring 180-2/8 points,
taken by Rylan Rudebusch in Larimer County, Colorado,
in 2007.*

High & Tight

Rylan Rudebusch

Introduction by Gordon Rudebusch

27th Big Game Awards Program

I KNEW WE WERE CLOSE, BUT WHERE WAS HE? THE WILLOWS WERE SO DENSE THAT MAKING OUT ANYTHING MORE THAN A FEW FEET AWAY WAS NEARLY IMPOSSIBLE. THEN, IN A BLINK OF THE EYE, HE APPEARED. THE FIRST FEATURES THAT CAME INTO VIEW WERE THE INCREDIBLY LONG PALMS. THEY WERE A MAGNIFICENT SIGHT, REFLECTING THE SUN WELL ABOVE THE WILLOWS. NEXT, THE MASSIVE, DARK BODY CAME INTO VIEW AT LESS THAN 50 YARDS. HE WAS ON A MISSION, MAKING TRACKS FOR THE OTHER SIDE OF THE DRAINAGE. I COULDN'T FIGURE OUT WHY HE WAS RUNNING. THIS WAS THE ONLY BULL THAT RYLAN HAD SHOWN ANY INTEREST IN DURING OUR ENTIRE SUMMER OF SCOUTING. THERE WAS NO WAY HE COULD HAVE SEEN OR SMELLED US, SO WHAT WAS IT?

"What happened? You didn't shoot," I said, half asking and half stating. Sometimes things happen pretty fast in the field, especially to a 14-year-old. My youngest son, Rylan, had drawn a coveted Colorado bull moose tag in 2007 at the age of 14—the first year he was eligible. I started putting him in for points when he was 11 and boy did it pay off! Here's Rylan's account of his hunt.

My dad is really into hunting, and he got me into it too. One day I came home from school and Dad told me that I had drawn a moose license. It was only my third year hunting, but I knew that this was a once-in-a-lifetime opportunity, literally. I was nervous. In the past, Dad had told me stories about people getting hard-to-get licenses but not getting anything or shooting something just to put a tag on it. If these experienced hunters couldn't find the animals they were looking for, then how was I supposed to? Luckily I had Dad to help.

One of the first people Dad called was a good friend, Scott Limmer, owner of Comanche Wilderness Outfitters, (my dad guides for Scott). Scott and his crew have guided numerous moose hunters to their trophies in Colorado and he was pretty excited to hear of my good fortune. He knew the potential of this unit in Larimer County and told us of a big bull that had been eluding his hunters over the past two seasons. Scott also said he would loan us two of his guides, Mike Williams and Fred Sell, to help out.

Late that summer, Dad and I helped Scott pack in and set up high-country elk camps for the fall hunting season. While en route to designated campsites, we would get the lay of the land and Scott would show us where he and his guides had seen some pretty nice bulls in the past. I'm not much into riding horses, so instead of riding, Dad and I hiked. This made for some pretty long, tiring days, but it was worth it.

We made several scouting trips into my unit. On one trip we hiked high up on a mountain together, and it wasn't long before I spotted a bull across a basin. Dad said, "That looks like one! What do you say we run over there to get a better look and some film of him?"

I thought for a second and said, "How about you run over there and I'll stay here and keep an eye on him in case he moves?" So off Dad went.

I kept an eye on Dad until he was out of sight. I then took

in the scenery and glassed until I finally saw Dad making his way back. When he got back, he was excited, telling me how close he got and the film he took of the "good" bull. It always seemed like every bull Dad saw was a "good" bull—still is, for that matter.

The next morning, I slept in while Dad went out to check a new drainage. A few hours later he returned and was again pumped about what he saw. He showed me some film he took of a couple bulls and pointed out a "good" one! For the first time, I agreed with him. It really was a good bull, and I made this my number one choice. We later found out this was the bull that had eluded Scott and crew. They had named him "High & Tight." As his name suggested he wasn't the widest bull, but he had super long and wide paddles, a lot of points and huge brows.

When hunting season finally arrived, the plan was for me to hunt for three days, then go back to school for two. Mom agreed to this part of the plan, but I didn't tell Mom the part about hunting the rest of the season if unsuccessful, and Dad wasn't about to say anything.

We headed out early, two days before the season. It seems like every time we do anything outdoors like camping, fishing, scouting, hunting, or anything else, Dad seems to think we need to get there before daylight. This time, we arrived where we wanted to be right at daylight, but it was raining, so we drove around scouting until it stopped. Mike Williams went up a couple days earlier to secure our camping spot at the edge of a big park. This enabled us the opportunity to hunt right outside of camp.

Not much later, my Uncle Marlyn showed up to tag along for the hunt. He had never seen a moose but Dad said his strong back would be needed later. Marlyn's day job is construction, but he was going to be my cameraman. I later found out that he swings a hammer better than he runs a camera.

On Sunday morning, we still had one day of scouting left. Fred Sell rolled into camp, ready to do some scouting. Marlyn went with Fred to check out some of the areas with less hiking so he could get used to the altitude. It had snowed a few inches and it was still moving and blowing around the landscape.

We headed up the drainage into the hidden basin we had scouted in August. Once we were close to the head of the drainage, we started seeing moose. We glassed a bull until he went into the timber and Dad said (you guessed it), "That's a good bull. That could be your No. 1 bull."

After lunch, we brought Marlyn with us so he could see the bull. Out of nowhere, we came face-to-face with a bull. He dropped his head and gave it a shake at 30 yards. Dad stepped back and told us to get some pictures. I fumbled for the camera and Marlyn snapped a few with his while the bull came forward. Again, my dad instructed us to "Get some more pictures." I finally got my camera going and the bull took a couple more steps forward, cutting our distance to him in half. I turned around and saw Dad running for cover, so Marlyn and I decided that it was a good idea to follow. The bull proceeded to move past us at 15 steps. You guessed it; Dad said, "Hey that was a pretty good bull!"

Dad wanted to see the pictures so Marlyn set his camera up but found out his card was full and hadn't recorded one picture. He told us that he borrowed the camera from my other uncle, Larry. The thought of him being my cameraman didn't seem that great. Whose idea was this—Dad?

Opening day finally arrived. Mike and Fred headed to check a drainage not far from where Dad, Marlyn, and I were headed. The morning was cold, really cold.

The vegetation was very tall and made a lot of noise as we walked through it. Finally, we cut through a little section of timber and emerged into an open park. From there we moved up the drainage to where it narrowed, staying just inside the timber, popping out now and then to glass.

The sun was just beginning to rise above the mountaintops.

After a few hundred yards of hiking the drainage, we stopped to glass. Immediately we saw the sun illuminating two huge palms just above the willow tops. We ducked into the timber, moved up another 100 yards, and the next thing I saw was a bull running across the drainage at close range.

Dad set up the shooting sticks and said, "There you go! That's your bull!" I was caught off-guard.

Later, Dad said he knew the first time we glassed him that this was my bull, but he didn't want to tell me because he didn't want to get me all worked up. I quickly got the gun on the sticks and got him in the scope but the shot just didn't present itself. I didn't want to take a shot just to shoot, no matter how much I wanted him. I also had the sun in my shooting eye.

The bull made it across and into the timber. "What happened? You didn't shoot," Dad asked.

I told him and he said, "You did the right thing. Good job; it's okay. We'll move up a little and set up again."

A little further up the drainage, Dad said, "There's a cow and a calf. That's why the bull went running across, to check out that cow!" Within a few seconds I heard Dad say "Here he comes, there's your bull Rylan." Dad ranged him at 167 yards. "Let him come. Get on him, 142 yards."

The bull stopped, turned, and looked right at us, his head held high and proud like he was king of the valley. Despite how cold I was, I was sweating. I put the crosshairs on target but I was shaking, so I took a breath and let it out easy. The sun was in my eyes, so dad took a step forward and blocked the sun. Now I could see him clearly. I took another breath, let it out, and fired.

At the sound of the shot the bull was off and running. He only went 10 yards and stopped, so I shot again. This time the bull only took a step and lifted his front leg. I fired again and the bull did a 360 and down he went. I put another round in the chamber, ready to fire again, but he couldn't make it to his feet.

All three of us watched intently to make sure he was done, but no one said a word. We just looked at each other in disbelief. Finally, Dad said, "You did it! That's your bull. That's the big bull. Great job!"

In no time Mike and Fred joined us, and Fred's first response was "Awesome! That's him, High and Tight."

The caping, quartering, and packing process were tough, but we had him all back to camp in two trips. Dad and I couldn't have been happier. I accomplished my goal and my dad was proud of me.

I would like to thank Scott Limmer of Comanche Wilderness Outfitters and two of his guides, Mike Williams and Fred Sell. Also, thanks to my uncle for taking time away from his job. He did a great job filming my hunt except for a couple sky shots. Finally, thanks to my dad, who made it all possible. 🦌

Photo from B&C Archives

Rylan Rudebusch accepting his youth award certificate at the 27th Big Game Awards Generation Next banquet. His moose was recognized the following night as the second award-winner for the Shiras' moose category.

Photo from B&C Archives

Mountain caribou, scoring 459-3/8 points,
taken by Paul T. Deuling in the Pelly Mountains of Yukon Territory,
in 1988.

Clancy the Caribou

Paul T. Deuling

21st Big Game Awards Program

A LOVELY BLONDE LADY FROM VANCOUVER WHO WAS VISITING OUR FAMILY QUIZZICALLY ASKED ME, "IS THAT A VERY BIG MOOSE YOU HAVE ON THE WALL THERE, PAUL?" SHE HAD SHOWN SOME INTEREST IN THE TAXIDERMY MOUNTS IN MY BASEMENT AS I HAD BEEN EXPLAINING WHAT THE VARIOUS ANIMALS WERE AND GENERALLY WHERE THEY WERE FOUND IN THE YUKON. I REPLIED THAT THE ANIMAL SHE WAS REFERRING TO WAS A MOUNTAIN CARIBOU AND THAT YES, IT WAS A FAIRLY LARGE ONE.

"Oh," she replied, "does he have a name?"

This took me by surprise until she followed with, "I'm a vegetarian and the only way I can deal with seeing these animals is by giving them a name. His name is Clancy. Clancy the caribou." And so it came to be that after all the years of roaming the Pelly Mountains and a few more [mounts] on my wall, Clancy finally received his name.

My hunt for Clancy was incidental to a Stone's sheep hunt that I had planned in late August of 1988 in the northern Pelly Mountains of the Yukon. All of my boys had either returned to school or hockey training camp so I decided to head out for a week's solitary Stone's sheep hunt before I, too, resumed my high school teaching duties. And I was frantic to go. That season had been a wet one and I had made several trips after sheep but either did not find them or sat in the tent for days before heading down the mountain for home.

With my old GMC 4x4 loaded down with my camper and extra gasoline, I headed for the Ketza country where I would have a walk of nearly a day before reaching my sheep area. The weather was absolutely beautiful with sunshine, a gentle breeze, and best of all, no bugs. Upon arriving that afternoon at my camp spot, a tiny side-hill bench, I kicked out a seat in the shale and chewed on some trail mix while watching a cow caribou in the basin below. She was foraging in the lichen, shaking her head and rubbing her back legs against one another in an effort, I supposed, to be rid of the bugs that were now appearing as the heat of the day dissipated. I watched her for a few minutes before she suddenly bolted off across the basin with head held high. And, just as caribou are apt to do, a few moments later she pranced right back to the origin of her fright. A wolverine was meandering in and out of the rocks and bushes, snooping into everything before loping off in his hunched-back fashion. The caribou was apparently fascinated by this, as she repeatedly ran off a short distance before turning, sniffing, and trotting right back to the disinterested mustelid, who just kept snooping for food. All this made great entertainment for a weary packer who was still sitting in sweat-soaked clothes and had yet to set up camp.

After pitching my tent, building a water pool from a tiny stream and setting out clothing to dry, I spent the next two hours having a snooze. Later that evening, I began to hike up the knob behind my camp where my boys had spotted rams on previous trips. Halfway up I remembered the silly cow and stopped to peer into the basin to see what she was up to. She had left the basin and climbed the very ridge I was on but was grazing about 900 meters north of me. About 50 yards away from her was a large animal that appeared to have a black oak tree growing from his head. The huge bull caribou immediately grabbed my attention and I set up my scope to have a better look at him. After a quick calculation of the number of days I had to pack this guy out if I shot him, I decided that he was worth taking home. Big sheep could wait until next year.

The hike down to the tent became a scramble, as the closer I got to the tent and my rifle, the more excited I became. I had seen a lot of good bulls in the Pellys over the years, but nothing quite matched what this guy was wearing. A quick drop off for the scope and a snatch of the .270 sent me on my way down the ridge formulating a plan of approach as I crept between boulders. Dropping off the ridge and paralleling it seemed the sensible thing to do, and the stalk became much easier with a distinct dip in the topography ahead. I was able to walk onto a ridge-cut that contained a pretty little tarn and then climbed about 40 feet to the rim where the bull was feeding. My last step was only enough to clear the ridge to allow viewing through my riflescope. Only 10 yards away, the large bull, resplendent in black velvet antlers and summer coat, could be heard munching as he tore up the lichen. I could see only a black mass through the scope, so I lowered it for a moment to assure myself that it was his shoulder that was filling up the aperture. At the shot, he bolted away and headed downhill toward the cow while I stood there dumbfounded that he would run at all. A second shot from 50 yards quickly brought him down.

I had not packed a camera since weight is an important factor in a solitary hunt, so I just sat beside the big fellow and stared at him. For how long, I don't know, but it was getting dark before I got around to caping and cleaning him. Few words can describe the feeling one has after killing such a magnificent animal, and I stopped many times just to stand back and view the scene.

The real work began the next morning when, loaded with meat, I began the first of three trips back to the truck. The loads were heavy, much heavier than I should have made them, but a 12-mile round trip up hills and over ridges is easier three times, rather than four. The next five days were spent pushing through willow brush and shin tangle with many a cuss word. "What a stupid, stupid thing to do!" was the most muttered phrase until I was done.

However, the trip was worth the effort and my family dined on very tender caribou the following winter. Tony Grabowski did a super taxidermy job on a shoulder mount and Clancy continues to impress hunters with his tremendous antlers.

And, from time to time, when the urbanites come to visit, I still receive a "that's a fine looking moose you have there!"

"A Yukon game officer told me that Paul was the only person he knew who would have tackled that job, as the area where Paul killed his caribou is extremely tough country to get around in," said Eldon Buckner, chairman of the Boone and Crockett Club's Records of North American Big Game Committee. "Along with being a hunter of the highest ethics, Paul also is an extremely modest man. It's a story in itself, but he was finally persuaded to strip the hardened velvet from the antlers and have the caribou measured."

Deuling was honored on June 26th, 2010, at the Boone and Crockett Club's 27th Awards Banquet in Reno, Nevada, where he received the Sagamore Hill Award, the highest honor given by the Boone and Crockett Club. Though Deuling harvested his World's Record caribou more than 20 years ago, he was unable to participate in the Club's triennial awards celebrations until this year. The Sagamore Hill Award was created in 1948 in memory of Theodore Roosevelt, Theodore Roosevelt, Jr., and Kermit Roosevelt to honor outstanding trophies worthy of great distinction. Only one award may be given in any three-year period, but the actual frequency has been even less often. Deuling is only the 17th recipient of a Sagamore Hill Award.

Deuling received the award for taking a World's Record mountain caribou in a hunt that exemplifies the sporting values that Roosevelt championed—fair chase, self reliance, perseverance, selective hunting, and mastery of challenges. The bull scores 459-3/8, more than 6 inches larger than the next-largest mountain caribou in Boone and Crockett Club's records book. 🦌

Deuling's story reprinted with permission from Of Man and Beast, *an Amboca publication.*

Mountain caribou, scoring 412-4/8 points,
taken by Jack E. Risner near Prospector Mountain in Yukon Territory,
in 2008.

Lucky

Jack E. Risner

27th Big Game Awards Program

I 'VE BEEN TOLD THAT I'M A LUCKY (EXPLETIVE) BY A FEW JEALOUS FRIENDS. MY RESPONSE IS THAT I'LL TAKE ALL THE GOOD LUCK I CAN GET.

In February 2007, my friend Lee Frudden called to tell me he was going caribou hunting in the Yukon in September. The trip was planned with Tim and Jen Mervyn of Mervyn's Yukon Outfitting. Lee said this was the place for the big ones. It sounded like a good hunt, so I called Tim. He didn't have any caribou hunts available in 2007 but he did have a moose hunt, so I booked it. The hunt went very well. It was the type of hunting and outfit I like, so when Tim took me to the airport to leave, I asked him about caribou again. He told me he had two hunts left for 2008. I knew that my hunting buddy Shawn Hullinger had always wanted to hunt caribou, so I told Tim that we'd take the hunts. (I called Shawn later when I got cell service in Seattle to ask if he wanted to go.)

Eleven and a half months later, we were off, double-checking everything ten times—guns, gear, etc. When we got to Vancouver, none of our gear made it (now that's lucky), so we went on to Whitehorse without it. We had scheduled two extra days just in case something like this happened. After our planned buffer days expired and countless phone calls, we still had nothing, and it was time to go into the bush. Tim told us he had guns that he would loan us, but we had to get going to keep everything flowing.

We had our boots, but that was it. About $1,500 later (there are no bargains in Whitehorse) we headed to Tim's to pick up a gun. It was a nice Steyr Mannlicher .30-06. Tim had it out and had run some rounds through it confirming it was hitting two inches high at 100 yards. It was good enough, but not having your own gun takes something out of you: confidence!

The flight to camp was exciting like all bush flights. Shawn pinched holes in the back of the seat, but all for naught—we made it just fine. When we arrived, the guides and horses were waiting for us. It was a boggy mile and a half to camp, and we were relieved to finally be there.

On September 14th at 5:30 a.m., I was up, chomping at the bit to go hunting. My guide Mike told me to chill out. Caribou hunting is similar to pronghorn hunting in that you can hunt all day long. After what seemed like far too long, we finally headed up the trail. About two miles up the creek we spotted a couple bulls about two miles away. We looked them over and decided they were immature bulls. Up to this point, the entire group had been together, but the canyon split into three different drainages. Shawn and his guide, Corey, took off up the right-hand fork and we went up the left. It was all uphill from there. Once we reached the top around 10 a.m., the view was spectacular—miles and miles of wilderness as far as the eye could see.

We hobbled the horses and headed down the ridge top on foot. In short order we had spotted seven or eight caribou about a mile away. There was what appeared to be a good bull in the bunch, but they fed over the top and out of sight. At that point, I really began missing my binoculars and spotting scope. Down the ridge, about a quarter mile across a canyon, we spotted caribou at the bottom. Mike set up his spotting scope and began looking them over. All of a sudden he got really excited and said, "There is the stud duck!" I tried not to knock him over so I could look. There was no doubt, the bull was a hog.

His tongue was hanging out as he was circling the herd; he'd been fighting and gotten whipped. He proceeded all the way around the herd, and lay down. He was still about 1,500 yards away and we could see about 10 cows and a couple of small bulls.

He looked good to me, and Mike agreed, so I headed off the mountain and Mike stayed to give me signals in case the bull moved. I did have a pair of 8X binoculars with me, but no eye cups. I crossed the bottom and climbed up on the point that was between us and the bull. The basin was covered with blueberry bushes about 18 to 24 inches tall. When I peeked over the ridge, he was still lying there. I guessed him to be between 400 to 500 yards away—too far, having never shot the gun before. The group of 11 had transformed into about 25 caribou. The group was intermixed, feeding and lying down on the wide-open hillside. I decided that 200 yards would be my maximum shooting distance with this borrowed rifle. Considering they were all much further than that, I started crawling down the hill. When I reached a point around 300 yards from them, I spotted another bull coming out from behind the hill. He appeared to be the boss and looked huge, but he was close to 450 yards and moving in and out of the cows. As I was trying to size him up with my borrowed 8X binoculars (and cussing the airlines), he turned around and headed back behind the hill. He stopped out of sight, but I could see the top of a tree whipping back and forth, so I kept crawling and slithered around the hill.

All this time, I was in plain sight of the first big bull and all the other caribou. I could just about see the second bull but some of the herd had spotted me. The first big bull stood up. I had already gone past him trying to get a good look at the other one. While he wasn't necessarily the biggest, he was still huge, and I decided I'd better take him before they all took off. It was at this point that I realized what a bad position I was in to take the shot. The hillside was too steep to sit down, so I lay down. This didn't work since there was too much brush to see facing downhill with my feet up, so I got on top of a bush and lay my arm out to rest the gun on top of. It was not the ideal position, but I had him in my crosshairs. Boom! He was down, and I was recovering from being scoped, but smiling through the blood.

Our gear showed up two days later. Shawn got to use his rifle to shoot his bull, also a 400-inch caribou. With my gun, I was fortunate enough to bag two wolves who were feeding on a kill of another 400-inch bull.

Good luck and a little bad luck—I'll take it all. My best luck is to be blessed with so many good friends and a wonderful wife, Lynette, who wishes me luck and tells me to shoot straight and be safe. I guess I am a lucky guy. 🦌

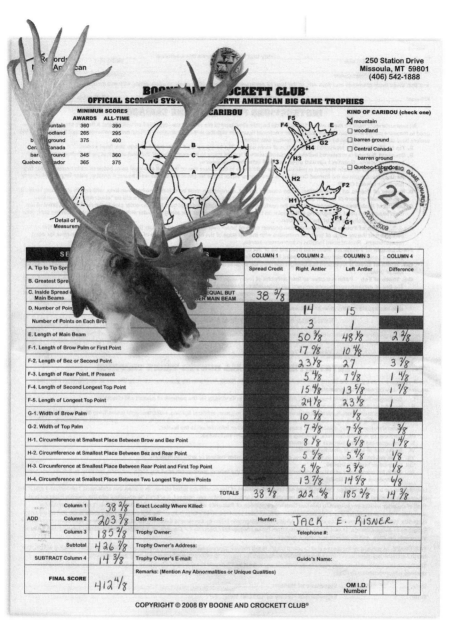

Final score chart for Risner's mountain caribou, which scores 412–4/8 Points.

Woodland caribou, scoring 340-5/8 points,
taken by Scott A. Trujillo near Sam's Pond, Newfoundland,
in 2006.

Keeping Up with Bob

Scott A. Trujillo

26th Big Game Awards Program

M Y TWO FRIENDS AND I HAD BEEN PREPARING FOR THIS HUNTING TRIP TO NEWFOUNDLAND ALL YEAR. I HAVE KNOWN BRAD SAUVE AND STEVE GARDNER FOR MOST OF MY ADULT LIFE AND WE HAVE HUNTED TOGETHER IN COLORADO AND UTAH FOR SEVERAL YEARS FOR ELK AND MULE DEER. BRAD HAD TAKEN A BIG CARIBOU ON A PREVIOUS HUNT IN QUEBEC, SO HE WAS SIGNED UP FOR A MOOSE AND BLACK BEAR COMBINATION HUNT THIS YEAR. STEVE AND I WERE PREPARING FOR WOODLAND CARIBOU.

Our outfitter, Bob Effords, was extremely helpful with all of the preparation for the trip. He spoke specifically of the wet conditions for which Newfoundland is famous. Per Bob's recommendation, we each made our investment in hip boots, new rain gear, and several other items that would help our equipment and our bodies survive and function in cold, rainy conditions.

When we arrived in St. Johns, however, it became clear that we were going to get conditions that none of us had prepared for — warm, beautiful weather! It seemed great on our first day. We spent that Sunday driving to Effords' headquarters, where Bob's team helped us pack our equipment into his floatplane.

At camp, we sighted in our rifles and demonstrated to our respective guides that we were familiar with our guns. We listened to amusing stories of hunters who came to camp having never shot their recently purchased rifles. The most common anecdote centered on hunters who came to camp with expensive, top-of-the-line hunting boots that barely covered their ankles. We would learn the importance of that lesson in days to come.

We listened while Brad hit bulls-eyes on a target he asked to set up about 600 yards away. Brad said he just wanted to make sure his gun was fine-tuned. I resisted the urge to explain to our hosts that Brad was the 2004 and 2006 United States National Marksmanship Champion in F-class shooting (rifles with scopes). The rest of the evening was spent speculating on how ironic and hilarious it would be if Brad missed at a trophy animal that week. These guys were great fun and shared lots of hunting stories with us.

The next morning, Brad, Steve, and I took off in separate directions with our guides. My guide Craig and I took a boat across the lake and spent the day trudging through miles of bogs and rivers. The land was difficult to describe. It was like walking across stacks of soaking wet bed mattresses covered in grass, surrounded by gorgeous landscapes. Standing water seemed to exist at any elevation. It made walking difficult and I was exhausted that first night, having covered so much area in warm weather. The most worrying part was that none of us saw any animals that day. Like elk and deer, caribou preferred deep timber when the weather is dry and above 40 degrees Fahrenheit. The weather was expected to remain like this all week. We all had some concerns.

The next day proved to be equally beautiful and equally void of wildlife. The following night, however, Steve came back to camp with his caribou. The next morning, Brad shot his moose. Yes, a perfect shot. I was still empty-handed and had only seen a cow and calf moose. Craig explained that he had never seen the land so empty. When Bob flew into camp later that week, he spoke with Craig, who assured him that we were covering miles of area together, from morning through sunset, but the animals were in deep cover.

Then came a curve in the experience I had not expected. Unfortunately, Craig was not able to guide me through all of my hunting. But as the outfitter and owner of the operation, Bob was dedicated to making sure I had an opportunity to see a decent caribou. Bob took me to an area I had not hunted earlier with Craig.

I soon realized why the guides hid their laughter when Bob offered to guide me. We started our trek into the wilderness and I struggled to keep up with him. Simply said, he walked very fast. The camp cook came along for the experience and struggled to keep up with Bob as well. We stopped for a minute when we reached some high ground about an hour from our starting point at the lake. The morning was cold but I was warm from the hike. I took out my spotting scope as an excuse to rest. About 10 minutes into our search, Bob nudged me and pointed to what looked like a large herd about two miles away. I knew Bob was up for it and I was excited about seeing a whole herd, so I packed away my scope and prepared for the walk.

Bob asked me again before we got started if I was up for the walk. He explained that this area would be even more treacherous and rugged than the area I hunted with Craig. He was right. We trudged through wetlands, bogs and thick timber, unlike anything I had experienced in my 20 years of hunting. I stayed right behind Bob from the beginning, as I was too excited to be tired. Two hours later, however, I began to worry about finding this herd. We were weaving in and out of bogs and patches of timber and had not seen any signs of the herd since we left the area where we spotted them. It had been about an hour since we were able to see more than 50-100 yards in any direction. I was convinced we had passed them or they had moved on to a different area. I looked for any indication that Bob was lost or confused about our location, relative to the animals, but saw no doubts on his face. The only time he looked back was when he checked on the cook, who was working to stay within sight of his boss. Bob was making no effort to be cautious or quiet during our hike. Then everything changed.

Without any indication of the herd, Bob told me to chamber a bullet from my clip, which I had not yet done for safety's sake. He started whispering for the first time since we left that morning. I kept looking around while he waited for the cook to catch up, but I was convinced that we had passed the herd an hour ago.

We followed him up to the next hill top and back down into a low area. Again, we saw nothing. Yet this time, he told the cook and I to move very quietly as we ascended up the next hill. Even the cook looked around in confusion. At the top, Bob seemed almost surprised when we again saw nothing. I caught the cook looking back in the direction that we came, as if he, too, thought we had passed the caribou. We followed Bob down the hill and this time he told me to get low as we approached the top of the next high area. I agreed, with forced enthusiasm on my face, but I admit I was worried that he was just trying to keep my interest, having lost the caribou. Before we reached to the top, Bob got down on all fours and crawled the last remaining distance to the crest of the hill. I put my gun on my back and did the same until I caught up with him.

I could not believe what I saw. There was the herd! I flattened out on the ground at the first glimpse of what must have been about 100 caribou on the next ridge. They were spread out all over. Females were bedded down on the next crest, while young caribou walked around feeding. Antlers were everywhere. I noticed that the cook stopped moving when he saw me flatten out, even though he couldn't see what we were hiding from. Bob signaled for him to quietly make his way up to us.

My first instinct was to ready my gun. In no time, I was looking through my riflescope as Bob directed the cook to take a position behind a bush to his left. Bob told me to crawl up a few yards to a small boulder where I could place my gun for stability. He suggested that we wait a while and scope the herd because they weren't aware of our presence and it might take a while to spot the largest animal. I handed him my video camera to give to the cook. I continued looking though my riflescope as Bob retreated a few feet away to the bush where the cook was. When they were still and silent, I crawled up to the rock. My heart was pounding and I was convinced the caribou could hear my breathing. I slowly organized my position, moving twigs out of the way and adjusting myself on the hard gravel ground.

The next five minutes were spent scoping the herd and thinking to myself, "How did he do that?" We had traveled two and a half miles through thick wilderness and he seemed to secretly know exactly where they would be two hours later. I felt guilty for doubting a man with such skill and experience.

I could hear Bob and the cook whispering while I looked for the best of the group. I strained to hear partial sound bites from them like "…what about that one on the right?" or "…the thick-antlered one toward the back is probably…"

I was calm now, having picked my animal. I spent the next several minutes scoping the different areas in front of me; frequently moving back to my favorite to make sure he was still there. I hadn't moved or taken my eye away from my scope in a while when I sensed intensity increase in the whispering behind me. I was sure I heard "@$#$^!" once or twice but I could not spot anything new. I swung my gun back and forth over the herd, looking for anything to justify the excitement. Seconds later, I could hear Bob crawling toward me. I hurriedly peeled my cheek off my gunstock for the first time in ten minutes and lifted my head, determined to see the what they spotted before Bob had to point it out to me. There he was, entering a low, open area in front of the herd.

If he didn't have such a white coat, I would have thought the rack belonged to a strange looking elk. I had not seen a real caribou before my visit to Newfoundland but his antlers were tall and distinctive and I could tell by Bob choosing to crawl toward me that this was the beast he had been waiting for.

My binoculars have a built-in laser rangefinder and I quickly scanned the caribou before Bob reached me. He was 255 yards away and I had my gun settled on the ground in perfect firing position. I put my face back down and clicked my safety off. Bob said, "Hold your shot; he's moving toward us."

As we waited, however, I had to pick my gun off of my resting spot in order to keep him in my sights. Bob positioned himself right behind me as if he was hoping to look through my scope. He kept whispering, "Just a minute… he's still too far… "

A few seconds passed and I had to completely raise my gun to a kneeling position in order to stay on him. Finally the caribou stopped and Bob gave the okay to shoot. In the time it took the caribou to move 50 yards closer, I had gone from a poised, calm, experienced hunter into a nervous pile of camouflage. I could feel embarrassment as I struggled to keep my gun from shaking and I knew Bob was positioned perfectly to see the end of the barrel moving all over the place. He was inches over my shoulder, whispering the common phrase, "Just calm down and take your time."

I actually started formulating excuses for a miss as I strained to keep the gun steady. There wasn't the time to explain that I have been target shooting with the best in the country for the last several years and 250 yards from a stable, prone position was a "gimme" compared to a 200-yard shot from a strained kneeling position. Because of my nervous shaking, Bob even felt compelled to put his hand on my shoulder and said, "Hold off for a second… just get comfortable before you shoot."

I took a deep breath, whispered back to him (but really for my own benefit), "Don't worry; he'll be dropping in about two seconds."

I relaxed, took another breath, put the crosshairs on him, and pulled the trigger. My ears were still ringing when I heard the cook yell, "He's down! He's down!"

Bob yelled, "Perfect shot; you got him!"

I chambered another round while I searched for movement. There was none. I picked up my bullet casing, quickly gathered up my pack, and started walking down to him. I noticed the cook filming as we were walking. "Did you get all that on camera?" I asked.

"I think some parts," he responded.

Later I found out that the video wasn't on during the excitement. Who cares? He was a great cook.

We took the rest of the day getting the animal back to the lake. The door to the plane had to be left slightly ajar, as the antlers wouldn't fit completely inside. I held onto them the entire ride back to the Effords' Outfitters base.

Bob recommended that I contact Boone and Crockett Club to measure the caribou. I had never taken an animal thought to be large enough for the B&C records book. He ended up scoring 340-5/8 points, within the top 25 in the all-time B&C records book. He had several points broken off from fighting, including every point on his right bez, otherwise he may have scored closer to 350. He was truly a remarkable and distinctive animal. 🦌

Central Canada barren ground caribou, scoring 382–3/8 points, taken by N. Guy Eastman near Northwest Territories' Point Lake, in 2002.

Bows on the Tundra

N. Guy Eastman

26th Big Game Awards Program

As a young man, I had the unique opportunity to travel western North America and Alaska with my grandfather, the late Gordon Eastman, during my summer breaks from school. On these trips, as we traveled to our next location, Gordon would tell me story after story of his lifetime of adventures in the outdoors. Some of my favorites were the tales of huge moose, caribou, and wolves of the Arctic in Canada's wild Northwest Territories.

I couldn't help but wonder if I would be fortunate enough to have some stories of my own to pass on to my grandchildren.

Perhaps I would now, I thought, as I sat in the airport with my brother Ike waiting for a flight to Yellowknife. We were filming the hunt for our television show, "Eastmans' Hunting Journal." Our destination was the wild Northwest Territories my grandfather had loved so much. Our bowhunting travels would take us a mere 20 miles short of the Arctic Circle in search of monster central Canada barren ground caribou.

After our plane ride, my quest began near the head of Esker Bay. It was about three miles wide and covered with tundra in brilliant shades of red, orange, and yellow. The sparsely scattered patches of Arctic timber provided a subtle contrast of green.

After we tied up our boat, we gathered all our gear and began hiking up the bottom of the valley along a small, rocky creek. The sand on the edge of the creek was covered with grizzly tracks. There had been at least five or six different bears in this valley during the past couple weeks. We didn't relish the thought of running into one.

We had only gone a couple of miles when we spotted two caribou on the mountainside across the valley. I pulled the spotting scope from my pack, rested it on top of a rock, and focused on the two feeding animals. Immediately, I could see substantial racks on both feeding bulls. I then dialed the Swarovski to full power and told our guide Paul Jones he had better grab a look at these bulls. Paul had his eye to the scope for about five seconds before he started putting together a plan to stalk the bulls. As we frantically packed up our packs, Paul said, "The bull on the left is one we really need to go after."

Soon we were off again, across the squishy tundra at full speed. The bulls were at least two miles away. We had to come down one side of the valley, cross the creek again and tromp up the other side. Fortunately, the big bull was in the perfect place for a stalk. He was feeding on a subtle ledge on the side of the mountain with the wind at his back. Just the sort of setup a bowhunter likes to see, because trophy animals seldom put themselves in a situation for a perfect stalk to within bow range. As we headed up the other side of the valley, we realized that because of the steep descent of the hillside, the bull could not see us coming from underneath him. It was going to be beautiful.

With 100 yards left to go, we shed our packs and all unnecessary items and stashed them in the brush. We put together a quick game plan, and I got Ike set up with the camera to film the action as it unfolded — good or bad!

Once we crept to within 50 yards, we began to see the velvet tops of his huge rack bobbing toward us in the skyline above the tundra. Ike started recording as the bull knocked another 25 yards off the distance between us. I knelt down and slowly drew my bow. The bull kept feeding closer and closer; his rack kept getting larger and larger. Paul ranged him at only 14 yards, but I didn't have a shot. He was coming straight at me, feeding with his head down. I knew we were going to have problems when his eyes rose to meet mine. I was a mere 11 yards from largest caribou I had ever seen, staring eye to eye with nothing between us but thin, crisp arctic air. I could almost see the wheels turning inside his head.

He then decided he'd had enough and instantly turned and ran. At about 40 yards, he suddenly stopped and turned broadside. I knew there was no time to range, so I estimated the distance, let the air out of my lungs, anchored my 40-yard pin behind his shoulder, and squeezed the release.

The shot felt good, and it sounded good when the arrow traveled cleanly through his body. The caribou turned and ran full blast across the tundra. His rack looked enormous as he was going away. I turned to Ike and gave him a slightly uncertain thumbs up.

Ike replied, "You hit him square behind the shoulder, and I got it all on film!"

It is a good thing the Arctic does not have much brush, because tracking a blood trail on the red tundra would have been a nightmare. Nonetheless, we had only walked about 60 yards and when we found the huge bull piled up on the mountainside overlooking Esker Bay.

He was absolutely tremendous. His shovel was over 17 inches tall and hung out beyond his nose — so far beyond, in fact, that the points on the end were worn down from scraping the ground when he fed.

One of his most distinctive features was the 20-inch "back scratcher" on his right antler. It turned straight into the center of his rack, and his spread was well over four feet. He is my trophy of a lifetime. 🦌

Quebec–Labrador caribou, scoring 407-3/8 points,
taken by Frederick B. Davis near the Caniapiscau River in Quebec,
in 2005.

Archery Trophy

Frederick B. Davis

27th Big Game Awards Program

I HAD DONE ENOUGH THINKING ABOUT CARIBOU HUNTING, AND I FINALLY DECIDED THAT IF I WAS GOING TO GO, I NEEDED TO START MAKING SOME DEFINITE PLANS. IT WASN'T LONG BEFORE I WAS ON THE PHONE RESEARCHING OUTFITTERS, AND I SOON HAD A HUNT BOOKED WITH JACK HUME ADVENTURES.

My trip began in early September 2005 when I drove to Montreal where other hunters and I would board a plane to Schefferville, Quebec, a town from which several outfitters operated. Shortly after arriving, I met the other hunters that I would be with for the next six days. We were all anxious to begin hunting after talking to other hunters returning from their adventures and seeing the caribou they brought back, including some nice bulls. The next morning, our hunting group boarded a floatplane that took us to a remote camp near the Caniapiscau River.

We had a camp helper, Alfred, and a cook for the week, which really helped things go smoothly since no one in camp had ever hunted caribou before. Our days began with a big breakfast, after which Alfred would take us by boat and drop us off at different crossings that caribou were known to use. In the evenings we would be picked up and brought back to another big meal at camp.

The first two days went by with only two bulls being taken by our group and very few sightings. The third morning was a cold sit by the lake, but I did see four bulls. The problem was that they had bedded on a distant ridge across the lake. When Alfred arrived at lunchtime to check on me, they hadn't shown any signs of moving, so I asked him for a ride across the lake so I could attempt a stalk. By the time I got to where the bulls had been, they were on their feet and just dropping below the ridge in front of me. I moved ahead to where I could see down the hill, expecting to see the four bulls nearby, but instead I saw another group of bulls working their way around the hill away from me. There was no cover to move directly in on them so I quickly backed off and swung around in an attempt to get in front of them. I was almost too late, but things started to get pretty exciting when I saw antler tops just in front of me. I just barely had time to move another couple of yards to a rock where I crouched down and nocked an arrow. In a matter of seconds I could hear the clicking sounds of moving caribou—that until this hunt, I had only heard about—getting louder and louder, and I had several bulls coming into view. One was only ten yards away, but I held off knowing that more were approaching. I was enjoying the encounter, though itching for a shot opportunity knowing that I could be busted at any second. The next two bulls that came into view were considerably larger than the others, and the decision to shoot was easy. I picked what I thought was the larger of the two, and when he stopped by a tree I had earlier ranged at 38 yards I made my move. He looked my way as I drew, but it was too late. My arrow was on its way. At the shot, he and the other 20 or so caribou bolted in as many different directions, but I kept my eye on him and I immediately knew the shot had been true.

I was excited and immediately got back to the top of the hill where I could radio back that I was going to need some help. I knew that I had shot a big bull, but I did not realize how big until we found him about 120 yards from where the blood trail started. Alfred was very surprised at the size of the bull and told me that it was very big. After stripping the velvet off back at camp we took some quick measurements, just to get an idea of the score. Even though I had limited knowledge of caribou antlers, I still realized that he was an exceptional bull. I never had him officially scored until three years later. I didn't personally know any measurers, and hauling him around was a hassle since I had a shoulder mount done as soon as I returned from my trip.

After the official scoring, I realized how fortunate I had been to take this bull. He ended up getting to be part of the display at the Pope and Young convention in Denver, Colorado, in 2009, and he was also sent to Boone and Crockett Club's 27th Awards Program Banquet in Reno, Nevada—both of which I expect to be once-in-a-lifetime honors. I may never get a shot at another animal as big as this; however, I will enjoy the memories from this hunt and the events that followed for the rest of my life. ❦

Horned Game

PRONGHORN

BISON

ROCKY MOUNTAIN GOAT

MUSK OX

BIGHORN SHEEP

STONE'S SHEEP

Bison, scoring 122-4/8 points,
taken by Robert D. Jones, in Custer County, South Dakota,
in 1995.

Big Buffalo Don't Come Easy!

Robert D. Jones

23rd Big Game Awards Program

I'VE ALWAYS HAD A FASCINATION WITH BUFFALO. AS A KID, IT WAS BUFFALO NICKELS. LATER ON, GRANCEL FITZ BECAME MY HERO WHEN I READ HOW HE HAD KILLED A TROPHY BULL AT FORT NIOBRARA, NEBRASKA, IN 1952. I BEGAN DREAMING OF COLLECTING A BIG, HEAVY-MANED BULL OF MY OWN.

My first buffalo was purchased from the surplus herd of the National Bison Range in Montana in 1977. This dandy old bull was hauled to Colville, Washington, and was put on live display for a couple of months. He was a real attraction. Everyone in the country came to see him, not to mention the senior citizen bus that came by twice a week. Finally it came time to butcher, and my first buffalo ended up as a life-size mount in the museum at Washington State University.

Then, in 1982, I drew one of 10 non-resident buffalo permits for the Henry Mountains in Utah. The Henry's are a rough piece of country, and a trophy bull was hard to find. Prior to my hunt, I spent 16 days on a backpack Dall's sheep hunt in Alaska; killing a buffalo at 10,200 feet elevation on Mt. Pinnell made the efforts of the sheep hunt look pretty tame. It took seven horses to pack out the meat, cape and skull. This Utah bull scored 113-6/8 points, and it was the biggest bull taken in Utah that season.

In the 1980s and early '90s, I outfitted buffalo hunts on the Triple U Ranch outside Pierre, South Dakota. I harvested several more bulls on the ranch, but these trophies, while probably the prettiest buffalo I had ever seen, were not eligible for the records book and just didn't get enough years on them to make them trophy-class. I was in on the kill of close to 200 mature bulls, and this led to my learning how to field judge buffalo with a little consistency. My advice: forget all about horn length and look for third-quarter mass only.

Finally, after a lot of research, I applied for a permit at Custer State Park in South Dakota. I drew a permit for a three-day hunt in January of 1995 and arrived at the park a few days early to scout the herd. I found a great old bull late in the afternoon the day before my hunt and photographed him until dark, confident that I had found a record-book bull. Unfortunately, my luck was about to take a turn for the worse. A truck's headlights came down the jeep trail. It was a park ranger guiding the only other hunter in the same three-day time slot. The old bull I had found was standing just off the road in a snowstorm. They came back the next morning and followed his tracks for five miles in the fresh snow until the other hunter filled his tag. That bull was a dandy, and should have scored close to 125 points.

I finally took an old, rugged-looking bull with horns that were broomed back so far that they are the shortest horns on record. They also have the largest third quarter mass, and score 118-6/8. He had character, and I finally had my record-class bison!

After my hunt, I stayed to photograph wildlife in the park and, after a few days, found the buffalo of a lifetime! I was one of the last hunters for the 94-95 season, and after the hunts were over I called the park office to see if this huge bull had been taken. He hadn't, so I put in again for the 1995-96 season. I also requested the first hunt of the season. I was drawn and my hunt was set for December 6, 7 and 8.

I arrived early and did a little scouting, but failed to find the old bull. Not unusual, since the park consists of 73,000 acres with a herd of 1,400 bison. On the first morning of my hunt I met Vern Ekstrom at the park headquarters. Vern is in charge of the buffalo program at Custer, and does most of the guiding on the hunts. We had a great time on my last hunt, and it was a pleasure to see him again. We immediately headed for a part of the park he hadn't been into for awhile. It wasn't a half hour after daylight when we spied a band of seven old bulls on a hillside, in heavy timber. A jeep trail leading into the area was blocked with downed trees, so we went on foot. The bulls spooked when they saw us, and went uphill and around into the bottom of a huge basin. They stopped there to feed and we glassed them from a high, rocky point. The tremendous old bull I had seen the previous year stood out like a sore thumb. Of all the buffalo in the park, and of all the country this bull could have been in, we had found him the first morning! I told Vern I would take him.

We had to wait for the meat inspector to come out before I could shoot. Under South Dakota law, all harvestable bison bulls must be observed by a meat inspector before they can be taken. Vern went back to the truck to radio this information to town, and came back with the bad news. The meat inspector was not available and we had to wait until the next day!

I told Vern I wanted to glass this band of bulls until it got dark so we would at least have an idea where they might be in the morning. There was no snow on the ground, so tracking was not an option. The weather was cool and very calm, which probably led to the buffalo holding tight. The lush feed in the basin didn't hurt anything either. They were still in the basin at dark when I left for the truck by flashlight.

After a long, slow night, Vern and I hiked into the basin right after daylight. The little herd was in the exact same spot. They hadn't moved more than 50 yards in 24 hours. Luck was on our side. Vern went back to the truck to call the inspector while I glassed the big bull with my spotting scope. After a couple of hours the okay was given, and I harvested the old bull with a 150 grain Nosler to the base of the skull from my .270.

This dandy old bull weighed 2,450 pounds (live weight), making him the heaviest ever recorded from Custer State Park. His horn measurements, after the required 60-day drying period, scored 130-4/8 inches. At that entry score the Records of North American Big Game, 10th Edition, would have listed this bull behind seven other entries: two of these were picked up, and four were taken from the wood bison herd in northern Alberta. My bull would have been the largest plains bull ever taken by a sport hunter. Unfortunately, when the Final Awards Judges' Panel in Reno scored my bull, the final score dropped to 122-4/8 points. This drop in points occurred because the base measurements were not taken in the correct place when it was initially measured.

Fifty years of dreaming, 40 years of big-game hunting, 20 years of experience with buffalo, and a lot of luck resulted in my taking this great animal. 🦬

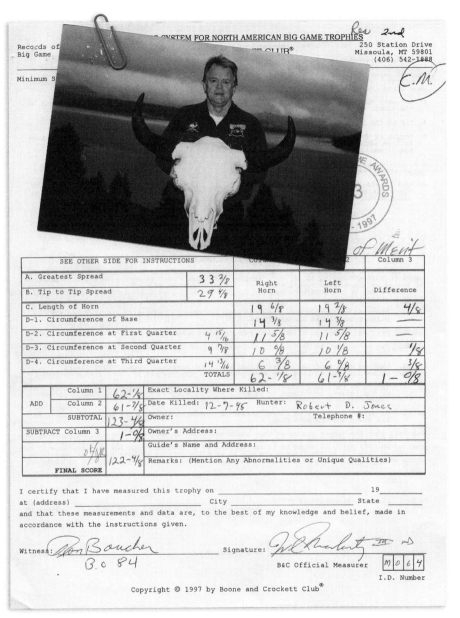

SYSTEM FOR NORTH AMERICAN BIG GAME TROPHIES

Records of
Big Game

250 Station Drive
Missoula, MT 59801
(406) 542-1888

Minimum S

SEE OTHER SIDE FOR INSTRUCTIONS			Column 3
A. Greatest Spread	33 2/8	Right Horn / Left Horn	Difference
B. Tip to Tip Spread	29 4/8		
C. Length of Horn		19 6/8 / 19 2/8	4/8
D-1. Circumference of Base		14 3/8 / 14 3/8	—
D-2. Circumference at First Quarter	4 15/16	11 5/8 / 11 5/8	—
D-3. Circumference at Second Quarter	9 7/8	10 0/8 / 10 1/8	1/8
D-4. Circumference at Third Quarter	14 13/16	6 3/8 / 6 0/8	3/8
TOTALS		62-1/8 / 61-3/8	1-0/8

ADD	Column 1	62-1/8	Exact Locality Where Killed:
	Column 2	61-3/8	Date Killed: 12-7-95 Hunter: Robert D. Jones
	SUBTOTAL	123-4/8	Owner: Telephone #:
SUBTRACT Column 3		1-0/8	Owner's Address:
			Guide's Name and Address:
FINAL SCORE		122-4/8	Remarks: (Mention Any Abnormalities or Unique Qualities)

I certify that I have measured this trophy on _____ 19_____
at (address) _____ City _____ State _____
and that these measurements and data are, to the best of my knowledge and belief, made in
accordance with the instructions given.

Witness: _Ron Boucher_   Signature: _____ III
B.0 84

B&C Official Measurer | m | 0 | 6 | 4 |
I.D. Number

Copyright © 1997 by Boone and Crockett Club®

*Original score chart for Jones' bison, which
scores 122-4/8 points.*

*Rocky Mountain goat, scoring 54 points,
taken by A.C. Smid near Kalum Lake in British Columbia,
in 2008.*

This Goat was for Pops

A.C. Smid

27th Big Game Awards Program

The first Rocky Mountain goat I ever harvested was in 2006. It was a beautiful goat, but it had a summer coat. So in September 2008, while hunting moose with my guide Roger, I mentioned to him that in some future year I would love to harvest a winter billy. He said that shouldn't be a problem, explaining that his good friend Bob Milligan, of Terrace, British Columbia, runs Milligan's Outfitting, and his area has some of the best goats in British Columbia!

"Great!" I said. "See what you can do for some future year." End of conversation.

In November 2008, my phone rang, and it was Roger. He said Bob Milligan had called about a trophy goat he had spotted, and they had been unsuccessful in hunting it for the last couple of weeks due to poor weather conditions. Bob was scheduled to take some needed time off, but instead called Roger and asked if I could get up there—now! The rut was coming, and Bob knew the billy would hang in the same general area with the nannies. This was a once-in-a-lifetime trophy, and the pictures that he took through his spotting scope would verify that!

I explained to Roger that in five days I was headed to western Montana on an elk hunt with my good friend, Ray Godin of Superior, Montana; and then over to Lewistown in central Montana to celebrate Thanksgiving week with my wife Melissa and my in-laws. Roger knew that my father-in-law Richard, who I fondly refer to as Pops, was dying of cancer, and I didn't think he would make it to Christmas. Roger understood the dilemma I was in, and just asked me to think about it and to get back to him as soon as possible.

After hanging up the phone with Roger, I opened my email and downloaded the pictures. No doubt about it—a trophy goat of a lifetime!

"Timing is everything" they say, but this time, there was no time for delay. I explained the situation to my wife Melissa and she understood the meaning of a trophy of a lifetime. She encouraged me that if I was going to go that I should get my butt in gear and not dilly dally around. She also knew that calling off the elk hunt would not be hard, but the call to Pops would be the tough one. At first he understood, but then he didn't, and I'll just leave it at that.

On November 18th Roger picked me up at the Smithers Regional Airport. The next day we sighted in my rifle, gathered Roger's gear, and prepared for the journey. He said there was no way in hell that he was going to miss this trip; he dropped everything he was doing to be part of my hunt. On November 20th, we boogied west to Terrace, which is about 70 miles from the coast.

Upon arrival, we were greeted by Bob, his wife Michelle, and their two boys Bobby and Billy. There was also Brodie Cardinal, one of Bob's guides who would be on the hunt as well.

After settling in at their home for the night, and going through the customary small chat, we got right down to the business at hand. Bob explained that the hunt was going to be a tough one. The weather won't cooperate, the climb will be long and steep, and the snow will be about 6- to 8-feet deep. The plan is basic: drive the pickup until the snow gets too deep, unload the modified ATV with its snow tracks, and drive it to the end of the logging road, pulling a sled. Strap on the 12x14-inch snowshoes and hoof it from there.

The next morning, shortly after 5 a.m., we were headed down the road and executing the plan that we discussed the night before. Over the last couple of days, the snow had been coming down heavily, and today was no exception. If we didn't have a break in the weather by 10 a.m., we wouldn't strap on the snowshoes because the day would be done. There wouldn't be enough time to make it to the goats even if we got a break in the weather. We sat waiting in the snow. Before long, 10 a.m. arrived, and our day was done.

Day two was the same drill, down the road until the end, snowing again just like yesterday, however much lighter, and there was something in Bob's facial expression that led me to believe that something was amiss. Last night when we Googled the weather forecast, there was a hole forming that might give us a short break before a new storm would hit. As we looked up into the morning sky, Bob turned to us and said, "Gear up, put on the snowshoes, and we are outta here."

Brodie led, followed by Bob, Roger, and me. After hiking for about two hours up a steep, tree-lined ridge, we finally came to the first—and last—opening on our way up. It was about 300 yards long and interspersed with trees. It was here where we would first have an opportunity to glass up the mountain and look into the bowls for the goats. Just as Bob had predicted there they were—about 15 in all—nannies and kids feeding while the three billies went about their power struggle. We took out the spotting scopes to find the one we were after. It was really difficult to determine who was who because of the distance until our billy stepped front and center. Not only did he have the horns, but the mass of his body dominated the others. He also had a red throat sash that was likely caused by another billy during a dominance fight.

The game plan was easy to figure out; it was the execution that would prove difficult. We needed to head to the thick tree-lined ridge that lay on the other side of this opening. The ridge looked like an inverted V, with bowls to the left and right. Our goats were in the bowl, above and to the left, and at the end of tree line. We guesstimated that the goats were over 1,200 yards horizontal distance and about 1,300 feet from the top of the mountain. Slowly we worked across the opening, trying to stay behind what trees we could, to avoid being spotted from above. After finally hitting the tree line, we headed straight up, angling to our right as we went, figuring the goats would be up and to our left.

It is hard to describe the entire journey, but the climb was surreal. It was like being on a StairMaster® with snowshoes in eight feet of snow for over eight hours. Being fourth in line, I had the advantage of placing my foot in a preformed cast, while all of the snow that had accumulated on the tree branches was being knocked down by the others ahead. Brodie had it the worst; he was leading and of course had to break trail. Numerous times we all offered to switch, but we all felt safe knowing that his young ego would get in the way. It was during this long climb that I started to mentally prepare myself for a long shot and the importance of remaining calm. Bob said that generally the shots are between 150 and 250 yards. I felt today was going to be different. I regularly practice shots at 400 and 500 yards with my Blazer .270 Weatherby Magnum that is scoped with a Schmidt

& Bender 3-12x42. I feel comfortable at that range but would definitely prefer closer. I do feel that I have a responsibility to the animal as well as to myself that if I'm going to shoot at that distance, I need to be confident and accurate.

By angling to our right, we kept the top of the ridgeline to our left and remained out of sight. As we finally broke through the tree line at the top of the inverted V, we found ourselves in scrub brush and stunted trees that stuck through the top of the snow. This was followed by small and large boulders as we continued up to a little knoll. We figured the bowl we had seen the goats in was to the left of the knoll, so we would stay to the right. As Brodie crested the knoll he immediately went prone, looked back at us and said, "The goats are 90 yards ahead in the bowl."

We all tried in vain to find them and we must have looked like bobbers in the ocean going up and down. Then over 500 yards away and about 100 feet higher in elevation, we spotted the off-white figures against the white snow! I guess I should have asked Brodie how he did in math, but in the end, it really didn't matter. The goats apparently drifted out of the bowl on our left and were now in the bowl to our right. Another group of about six goats appeared above us about 700 yards away, and they definitely had seen us. Fortunately, our billy was not among them. Bob crawled up and out to get a better view of the billy we were after. As Bob lay there and glassed, time went by and we could tell by his body language that he hadn't spotted our goat—no movement, no nothing.

During the climb, the temperature hovered about 20°F with about a 20 mph wind, light snow, and overcast skies. The wind, thank goodness, had been blowing from our right to the left, so we knew they hadn't winded us. As we lay there, chill factor came into play, and I knew I would have to layer up. We all layered differently. Bob chose to stay fully dressed as he hikes from the bottom to the top and then change into dry clothes. On the other hand, I layer as I go, and now was the time to get warm so I wouldn't have the shakes when it would be my time to step up to the plate.

After getting the right amount of clothes on, we went back to the binoculars and continued to look at the goats that were on a little bench across from us. As we continued to glass, suddenly we saw tips of horns coming our way from the far side of the bench. As if on cue, there he was, with the red throat sash and significantly larger horns and body mass when compared to the other billy in the group. Bob immediately turned around and said, "Charles get ready. It's him."

Then Roger chimed in and said, "Please Bob, put the spotting scope on him and make sure." Bob complied and no doubt about it, this was our billy. We couldn't tell by their mannerisms if they had made us yet; they just kept pawing and feeding to the right.

We had to get closer, so Bob and I would go it alone. We couldn't go back around, then up and back down. It was already 3:30 p.m., and we would be out of light by the time we made it. Our only option was to angle up and to our right to the remnants of a scrub tree that lay about 100 yards away, and from there I could take the long shot. I turned and shook Brodie's and Roger's hands as they wished me luck, and off we crawled to about 40 yards away. There we paused to ensure that the goats would not go into panic mode by what we were doing. As I found out later, the only meltdown was happening with Roger who was having an anxiety attack over the improbability of success. Thankfully, Brodie shook him out of it.

We continued to crawl until we reached the 30-inch scrub tree. Trying to find a shooting position when the hill is so steep was a trick—thank goodness for the tree. I had to lay my pack on an angle against it so I could get a steady rest. As I was going through all these contortions, Bob kept fidgeting to my right.

"Bob, what are you doing?" I asked.

"I'm trying to get this damn video camera to work, but I think it is frozen."

"Forget the camera. I've got the distance, and let's get this goat," I said.

"Charles, are you on 12x power?"

"Yes I am, and he's in my crosshairs."

"Whenever you're ready, Charles."

The first shot rang out, and the goat buckled.

"Nice shot. Shoot him again—you got him in the guts," Bob said.

Second and third shots rang out. At the sound of the first shot, the goats were confused as to where the sound was coming from and what was going on. As they continued to move to the right, we lost sight of them once again because of the angle. Then all of a sudden they reappeared about 500 yards away as they were making their way up and out of the bowl going to our right. One by one they left, a few of the nannies would stop and look back to try and figure out what happened. When the billy wasn't among them, Bob and I knew for sure that our billy was hit well.

At the sound of the first shot, Roger and Brodie sprang to their feet and eventually made their way up to us. We informed them that we thought the billy was down over the bench and we needed to make our way through the bowl and up to him.

As we crossed the bowl, Brodie asked Bob if we were in an avalanche shoot. Bob said, "Just keep walking." I think we all got a bit more of a hitch in our giddy-up at that response.

As we neared the edge of the bench, Brodie was right in front of me and he professionally waited so we would go shoulder to shoulder and be ready for whatever would happen next. We just kept looking ahead and looking down for any sign of the goat. Then, just ahead, there he lay, completely still. We figured that he probably traveled no more than 30 yards before he expired, at an elevation of about 5,100 feet. No doubt about it, this billy was big, and his score in the records book would verify that.

After all the backslapping and picture taking, we settled into the task of caping and boning out the meat. As we figured, the red throat sash was caused by a dominance fight with another billy just missing his jugular by about a half inch. The chance of him surviving the winter was doubtful due to the severity of the wound. The shots all turned out to be well-placed, right behind the front shoulder. Our descent was the same way as we had come up, but now with head lamps on all the way down.

Before we left, and as I always do, I gave a prayer of thanks for having the opportunity to harvest such a beautiful animal.

I gave a special prayer for Pops.

We made it down in about half the time it took us to climb up. Basically we skied the whole way down with our snowshoes on. The only person that had difficulty was Roger, and seriously, he went end-over-end at least 40 times. Tired and exhausted, we finally made it back to Bob's domain.

After a good night's sleep, we said our good-byes with handshakes and hugs, just a bit more bonded by the experience. I cannot say thanks enough about Brodie and the effort he made in the hunt. He is a true professional guide with a lot of toughness. Roger is just Roger—a great man and an important person in my life. As for Bob, he is one talented individual with a deep respect and knowledge of the land and the animals. He is a very congenial person that makes one feel at ease in his home as well as in the mountains. It was a special journey, in a special place, with special people!

Roger got me back to the Smithers airport and back to Montana in time for Thanksgiving and special days with Pops. After telling the story to Pops, he relived the hunt with his numerous friends that came to visit and told the story like the hunt was his. In many ways it was. I believe that he now truly understood the meaning of a trophy of a lifetime!

Christmas came, and on that day, Richard T. Orr went to the higher spiritual hunting ground and I feel fortunate to say that "this goat was for Pops."

Musk ox, scoring 122-6/8 points,
taken by James D. Mierzwiak near Gjoa Haven, Nunavut,
in 1995.

The Oncoming Beast

James D. Mierzwiak

27th Big Game Awards Program

"JIM, THAT'S THE BIGGEST *OOMINGMAK* (MUSK OX) THAT I HAVE EVER SEEN," SAID MY GUIDE ANDY KAMEEMALIK. THESE WORDS DIDN'T HAVE THE IMPACT ON ME THEN THAT THEY WOULD LATER.

The reason I didn't get too excited was really simple. I had hunted Central Canada barren ground caribou on eight previous occasions with Andy, and he, along with most of the other Inuit guides and hunters I have met, are wonderful, happy people. There were always praises for well-placed shots and the animals harvested. It wasn't until I found out later that I had taken a B&C musk ox that I fully understood the significance of his statement.

My partner for this hunt was Gary Solomon, a friend and hunting companion for many years. We were invited guests of our Inuit friends Andy Kameemalik and George Konana.

We left Los Angeles for the town of Yellowknife, Northwest Territories, Canada, on March 27, 1995. After an overnight stay in Yellowknife, we departed for the hamlet of Gjoa Haven, which is located on King Williams Island within the Arctic Circle. Due to the severity of the weather and frequent stops to deliver supplies to other outpost towns, we did not arrive in Gjoa Haven until March 30th. There are no direct flights to most of these hamlets.

Coming from Southern California, it is almost impossible to describe the Arctic cold in March. Let it suffice to say that after the plane landed in Gjoa Haven, it did not leave again for seven days due to the starter motor freezing solid, along with other moving parts on the plane. The temperature was -40°F, plus the wind-chill factor was significant. We had purchased the best clothing for Arctic exploration available, but nothing keeps you warm and comfortable in these extremes.

The best was yet to come. Our transportation on this hunt was a 16-foot wooden sled with a box attached to one end. There were no shocks or other attachments, and it was 10 hours of bone-jarring, teeth-crunching, back-breaking, skin-freezing hell to our camp!

What the heck were we thinking?

We finally arrived at our Hilton Hotel (igloo), much the worse for wear. After three days of isolation in our ice home, I became aware of this horrible feeling of doom in the form of claustrophobia coming over me. I casually informed our hosts that if they did not get me outside by tomorrow, I could not be responsible for my actions.

The next day dawned bright, clear, and of course, cold. After what seemed like hours, we arrived at an overlook with a view of forever. Way out there were several black dots in a sea of white. After looking through a spotting scope, Andy informed us there was indeed a herd of musk ox with some good bulls in the group. We immediately took off, arriving on the backside of the hill where the animals had been spotted. After a careful stalk, Andy set me up about 100 yards from the animals.

After some shifting of the herd, we both spotted what looked like an enormous bull. Keep in mind that I had never seen a live musk ox until this very minute, so they all looked big with shaggy coats of long hair! Only after Andy pointed out specific parts of their anatomy did I understand what to look for.

The .300 Winchester Magnum and the 180-grain Federal bullets did their job, and I had my first musk ox bull. The rest of the herd did not wait around and immediately got out of Dodge!

We made our way back to where our friends were waiting, and informed them my bull was down. Much celebrating and congratulations were exchanged, after which Andy and George took off with one of the sleds, both snowmobiles, and the only rifle to retrieve my bull.

This is when things began to get exciting. While we waited, Gary pointed out a dark shape moving towards our position with great haste. A look through the binoculars confirmed it was a musk ox bull running at full steam towards our position. We joked with each other about how we had heard that musk oxen are almost never aggressive unless provoked. Well it appeared that nobody had bothered to inform this oncoming beast of this fact!

This animal hit the box on our sled with such force that he put one of his horns through the plywood and almost knocked it off the sled. After chasing us around the sled a couple of times, he headed off into the white wilderness. Stunned, we looked at each other and started laughing hysterically.

As soon as Andy and George returned with my animal, George and Gary took off with the gun after the crazed musk ox. They followed him for quite some distance into a small valley where Gary was able to finally put an end to his rampaging. After some hot tea and a bite to eat, we packed up our animals and headed back to our ice Hilton.

During our hunt, we learned many survival techniques from our Inuit friends, including spear hunting seals through the ice; how to quickly build an igloo shelter; ice fishing for Arctic char with handmade soda pop-can lures; how to make emergency clothing, etc. I do not believe more caring, giving people exist on this earth. Hopefully, the Inuit people will continue to retain their current values as modern civilization invades their way of life in the far north.

One last thought: If you have a desire to hunt *Oomingmak* in his arctic home, go during the fall season before the snow and cold makes this hunt more of an exercise in survival than enjoyment! 🦬

Bighorn sheep, scoring 200-7/8 points,
taken by Jack M. Greenwood in Sanders County, Montana,
in 2001.

Grateful

Jack M. Greenwood

25th Big Game Awards Program

THE SUMMER OF 2001 FOUND ME WORKING IN ALASKA. ON ONE OF MY WEEKEND PHONE CALLS, I HEARD, "YOU WILL NEVER GUESS WHAT YOU GOT IN THE MAIL."

After several wrong guesses, I refused to guess any more and made my teenagers tell me. This is how my bighorn sheep hunting season started. It was a combination of surprise and excitement that erupted from my mouth. After 17 years of getting refunds, this was truly a dream come true.

In August, I was able to get a week off from work. Back to Montana I went to do some preseason scouting. Not being familiar with the hunting district, my first stop was the Forest Service office to buy a map of the area. My second stop was the Montana Department of Fish, Wildlife and Parks office where they gave me the name of the local biologist to call for more information.

Finally, my dad and I were off to do some leg work. The morning was spent driving the back roads to get the lay of the land; the afternoon found us hiking a trail and doing a little glassing of the steep, rocky terrain. No sheep were sighted, but we were still excited. My time was up, however, and I had to fly back to Alaska.

On September 6th, I was once again in the air, this time home for the fall and winter. I was anxious to get to my hunting district as soon as possible. On September 10th, my wife and I drove the 90 miles from our home to the hunting district, with the plan of me doing some hiking and her picking me up at a prearranged destination. Everything went according to plan, except that, once again, I was not able to locate any sheep. There was a lot of sign, but the weather was hot and all the animals were moving as little as possible.

Saturday, the 15th of September, was opening day. My 15-year-old son, Jerry, was able to go with me and we were expecting a great day. Using binoculars, we were able to locate some sheep at first light. It looked like they were returning from the river and climbing back to their daytime haunts. Using some landmarks, we determined where they bedded and also the best route for us to approach.

Donning our backpacks and my Ruger .30-06 rifle and Leupold scope, we were off. A couple of hours later, we found a good vantage point and began to glass the opposing rockslide. My son found three sheep, all rams. Now we were really excited! We set up the spotting scope for a better look. The rams turned out to be little guys — one yearling and two not quite 3/4-curls. We were able to watch them for five hours undisturbed at a distance of 345 yards.

Toward evening, I asked Jerry whether or not I should try for the largest ram (my tag was good for either sex.) Due to school and sports, this would be the only time he would be able to hunt with me. He looked the ram over again and said "I wouldn't shoot a ram that little on opening day."

I took his advice, and we began to load up our gear. As we were getting ready to leave, a clatter in the rocks got our attention. We watched as a band of ewes and lambs came around the hillside. It was a nice finish to a great day.

I wasn't able to make it back to hunting for 10 anxious days, but my calendar was now open for as long as it took. I loaded my backpack with five days worth of food and gear, grabbed my rifle, told my family good-bye, and off I went.

The morning of the 25th, I hiked down an overgrown road. After a couple of hours of fruitless glassing, I decided to return to the drainage where my son and I had observed the rams on opening day. It was near evening when I reached the area and set up to glass. Almost immediately, I was able to locate 23 ewes and lambs working their way down the mountain toward the river. It was fun to watch them fearlessly jump from rock to ledge. Just at dark, I found a group of seven sheep high on the mountain. However, the light was too poor for a good look. I went to sleep that night wondering what they were.

On the dawn of the 26th, I was searching the mountains for sheep. The ewes and lambs were still there, but where were the rams? I moved to glass another spot and movement caught my eye; it was a bunch of rams! The spotting scope revealed three rams. Two were little guys, but one needed a closer look.

I headed back to the exact spot where my son and I had watched the rams on opening day. As I was climbing up the now familiar mountain, I paused for a breather. I happened to glance up at the mountain that was at my back. On opening day, my son had brought to my attention some large, white boulders on this particular mountain. As I looked up at them, one of those boulders ran down the mountain a little ways.

I grabbed my binoculars and instantly found the ram of my dreams! It was in a group of four rams and was lying down apart from the others. I quickly changed plans, abandoning my back-pack for my fanny pack. I shouldered my rifle and began to climb.

It was 11:30 a.m. when I first saw the rams. It took a little over an hour to gain the necessary elevation to begin the stalk. In my haste to get to the ram, I neglected to get a good landmark for reference. Due to the wind, I had circled around the back of the mountain. I was now attempting to come around and locate the rams. I crept around the mountainside with my eyes peeled.

After a short distance, a patch of white caught my eye. I dropped to the ground and maneuvered to get a better look. It was a ram, lying down under a big fir tree. It was facing away from me, chewing its cud with not a care in the world. I retrieved my laser range finder from my fanny pack and focused; it was 142 yards. I looked the ram over thoroughly. It was nice, but I didn't think it was the big one.

Suddenly, the ram was on its feet. It stretched and wandered out of sight. While I was wondering what to do, another smaller ram appeared and bedded down in the first ram's vacated bed. This second ram was facing me. I was able to watch it doze at such close distance that I could literally watch the ram open and close its eyes. This ram was also undisturbed by my presence. But just like the other ram, this one decided it was time to move. It got up and followed the exact route of the first ram. I had now been on the mountain for nearly two hours, viewing two rams for most of that time at less than 150 yards. It was truly incredible.

For the moment, there were no rams in sight. I was confident, however, that the rams were close and that my presence was undetected. I looked at my watch, which said it was 2 p.m., and debated what would be the best course of action. Should I move and try to find the rams and thereby run the risk of spooking them? Or sit tight and wait for them to move? I opted for the latter and spent the next two hours second-guessing my decision.

At 4 p.m., a clatter of rocks brought me to full attention. Through the brush and trees, I could make out the rams as they began to feed. I was able to identify three rams momentarily; two were smaller rams, a third was a nice ram (the one I had watched earlier) but the fourth had its head down and was facing away from me. It seemed liked 10 minutes before it picked up its head. When it did, I said, "That's the one."

The rams continued to feed, wandering in and out of view. I sat tight, hoping for a shot. The second-largest ram began to feed directly toward me. I figured it would come out in the open in about five more steps, and I decided I would take it. I thought to myself that it was too good of a ram to pass up at 120 yards. But for some unknown reason, the ram turned in its tracks and went back the other way. My opportunity was gone. I watched and listened for several minutes, but the rams seemed to have moved.

Cautiously, I began to make my way across the rocks to the point where I had last seen the rams. Peeking over the edge, I noticed that I had a good field of view, but that there weren't any rams in sight. I kept scanning closely.

All of a sudden, out of a little fold in the hillside, the rams bolted into view. They were above me and running away. I had my rifle up, trying to find the big one. It was up front, followed by the others. They bunched up together behind a big Ponderosa pine tree, hesitating a moment before emerging on the other side. The big ram was once again in the lead, but they were now quartering away. I don't remember taking my safety off; it was like second nature. The ram was in my cross hairs, and then I remember the recoil and looking for the ram, which was now rolling down the mountain. I reloaded, picked up my empty, and watched as the ram came to rest against a small tree. Then I noticed the other three rams. I quickly looked them over and then focused my attention on the downed ram. I made my way over to it and when I approached the ram, I thought, "It's a monster."

I had to maneuver the ram down the mountain to a flat piece of ground, 400 yards through the rocks and shale, trying to be as careful as possible. It took nearly 45 minutes. Now light was fading fast, and I needed to get it caped and field dressed. I worked both fast and furious. When I finished, I thought about taking some pictures. Unfortunately, in my hurry that morning, I had left my camera in my backpack. Oh, well. I hung the head and cape up in a tree as high as I could and made my way toward my pack. I was able to hike back to my truck, arriving about an hour after dark.

I called my family on my cell phone and made plans for my wife and son to come the next day and help me bone and pack out the ram. It took most of the day for us to get the job done. By the time we got to a Montana Fish, Wildlife, and Parks office for the necessary check-in, it was past quitting time. Luckily, someone was still there and was able to check it in. This was the first time that a tape was placed on the ram. The bases measured 16-7/8 inches and 17 inches, and the horn length were both 44 inches or greater.

It is hard to describe how I felt because I do not consider myself a trophy hunter. I had hoped to harvest a nice ram, but this was beyond my dreams. After the 60-day drying period, I had the ram officially scored. It ended up scoring 200-7/8 B&C points.

I had always felt that bighorn sheep hunting was a dream — something other hunters got to do. I was grateful just for the opportunity to hunt such a magnificent animal. To harvest such a trophy was the culmination of my dreams. 🦌

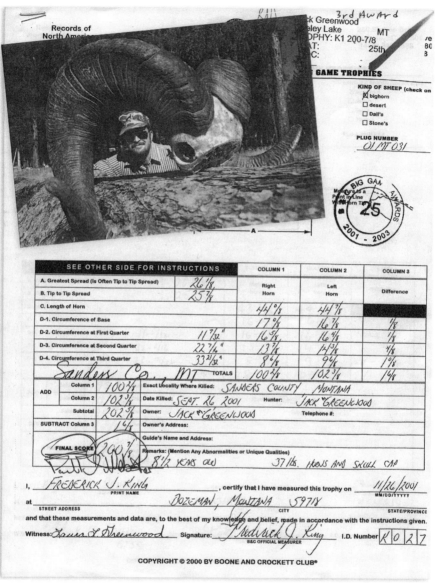

Original score chart for Greenwood's bighorn sheep,
scoring 200–7/8 points.

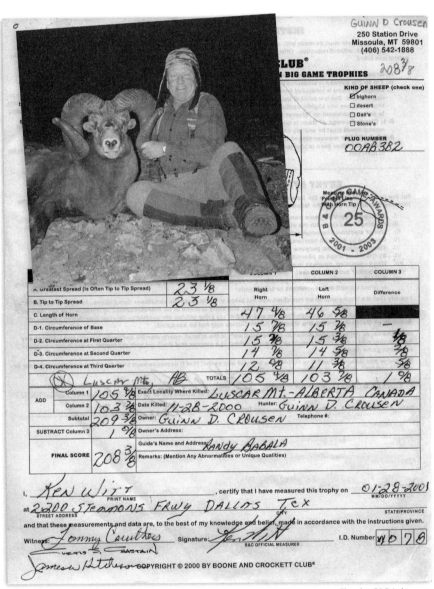

*Score chart for Guinn D. Crousen's bighorn sheep,
scoring 208-3/8 points, taken near Luscar Mountain, Alberta,
in 2000.*

New World's Record

Guinn D. Crousen

As told by Craig Boddington

25th Big Game Awards Program

IT WAS LATE IN THE AFTERNOON ON NOVEMBER 28, 2000, ON LUSCAR MOUNTAIN IN ALBERTA'S ROCKIES. THE ECHOES OF GUINN CROUSEN'S .270 WEATHERBY MAGNUM HAD DIED AWAY AND THE GREAT RAM WAS DOWN. MANY MEN WOULD HAVE RUN FORWARD TO SEE THEIR PRIZE UP CLOSE. BUT GUINN CROUSEN IS BOTH PATIENT AND PRACTICAL. HE'D WAITED MORE THAN A DOZEN YEARS TO FINISH HIS GRAND SLAM WITH A ROCKY MOUNTAIN BIGHORN—NOT JUST ANY BIGHORN, BUT THE RIGHT ONE.

He'd tried to obtain this particular tag for four years, believing that Alberta offered the best opportunity for the kind of ram he wanted. With the right tag finally in hand, he'd tried for 15 days to get a shot at this particular ram. Now it was getting dark and cold in the Alberta mountains. He was tired and his bad knees hurt. The ram could wait a little bit longer. So while his hunting partners sprang forward, Crousen turned back to retrieve his pack and jacket, dropped during the final moments of the stalk.

A few minutes later, moving more slowly with adrenaline levels dropping, Crousen approached his ram. His hunting team

— Randy Babala, Ron McKenzie, and Lyle Moberly — were sitting quietly, looking at the downed monarch. Crousen approached from the rear, seeing the full curl of the ram's horns. "My gosh, boys, he's big," he said.

Randy Babala looked up and spoke quietly in the silence of the moment. "Guinn, you may have a new World's Record." And Guinn Crousen sat down and cried a little.

Few among us have the dream of taking a World's Record of any species, and even fewer come to believe that it might actually happen to them. Guinn Crousen of Dallas, Texas, was not among either group. His father was a retired Marine Gunnery Sergeant who saw service from Nicaragua to the island campaigns of World War II. Guinn grew up with his Dad kicking his tail in true Marine Corps fashion—and teaching him a strong sense of ethics extending from the field to the work place. As a hunter, Guinn Crousen learned to hunt hard and hunt fair. Like most hunters, he dreamed of someday taking a really great trophy—which meant, as it does to most of us, an animal that would make the minimum in the All-time records book *Records of North American Big Game*. As a businessman, he built up a successful corporation, which in time allowed him to expand his hunting horizons.

In 1985 his friend, Don Harold, persuaded him to attend the Foundation for North American Wild Sheep convention. As a result he booked his first sheep hunt, taking a nice Stone's ram with Myles Bradford in northern B.C. He followed up with a Dall's sheep with Stan Stevens in the Mackenzie Mountains of Northwest Territories. Then, in 1989, he took a desert sheep in Baja Norte. Now he had three-fourths of a Grand Slam, all nice sheep but no record-class trophies. He got to thinking that he'd like to close out his Slam with a really big ram, one that would make the book and stay there.

As a measure of Guinn Crousen's patience and persistence,

he didn't just book a bighorn sheep hunt. He did his homework, deciding that western Alberta, near Jasper Park, offered the best available opportunity for the kind of ram he was looking for. And he booked four hunts simultaneously, four years in a row, with Gordon Utri's Whispering Pines Outfitters.

He only hunted two of the four years, allowing friends to take his other two bookings. He was hunting Unit 438, and during those two lengthy hunts he never saw a good ram in his hunting area. But from a favored vantage point he could see the Cardinal River Mine, an area closed to hunting, and in that promised land he frequently glassed good sheep.

When the Alberta auction tag first came out he recognized the opportunity. Six of the ten largest bighorns in the record book and half the top twenty came out of Alberta. Crousen was sure Alberta offered the best opportunity for a really big ram. Starting in 1995 he bid on the Alberta tag for four out of the next six years, losing the bid three times. In 2000, at the Rocky Mountain Elk Foundation gathering in Denver, after dreaming of a good bighorn for a decade, he walked away with the Alberta sheep tag.

What to do with it? Crousen knew he wanted to hunt Unit 438, between Jasper Park and Cardinal River Mine. He also knew that no human being knew the area better than veteran sheep outfitter Randy Babala. Babala grew up in nearby Cadomin, Alberta, roaming the hills as a youngster and eventually guiding in the area for his uncle, Jim Babala. After guiding and outfitting Alberta bighorns for years Randy Babala eventually sold out, relocating to sheep country in the Yukon, but he still knew the area better than anyone.

Crousen called him to ask him to guide the hunt. After the preliminaries Babala, bluntly asked him, "What do you want with the tag?"

Without hesitation Crousen answered, "I want to join the '200 Club'."

Babala didn't know what that meant, so Crousen explained that he wanted to join the tiny group of sheep hunters who had taken rams that achieved a final score—net and dry—of 200 points or better.

Long silence, then Babala said, "There are thousands of sheep hunters who have died, and thousands more that are gonna die, without ever seeing a ram that big—let alone connecting. But if you want to try, come on up and let's go hunting!"

Crousen's team would consist of Randy Babala, assisted by Ron McKenzie and Lyle Moberly, with Lenore Vinson acting as camp cook. "Camp" and headquarters would be Babala's house in Cadomin. Crousen set aside the whole month of November for the hunt, but the agreement was that there was no point beginning until the rams started to move. Interestingly, they did no scouting; everyone involved knew there were big rams on the old mine, or across the area in Jasper Park. With rutting activity the rams would move—and maybe a really big ram would show. On about the seventh of November Babala called Crousen, telling him the rams were starting to move a bit. It was time.

Crousen arrived on the 9th of November, and from that evening onward they hunted all day, every day except Sundays, dawn to dark. The weather was cold, with highs in the teens, occasionally reaching above freezing, but strangely dry. Early on they got seven or eight inches of snow, but for most of the hunt it remained clear and cold, with occasional snow flurries and periods of high winds. Crousen remembers one day when "nickel-sized rocks were blowing through a drainage."

On the third day, late in the evening, they glassed a very big ram, unique and recognizable because of his exceptional length, but much too far away to see clearly. It was too late to move closer that evening, but the next morning they picked the ram up again on the old mine. Crousen knew instantly this was the largest ram he had ever seen. Babala was noncommittal; he simply said, "He'll net/dry 200." From that moment this ram became the quest, but they never again attempted to precisely call its measurements.

On the fifth day they lost the ram and didn't see it again for six long days. During this period they separated, going in different directions to glass, then meeting back up to discuss what they had seen. Ron McKenzie and Lyle Moberly went up to Mystery Lake, while the rest of the team took up different vantage points along Luscar Mountain, glassing down into the mine and west toward Jasper.

By now the rut was in full swing, with rams moving everywhere. Rams from the mine area seemed to have extremely dark horns, almost certainly because of the coal dust. Jasper Park was only four or five miles away, but the Park rams were identifiable because of golden-colored horns.

Eventually, about the 19th of November, they found the long-horned ram again, still in its sanctuary on the old mine. The rams were fighting heavily, and Crousen was afraid to look through the spotting scope. He would ask Randy, "Has he broken anything?" No, it had not. The ram was still pretty, was still the "net/dry 200" they sought—and it was still as safe as if he'd been on the moon.

Early on Crousen had told Babala, "Randy, consider this tag yours. Tell me when you would shoot a ram."

One afternoon they worked in behind some cedars, coming up just 35 or 40 yards above three ewes. A big ram came out of the draw below and stopped just 40 yards below them. Randy Babala whispered, "I'd shoot that ram."

Crousen just looked at him, so Babala went on, "You told me to tell you when I would shoot a ram. I would shoot that ram."

"How big is he?"

"He's 196 or 197, no deducts, a gorgeous ram. I would shoot him."

Crousen passed it, with Babala saying, "Gosh, that ram sure is pretty!"

By November 27th, with time growing short, they had the long-horned ram pretty well located—but it was staying well within the sanctuary. After they came off the mountain Crousen took a shower, then came into the main room. Nobody was saying anything, so Babala broke the silence. "Guinn, we better have a talk. Maybe that ram isn't gonna come out. We should start thinking of a different ram or you might be going home in four days with nothing."

Crousen thought about it for a moment, then replied, "Well, that's all right. It's going to be that big ram or nothin'."

"Okay, let's have supper," said Babala, and that was that.

The ram was still there that morning. Crousen and his crew spread out on the backside of Luscar Mountain, glassing down along the mine's sawtoothed boundary. In the late afternoon a pack of coyotes—at least three, maybe more—dashed into the herd of sheep down on the mine's flat, reclaimed meadows. Suddenly sheep were running everywhere, moving out of the flat and up into the rough rocks. Babala appeared at Crousen's side. "He's coming out. Let's go!"

They left their gear and ran, pulling up short as Babala said, "There's the ram, there's the boundary stake. He's out. Take him!" It was a going-away shot at just about 70 yards, and the ram that would become the new World's Record bighorn belonged to Guinn Crousen, his team, and all of us who care about such things.

In 1911, in Blind Canyon, Alberta, Fred Weiller took a ram that stood as the World's Record for 90 years. Among all of Boone and Crockett Club's categories for North American big game only the World's Record woodland caribou has stood for a longer period. As Guinn Crousen and his ram have proven, records are made to be broken, but few of us who have studied the record book ever believed that Fred Weiller's ram would be beaten.

The reasons for this are obvious. Our bighorns have made a wonderful comeback in many areas, so it isn't necessarily clear that there are fewer bighorns today than there were in 1911. But in today's well-managed herds the permits are carefully allocated for a sustainable yield, not necessarily to allow the maximum growth potential. Few herds have the genetics and the feed and minerals to produce "net/dry 200-point rams," and among those that do very few rams escape predators, hunters, hard winters, and other natural calamities long enough to reach their maximum potential. Were I a betting man, I would have bet that Fred Weiller's Blind Canyon ram would stand forever as the largest-horned bighorn sheep known to have ever lived. I would have been wrong. Guinn Crousen's Luscar Mountain ram, taken on November 28, 2000, officially scored on August 15, 2001, in Missoula, Montana, by a B&C Panel of Judges at 208-3/8 points, is the new World's Record bighorn by two eighths of a point.

It's interesting to note that Crousen's ram achieves its fabulous score in unusual fashion. With bases of 15-7/8 inches, it is not particularly heavy-based as bighorns go. Crousen and his team were absolutely correct when they recognized its incredible length; at 47-4/8 inches on the right and 46-5/8 inches on the left its horns average the second longest of any bighorn sheep in the All-time records book. And while the bases are not huge by bighorn standards, it carries the mass very well into the first, second, and third quarter measurements. It is a great ram, well-judged, well-hunted, and well-taken. Now it's a part of hunting history, and I think I would have cried a little on that mountain as well. 🦌

Bighorn sheep, scoring 201-2/8 points,
taken by Larry Strawson (right) in Alberta's Nikanassin Range,
in 1997 (pictured with Ken Williamson).

No Fire, No Blanket

Larry Strawson

23rd Big Game Awards Program

AUGUST 7: It was a smoldering hot day in August, three weeks before the opening day of sheep season. The temperature was 30°C, but climbing in and out of some of my favorite sheep basins made it feel more like 40°C. In one of these basins, I spotted what looked like sheep. I dug into my backpack for my spotting scope—yep, they are rams. I had to get a closer look. Five miles further up the valley, there were more rams—10 rams and twelve ewes to be exact. Four of the rams were legal, and one was a real dandy. This second group of sheep was between me and the rams I originally spotted. Not wanting to spook any of them, I decide to leave the area, knowing I would return on opening day.

Saturday, August 25: Dwayne Huggins, a good friend of mine, and I headed into Notellem Basin in Alberta. We were hoping to find the rams I had spotted there a few weeks earlier. When we finally reached the basin, we came up empty, so we decided to split up. After several hours of searching, I spotted the ram I was looking for. When I finally managed to catch Dwayne's attention, I waved him over to figure out our game plan. He would stay and watch the ram, while I hiked back to get our camp supplies. Upon my return, Dwayne informed me the ram moved into a neighboring basin. By this time, it was too late to try and relocate the ram, so I decided to set up camp for the night. Dwayne went back to our main camp to pick up another one of our hunting partners, and a video camera. We planned to meet again at our makeshift camp, sometime the next day.

Sunday, August 26: The temperature dropped during the night and my sleeping bag was covered in frost when I awoke. The sky was clear and I headed toward the basin where Dwayne had last seen the ram. Several hours later, when I found a good vantage point, I began searching. Anyone who has ever tried to find one ram, in a basin full of rock, can appreciate just how much time and patience it can take. Fortunately, I found my ram at 10 a.m.

I spotted the ram, bedded, in a field of big boulders. Since it was still the day before opening day, I decided to leave the area for a catnap, not wanting to risk spooking the ram. When I woke up, and went back to check on the ram, he was gone! The ram was gone! I couldn't believe my eyes; the search was on again. After an hour of continuous glassing, I relocated the ram, bedded in a different pile of boulders. Not wanting to go through all of this again, I decided not to return to camp. I stayed up on the mountain, with the ram, until morning.

While I waited, I spotted another hunter, Ken Williamson, and he was also looking for sheep. I was going to ask if he would let Dwayne know where I was, and send him over with the video camera. Right about then, we noticed a husband and wife, heading toward the ram. Afraid that they might spook him, I asked Ken if he would stay with me, so we could cover more area if the ram took off.

Ken and I were situated in a saddle I expected the ram to use. Suddenly, Ken whispered, "Hold it." Sure enough, just 30 yards away, in walked the ram. The couple down below had startled him, as we had anticipated. Unfortunately, there was nothing we could do but watch him, and hope like crazy he didn't go far. Luck was with us that night. He only traveled 300 yards, and bedded down within sight. Now we were stuck for the night.

It was dark and getting cold, and there was no way we could light a fire without scaring the ram, so we had to make do. We both had survival blankets in our packs and figured we might as well use them. After spending a half hour unfolding our blankets, we could hardly wait to crawl in and warm up. Unfortunately, we found out are "survival" blankets had been in our packs so long they had deteriorated and fallen apart. No fire. No blanket. No way we could move. It was going to be a long, cold night.

Monday, August 27: I had just completed jumping jack number 5,000 when I could feel a tingle in my feet again. Apparently, they didn't freeze off during the night. To the east, I could see a hint of gray in the sky, indicating that dawn was approaching. Opening day was finally here. Ken and I made our plans for the hunt. I had noticed a steep draw, and felt that if I could get into it before daylight, I would have a good chance to make a stalk on the ram. It was 6 a.m., and legal shooting time was 6:40 a.m.

I started up the steep shale draw, slipping and sliding my way up toward the ram. A glance at my watch revealed 6:30 a.m., but I still had a considerable way to go. Finally, I arrived at the spot where I thought the ram bedded the night before. Slowly, I released the waist belt on my pack. Wrong buckle! I had undone the buckle on my utility belt. Not wanting to leave it behind, I had to set down my rifle to get it back on with both hands. In the steep shale, my rifle took off sliding, bouncing, and rattling down the mountain. Thoughts of a ruined stalk raced through my mind, since I was sure the clattering rifle spooked the ram. Fifty yards down the draw, my rifle came to rest against a big rock. A quick examination showed nothing more than a few scratches. My watch now read 6:40 a.m.

As I made my way back to where I wanted to exit the draw, my thoughts were running wild. *"Is the ram still there, are my rifle scope still true?"* These thoughts vanished as I came out of the draw, and there was no sign of the ram. Not knowing if my rifle had spooked him, or if he had simply changed beds during the night, I had to go slowly. As I proceeded along the mountain, I spotted a sheep below me. A quick look through my binoculars confirmed he was the one. The ram was now bedded 200 yards below me, at a steep angle. He didn't know I was there, so I tried to get closer. I shoot a .300 Weatherby, and felt comfortable shooting from a rest out to 350 yards. But, this was what I figured to be a 190-plus bighorn, and I wanted to be sure. After I wormed my way to within 100 yards, I laid my pack in front of me for a solid rest. It was still a steep angle, so the shooting position was less than comfortable. The thoughts of my rifle bouncing down the mountain were still on my mind as I racked a shell into the chamber. A look through my scope revealed the ram had gotten up, and started to feed. Since the ram was still unaware of my presence, I took my time to steady the cross hairs behind his shoulder.

The shot was loud on that clear August morning, but not near as loud as the "yahoo" I let out as the ram went down with one shot. As I worked my way down to the fallen sheep, I couldn't help but notice the beautiful surroundings, crowned by the rising sun. When I got to the ram, I noticed Ken working his way up, so I had time to sit down and reflect on what I had done. I knew three things for sure. One, I had taken one heck of a ram. Two, I had blisters on top of blisters from the two previous days of following this ram. And three, I still had to pack this bruiser out of a basin that I think is impassable, unless a huge detour was taken to get back to main camp.

A story an old-timer told me about packing a sheep out of this same basin kept going through my mind as Ken walked up with a big smile. A handshake and congratulations were in order as we stood there, admiring the great trophy. After taking field photographs, the job of caping and boning began. When I told Ken of my plan to pack the ram out the back of the basin, he said I was crazy. I was determined, because if someone else could do it, then so could I. With all the meat and the horns on two packs, we headed up the back of the basin. After three hours of white knuckles, dizzying heights, and falling rock, on legs that would barely support my weight, we made it to the top, grinning at each other. We were both thinking the same thing, *"this sheep hunting sure is fun."* Am I nuts or a little bit crazy, but as I looked down to the emerald green lake nestled in the long green alpine basin, crowned by towering snowcapped mountains, with a ram tied to my pack, it all began to make sense. Also, the fact that the ram's Boone and Crockett score would be around 200 points helped to make it all seem worthwhile. He is the ram of a lifetime.

This story is a brief overview of the events prior to and the actual harvesting of my ram. But it doesn't touch on all the events, sights, smells and camaraderie that make hunting a complete experience. It doesn't describe all the sweat, and numb fingers and toes, when the temperature drops below zero. Nor does it include the fording of those icy cold creeks, and the water coming over the top of your boots. Sheep hunting is always in the most incredible scenery in the world.

The enduring friendships are also part of a enjoyable hunting trip. I would like to say thanks to a few people who made this whole trip possible: to Donovan, my boss who gave me the days off; to Dwayne, who was always trying to catch up, thanks for honoring the unwritten code of "first spot, first shot;" to Ken Williamson, a man I talked to maybe six times before this hunt, thank you for also honoring my right to the first shot. Ken also packed more than his share up that cliff, never once questioning or complaining. Thanks also go to Rick Stelter, who looked after the preservation of cape and horns so they may be admired for many years to come and to Rick Alkire, of H.O.R.N.S, who did reproductions of the horns, so that they may be protected from theft and fire. And finally, Leupold rifle scopes: it's amazing that a rifle was right on after the tumble it took down that slide. Thanks again for a quality product. 🦌

*Original score chart for Strawson's bighorn sheep,
scoring 201-2/8 points.*

Bighorn sheep, scoring 204–2/8 points,
taken by Toni L. Sannon in Fergus County, Montana,
in 2008.

Every Sheep Hunter's Dream

Toni L. Sannon

27th Big Game Awards Program

After a decade of applying, 2008 was my year to be one of the lucky ones to receive a Montana bighorn ram permit for the much sought-after Missouri River Breaks. It was just two years earlier that I had drawn a coveted bull elk tag for the same area. While the Breaks tag for bulls isn't as desirable as the sheep permit, it is a very close second. After harvesting a six-point bull that year, I thought I had used up all of my luck. I knew this area has a well-deserved reputation for producing huge rams year after year, and to say I was excited would be a very big understatement.

When it finally sunk in that I would be going on the hunt of my lifetime, the next three months were filled with much preparation. My hunting partner Randy Latterell and I spent countless hours obtaining landowner permission, purchasing and studying maps, talking to biologists and anyone else who had information on the sheep and this very unique country they inhabit. That summer, like several recent years, was extremely dry, and we figured the sheep would be concentrated close to the river. Access to this sheep area is limited at best, so we decided to put all our eggs in one basket and buy a river boat so that we could hunt from the water.

We knew there were outfitters that we could employ but I wanted this to be a true do-it-yourself hunt. I was confident that when the season was over, I would have a nice ram to show for all our efforts. I had arranged a full month off at the beginning of the season for the hunt, and more time later if necessary. I didn't really know how long it might take. My goal was to take a ram with my bow, though if I wasn't able to get a bow shot I would use a J.C. Higgins .270—a 1952 purchase for Randy's mother. He had killed his ram 12 years earlier with it, and I had used it to take my bull in 2006.

We planned to camp as close to the sheep as possible, but a rainstorm just hours before our arrival made access to the camp area impossible. We would have to base camp 20 miles further downriver than we had planned. This would require two hours of unplanned travel time on the river each day. It did cut into the time that we had planned to be hunting, but we weren't going to let that get us down at the start of my bighorn adventure!

Montana recently began to allow a 10-day archery-only season prior to the regular season. Unfortunately I only had one day to hunt during this time. The rest of the season I would be hunting with both rifle and archery hunters.

The first morning, Sept 14th, started out with extremely thick fog that didn't lift until 10 a.m. When it did, it was a beautiful sunny day that topped out around 70° F—not the type of weather that one thinks ideal for sheep hunting in Montana. This was our first look at this breathtaking country. Most of the river corridor is just as Lewis and Clark saw it 200 years earlier. The unique and varied rock formations throughout this badlands terrain were spectacular, as were the numerous other wildlife species we encountered. We saw deer, elk, eagles, badgers, beavers and thousands of geese and other waterfowl. We spotted a few rams the first day, with the biggest being about 180 points.

At 10 a.m. on my second day, we spotted two rams laid up under a ledge on a cliff. From 1,200 yards, we could tell one of them was worthy of closer inspection. We videotaped and tried to judge him from 450 yards for an hour, but he would never turn his head. We needed to be closer. Just as we got to 250 yards, they stood and walked out of sight. As we waited for them to show again, three younger rams grazed on another nearby hillside. While we were watching them, much to our surprise the two big rams joined them at 600 yards. We conservatively estimated the biggest to be at least in the high 180s with both horns flared far to each side and appearing to be about the same length. He was a very pretty ram. We videotaped and studied them with the spotting scope until they got up and grazed away from us. Not wanting to spook them out of the country, we decided that it would be best to find them the next morning. That evening at camp, we reviewed the footage, and I thought this was the one we should concentrate on getting within bow range.

On our way upriver the next morning, we spotted two mature rams in a group of eight. We studied them for a while but continued upstream to try to find the big flared ram from yesterday. We didn't find him and decided to put a sneak on the previous rams. The temperature was in the 90s, but we were able to get within bow range of the group. The two larger rams were pushing 190, but I couldn't get too serious about them this early in the hunt, especially since I needed to get a better look at the flared ram.

Each day we would see this group of eight, but we couldn't find the flared ram. I was quite concerned that maybe he had already been taken by another hunter, as we had seen sheep hunters every day in the area.

At 9:30 a.m. on September 21, the eighth day of my hunt,

we finally found him. He was all alone near the top of a terribly steep ridge. After sizing up the terrain and taking into consideration the other hunters in the area, it was an easy decision to forego the archery equipment and take him with the .270. This was too nice of a ram to chance losing him again if the archery stalk spooked him out of the country. We had to motor across the river to his side and were scared that he might run. He continued to graze in the open while we closed the distance to 300 yards.

I wasn't used to shooting on such a steep incline so it took me about 15 minutes to get comfortable with the shooting sticks. Randy was busy filming and watching him through the spotting scope. My first shot hit him hard and a couple more anchored him. He rolled a good 100 yards down the hill before he hung up on sagebrush. It was a steep climb up to him, one filled with anticipation to see my ram. When we got up to him, we both knew instantly that I had just taken the ram of every sheep hunter's dreams. We put a quick tape on him and were sure that this was the largest sheep to ever come out of the Breaks. We had time for a couple dozen pictures but knew it would take the entire day to bone the meat, cape him for a life-sized mount, and get back to camp by dark.

The ram's score is 204-2/8 points. His horn lengths are 44-4/8 and 44-2/8 for his right and left horns, respectively. Both bases measure 16-4/8. He has unbelievable symmetry with only a 1/8-inch deduction on one circumference measurement. Boone and Crockett Club's 27th Awards Judges Panel verified the entry score of the ram. This is the second largest bighorn ram ever taken in the United States and the largest bighorn sheep ever taken by a woman in Boone and Crockett Club records.

I feel truly blessed for the opportunity to hunt these magnificent animals in such a rugged and remote environment and to come away with such a truly remarkable trophy. 🦌

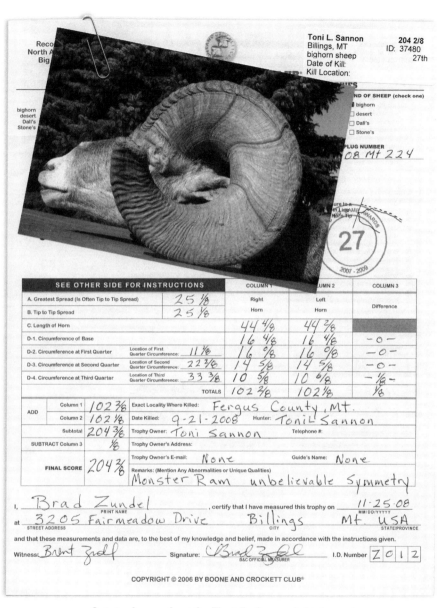

Original score chart for Toni L. Sannon's bighorn sheep scoring 204-2/8 points.

Bighorn sheep, scoring 198-3/8 points,
taken by Stephen C. Morrical in Blaine County, Montana,
in 2006.

True Connection

Stephen C. Morrical

26th Big Game Awards Program

MOST SUCCESSFUL HUNTS START WITH A LOT OF PLAN-
NING AND PREPARATION AND END WITH A LOT OF LUCK.
IN THE CASE OF MY 2006 MONTANA BIGHORN SHEEP HUNT,
A GREAT DEAL OF THE LUCK TOOK PLACE BEFORE THE HUNT
EVEN HAPPENED.

For over 20 years, I had been applying for a bighorn sheep permit in my home state of Montana, with no success. Finally, this past year in June, I received notification from the Montana Fish, Wildlife & Parks that I had finally drawn a tag. I didn't draw just any tag; I drew one of the coveted Missouri Breaks permits. This permit is highly desired by big game hunters because this district, home range to the now extinct Audubon sheep first re-corded by the Lewis and Clark expedition, is known to contain a very healthy herd of transplanted Rocky Mountain bighorn sheep, with many older rams capable of scoring high in the Boone and Crockett Club's records book.

Aerial surveys conducted by Montana Fish, Wildlife and Parks in the spring of 2006 reported the Missouri Breaks herd doing well. In addition to a healthy herd, biologists conducting the surveys observed many trophy-class rams.

With tag in hand and reports of excellent sheep populations, the stage was set. I could hardly contain my enthusiasm through the summer months. Being a first-time sheep hunter, I read as many books and articles on bighorn sheep hunting as I could get my hands on, focusing my study on field judging horn size. I knew this was going to be the best opportunity I would ever get to harvest a Boone and Crockett animal, so I set out to learn what a 180+ set of horns looked like.

Although I had not spent much time in the area I would be hunting sheep, I was no stranger to the Missouri Breaks. During the last 10 years, I had spent a lot of time bow hunting for elk, rifle hunting for mule deer, and exploring the terrain of the Missouri River Basin from my jet boat. I was all too aware of the challenges hunting the Breaks can pose. As it is in much of the western United States, the weather here can be fickle. In the Breaks, however, rain or snow means "gumbo clay" which in turn means "You're not going anywhere until things dry out." My sheep district would be accessible by either the river or a network of unimproved BLM roads, totally at the mercy of the weather.

The Montana sheep hunting season is long (Sept. 15-Nov. 30) and the hunter can choose to hunt with either a bow or a firearm. Being both an avid bow hunter and a gun hunter, selecting which method became a dilemma. In the end, I decided to conduct my early hunts with the bow, keeping my .30-06 in camp if I felt the need to use it. Because my hunting district was about five hours travel time from my home, I set aside numerous vacation days with the intent of spending three to four days at a time hunting, distributing several of these hunts throughout the season.

Opening weekend found my friend Mike Killian and I running 25 miles upriver in the jet boat to hunt the steep cliffs and lower coulees of the Missouri River. The weather was wet and miserable and fortunately we did not need to rely on vehicle travel to access the hunting areas because, as earlier mentioned, the roads were impassable due to the gumbo. Even the hiking proved difficult as, with every third step, five pounds of clay would stick to your boots.

Most of the hunting that weekend was confined to glassing from the river. Even the sheep seemed to be hanging low as we only spotted a few bands of rams over the course of the first three days, with nothing that appeared to be an eye-popper.

A few weeks later I was back at it again, this time solo, and hunting by truck off the BLM road system. The weather was more cooperative and I did manage to spot a fair number of sheep, including one magnificent ram that I guessed would go in the high 180s. He was lounging with three smaller rams on a hanging bench in a steep canyon. I was still carrying my bow and planned a stalk that would put me within 50 yards but, as is often the case, something happened and the sheep slipped across the canyon, casually observing my stalk from a safe distance. I did get a great opportunity to sit and study this ram at 150 yards for over an hour, piecing together the aspects of horn size and learning a lot about judging a trophy-class sheep.

One of the highlights of my sheep hunting experience came on this trip when I woke at 4 a.m. to a spectacular northern lights show. It was close to wake-up time, so I decided to brew coffee and sit in my camp chair watching the show and listening to the coyotes.

The 2006 sheep season was nearly at the midpoint when I embarked on the third hunt. On this trip, my very good friend, fishing buddy and bowhunting mentor Mike Ellig accompanied me. Although being a sheep-hunting novice like me, Mike has as much experience hunting North American big-game animals as anyone I know, and I looked forward to his help and companionship. We would again be accessing the area by vehicle but chose to hunt a part of the hunting district that had so far been tough to get to because of weather conditions.

On the evening of our first day, we spotted a lone ram feeding on a grassy knoll. He looked good at 800 yards through the spotting scope, so I decided to stalk in for a closer look. As I got closer, the ram moved just out of sight below the grassy knoll, a perfect condition for a bow stalk. I slipped off my pack, nocked an arrow and carefully closed to where I thought he should be.

At that moment I heard Mike, 500 yards away, whistle my attention. As I turned to see what he was telling me, I noticed a movement to my left. There he was, 40 yards away, head concealed by a juniper bush, body fully exposed. I didn't want to shoot because I wasn't sure how big he was. After about 15 seconds, the sheep had enough and bolted to about 70 yards before stopping and looking me over. I was heartbroken and awed at the same moment. He was a massive ram with huge bases, horn clearly below the jawline and mass extending along the horn length to the broomed ends. An interesting thing about this animal was that he carried a radio collar. We stared each other down for at least 30 minutes before he again had enough and disappeared down into a maze of steep clay cliffs and draws. The shot was too far for me to take with the bow, and my gun was safely stowed back in the truck. I learned a valuable lesson from this experience: Decide whether or not you are going to shoot before getting too close, especially on sheep, where careful study is required if you want to be sure.

That night in camp I made a pivotal decision; I was going to start carrying the rifle. My main goal was to shoot a ram that would make the records book and I didn't know how many opportunities I would get for a sheep like the collared ram. I love the challenge that archery presents but, more than that, I wanted a trophy sheep.

We spent most of the next day trying to find the collared ram with no success. Toward late afternoon, we glassed four rams in a jumbled canyon. As we looked them over, it became apparent that one looked exceptional. At 600 yards, you could see the length of horn and what appeared to be good mass. This sheep didn't appear to be broomed at all.

After some on-again, off-again decision making, I decided that he didn't look as massive as the collared ram and that we should keep looking. I had half the season ahead of me plus the rut so I was very nervous about making a hasty decision. Still, that night in camp I seriously wondered if I had not made yet another mistake.

The last full day of this hunt broke clear, cool, and calm. We again spent the day looking for the collared ram with no success, ending up the day back where we had seen the other big ram the evening before. After splitting up and doing some careful spotting, I found the band of rams seen the afternoon before about a mile across the canyon feeding. Mike and I decided that with only an hour of shooting light left, our best option was to jump in the truck, drive around to the opposite ridge, and try to approach these sheep from above. It took us 40 minutes to get to where we wanted to park, so time was dwindling fast.

As we stalked down off the ridgetop and closed in on landmarks guiding us to the last known whereabouts of the rams, I could feel my pulse quickening and throat tightening. The wind was dead calm, so every step was made as quietly as possible. As I inched closer to an overlook, I couldn't figure out where the sheep has disappeared to. Finally, on the last step, I noticed the back of a sheep no more than 45 yards straight below me. I quickly ducked, hand-signaled Mike the situation, and together we belly crawled to the edge of the overlook.

On the hanging bench, totally unaware of our presence, were three of the rams, including the biggest one I had agonized over. At such a close distance, I didn't need the binoculars or the scope to confirm horn size. His bases were much more massive than originally thought and the horn extended well below the jawline and back up over the bridge of the nose. The mass at the midpoint appeared to be equal to the base. A lot of things were going through my mind those last few seconds, but foremost was the underlying question: *Was this going to be it?*

A few seconds of viewing this tremendous animal and the answer was clear. I whispered to Mike that I was going to take him. The huge grin on his face was all I needed to confirm his approval. From our position above the sheep, I elected to take the shot straight down through the top of the back. The 180-grain Nosler partition bullet hit the mark, resulting in a clean, quick kill. The rangefinder verified the shot at 41 yards.

After waiting a few moments to make sure he wasn't going anywhere, we picked our way down to him. As we got closer, I couldn't believe the beautiful and massive animal before us. The horns were much heavier than we had first thought and the tips were hardly broomed, curling above the bridge of the nose. We spent those first several minutes just taking in the moment, admiring our trophy, and thanking our good fortune.

The next few hours were spent caping and skinning the ram by headlamp under a clear October night sky. We then ascended the canyon with the head and cape. We retrieved the quarters early the next morning and headed straight to the nearest ranch to contact Fish, Wildlife & Parks to obtain the necessary transport permit. The wardens that checked us were not only impressed with the size of my ram but were also awed by the fact that he was aged at 5-1/2 years old! What a tribute to the quality of habitat and genetics of this sheep population.

When I reflect back on my 2006 sheep hunting experience, I realize how fortunate I was to draw the permit and hunt such a magnificent animal in the unspoiled setting of the Missouri River Breaks. In listening to my account of the hunt, one may think that my only measure of success was to harvest a "book" animal.

But hunting is not only about killing a trophy animal. It's the thrill of the hunt, the companionship, and the true connection that hunters have with the natural world that really matters. 🐾

Stone's sheep, scoring 177-2/8 points,
taken by R. Terrell McCombs near the Stikine River in British Columbia,
in 2007.

A Stone for the Ages

R. Terrell McCombs

27th Big Game Awards Program

SHEEP HAVE ALWAYS HELD A SPECIAL FASCINATION FOR ME. MAYBE IT'S BECAUSE THEY LIVE IN SUCH SPECTACULAR, HARSH ENVIRONMENTS. MAYBE IT'S BECAUSE THEY REPRESENT SUCH A TREMENDOUS PHYSICAL AND MENTAL CHALLENGE. HOWEVER, I THINK THE REAL BASIS FOR MY FASCINATION IS SIMPLE: IT'S THOSE HORNS! I DON'T KNOW MANY HUNTERS WHO AREN'T IN AWE OF HOLDING A REALLY GOOD SET OF HEAVY, MASSIVE SHEEP HORNS IN THEIR HANDS.

It was in September 2007 that I set out to find a Stone's ram to add to a fine Dall's ram I had harvested in Alaska's Chugach range. That was in 2004, and although I hunted these "rams of the rocks" in 2006, I had been unsuccessful. Now at 52, I can see the horizon of my sheep-hunting career much clearer than I could a decade earlier. We only have so much time to do what we love, and I was determined to take a good Stone's ram, arguably one of the most beautiful and coveted big-game animals in North America.

The final floatplane ride into Jerry Geraci's Stikine River Lodge was smooth and the scenery spectacular. After touching down, I ate a fine meal of sheep ribs prepared by Ruth, the lodge's cook, and sacked out for a good night's rest. The following morning would find me in the saddle for a 25-mile horseback ride with a pack string into some of the wildest country in North America.

My guide was Rod, a 33-year-old fireman and mountaineer from Vancouver, British Columbia. Rod enjoyed taking a month's vacation every year to guide for Jerry. He was athletic, offered intelligent conversation on a wide variety of subjects, and was well-versed in sheep behavior and ecology. While Rod had guided many hunters to moose, caribou, goat, and even grizzly, he freely admitted that this was his first opportunity to guide a sheep hunter. Normally this would concern me, but not with Rod. While I have a decent amount of sheep- and goat-hunting experience, his attitude and confidence was infectious.

He said, "Terrell, all you and I have to worry about is the weather. We'll find a ram because I saw a real good one up here last week when I was glassing for moose down in the valley."

"How good was he?" I asked.

"Oh", Rod replied, "He was good alright. It looked to me like his horns came two or three inches above the bridge of his nose and he looked plenty heavy."

He curled above the bridge of his nose? What a ram! I thought. Now I was excited and in the game. Later that evening we arrived at our campsite, and I stole some time to glass for sheep while helping set up camp. Nothing motivates a sheep hunter like sighting a big ram.

The next morning Rod and I left Earl, our young wrangler, in camp as we backpacked two or three miles to a good spike camp location to glass for the ram. We hunted and glassed hard for nearly three days, climbing up to look over several basins and an untold number of shale slides. No sheep. The fourth and final day found us tent-bound as the weather cooled considerably and six inches of snow greeted us at dawn. It snowed all day.

When you are 6-foot-5, spending the day cramped into a small backpack tent with your guide is a challenge to your commitment. Little doubts and questions enter your mind as to why you are really there. It also offers you too much time to think about your responsibilities back home. I tried to keep my mind busy by reading or simply sleeping. Bad weather is the curse of sheep hunting.

I have always thought the greatest challenge with hunting sheep is the mental aspect of it. You begin asking yourself too many questions when you are confined by the weather. How many days are left? Will I find a good ram? Will the weather ever clear up? Will that head cold turn into something worse? What if the shot is too far? How's my family? That is why I'll glass and trek to the top of every visible mountain before I'll spend one daylight hour in a tent. The problem is you never have any choice in the matter. Weather dictates everything. If you don't have the visibility to glass, you can't hunt sheep.

We glassed for an hour the next morning before bad weather descended upon us again. All we saw was one lone billy goat, but no sheep. At that point we decided to return to Earl and the horses. We at least had a larger tent there. We approached camp and called out for Earl around mid-morning. The 18-year-old was ecstatic to see us. I don't think Earl enjoyed those lonely days by himself! However, he offered good news. He had been riding up to a nearby pass early that morning and had seen a good ram feeding. We excitedly asked him for more details. After listening to Earl and asking several questions about the animal, Rod concluded that it was the same ram we had been looking for. The weather was clearing some, and we decided look for the ram that afternoon.

We hunted very hard, glassing into high mountain basins, while sitting out wave after wave of snow and sleet descending upon us from the northwest. It was strange. There were periods you could see a mile or more, closely followed by periods where you could not see 100 yards, coupled with high winds. We stuck it out all afternoon in search of the ram. We glassed and hunted over the high mountain pass and the adjoining mountains and deep cirques for nearly seven hours. Only the approaching dusk pushed us back toward camp. While the scenic vistas had been beautiful, we hadn't seen any sheep.

That evening, a serious storm blew in, dumping more than a foot of snow on top of an already hefty accumulation. The temperature dropped into the high teens and the next day was spent in the tent. No one, as I mentioned earlier, likes being confined to a tent because of weather. The time passes slowly and cabin fever can build up in hunters and guide alike. Earl and Rod were singing the blues that evening. Now, with only two full days left to hunt, the warm fires of Jerry's Stikine River Lodge were becoming more and more appealing. In fact, the idea of heading back early was even mentioned. I can't blame the guys. We were all a little down over the weather. That's when I reminded them to maintain a positive attitude.

I said, "Many great animals have been taken on the last hour of the last day of the hunt. We are going to tough this thing out. Who knows? The weather could clear up tomorrow and we could climb up to that pass and take the ram of the century."

I had no idea how prophetic those words would become.

The next morning dawned with fog, snow, and a gray overcast but there was a hint of blue in the western sky. Sure enough, it cleared enough by 11 a.m. to hunt. We busily packed our gear and began climbing toward the pass.

The going was slow as we pushed through snow two to three feet deep. I was in the lead and stopped to glass often. After an hour, we were a little more than halfway to the head of the pass when I noticed something unusual about 1,200 yards away on a south facing slope. Any big-game hunter knows what I am talking about. It just looked out of place. Slowly and quietly I held up my hand to stop our progress. I pointed toward the slope, and three pairs of binoculars went up at once. My breathing stopped for a moment as I realized I was looking at a very good bedded Stone's ram. He had not seen us and we slowly dropped out of sight into a side canyon.

I can't exactly describe the next few moments except to say the debate over stalking strategy was heated and intense. Finally, Rod and I agreed on the most conservative approach to the ram. After my disappointing experience the prior year, I had developed a deep respect for the powerful vision of these animals. I would not make the same mistake twice.

We lunged through the deep snowdrifts, my lungs burning as we pushed up an adjacent slope to reach a good shooting position. Although we were only at a little over 6,000 feet, the steep slope and deep snow made every step feel like 30-pound weights were strapped to each leg. Earl was paralleling us, peeking around the edge from time to time to keep an eye on the ram as we ascended. Suddenly, he motioned that the ram was up. He could not have seen, heard, or smelled us. Regardless, he was headed straight up the slope toward the crest of the adjoining drainage. We shifted into high gear as we cursed the snow and the icy mountain as we slipped and struggled the last 50 yards to the crest.

I had wanted a shot under 300 yards, but there was no hope for that now. I flopped down into the snow and grabbed Rod's pack for a rest. I was still heaving from the hard climb and took several deep breaths to calm my nerves as I tried to prepare for the shot of my life. I settled down as the ram continued toward the crest of the ridge, now less than 25 yards away. He was moving with purpose and there would be no way to keep up with him under these conditions. It was now or never.

"Earl, give me the range."

"476 yards," he replied.

Rod urged me to hurry before the ram disappeared over the ridge. However, I ignored his urgings, as I concentrated fully on the shot. It was still and silent, nearly solemn, like being in a cathedral. I was in a deep zone of concentration now, and my world went into slow motion. I took two more slow, deep breaths and acquired a solid, steady sight picture. Earl was saying something to me, but I didn't hear him. Every ounce of concentration was on the ram. I slowly began my trigger squeeze and I remember being surprised as the loud report of the rifle disturbed the deep stillness of the wilderness.

I saw the ram fall as I recovered from the recoil. I was turning toward Earl, with a look of triumph on my face, when he screamed, "You killed him!"

Earl, his face showing a combination of shock and elation, leaped on me, driving us both down into three feet of snow. It was an act of pure joy. Suddenly, Rod joined the dog pile and the three of us laughed and shouted in victory as we rolled through the deep snow like schoolboys on winter vacation. We had been three men, thrown together as strangers in the intense crucible that is sheep hunting. Now we were laughing, screaming, and even shedding some tears in pure celebration of the hunt. It was a scene as old as mankind itself, and we continued to hug and shake hands, delirious over our success. We thought we might be shut out, but in the last inning, grasped victory! It is a feeling I cannot explain, but will never forget as long as I live.

We approached the ram together, for through this bonding experience we were now a team. I pulled the trigger but each of us owned a piece of that ram. No one had to say anything. We all knew it. I observed that his bases looked larger than 13 or even 14 inches. A tape measure was back at camp, but we weren't too concerned about it. We were just thrilled to have harvested such a fine animal. After plenty of pictures, we began the long pack down to camp.

I took out a vinyl tape measure in camp and casually measured the horns, mostly out of curiosity. The tape said 43 x 15 inches. Earl, ever the skeptic, insisted we measure them again. The results were the same. His horns didn't look that long due to their heavy mass. No one said anything for a few minutes as we began to realize the true size of this magnificent animal before us. I told Rod it was a heck of a way to begin his sheep guiding career and then kidded him that it would be all downhill from here.

Later, Jerry said it was the largest ram to come out of his area in nearly 25 years. No one had seen him before, strong testament to the fact that it is very hard to hunt every inch of a 4,000-square-mile hunting concession, even over 25 years. We carefully green-scored him at around 180 points. Roger Britton, the government inspector and a local taxidermist in Smithers, said it was the largest ram he had seen in more than 20 years on the job. He aged the ram at 13½.

Large rams are where you find them. I have heard it said that all the great Stone's sheep were taken in the 60s and 70s and none are left in British Columbia and the Yukon today. Great sheep are still there and more probably die from worn teeth and wolves than most of us would care to admit. However, with recent commodity prices at historic highs, more resident hunting pressure is put on sheep today than in the past. Once-formidable wilderness is being carved up and penetrated with easily accessed mining roads. High prices, due to the world's growing demand for energy and minerals, are a fact of life today. No outfitter can control that fact; he can only work to gain the cooperation of these natural resource companies in order to respect the wildlife that is his living. Let us hope this sense of cooperation in land-use management is successful. It is important because today more than ever, we need to know that great rams still roam wild and steep mountain basins.

Fortunately, this hunt proved to me they still do. ☙

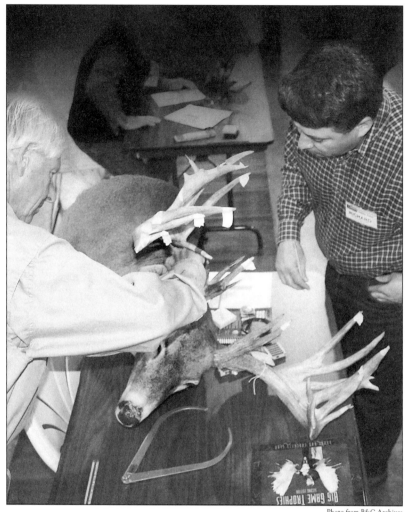

*Long-time Official Measurers and Club members Frederick J. King (left)
and Richard T. Hale (right) take part in the 27th Big Game Awards Judges
Panel held in Reno, Nevada, in 2010. The top scoring trophies for each
Award Period are invited to have their scores verified by the panel, which
makes them eligible for B&C Awards.*

Entering Your Trophy

Jack Reneau

Boone and Crockett Club

I F YOU ARE FORTUNATE TO HAVE TAKEN A ONCE-IN-A-LIFETIME TROPHY LIKE THOSE FEATURED IN THIS BOOK, YOU OWE IT TO YOURSELF, YOUR TROPHY, AND THOUSANDS OF HUNTER-CON- SERVATIONISTS TO ENTER IT INTO B&C'S PRESTIGIOUS RECORDS BOOK. NOT ONLY WILL YOUR TROPHY RECEIVE THE RECOGNITION IT DESERVES, BUT THE CONSERVATION RECORD ATTRIBUTED TO THE EFFORTS OF HUNTER-CONSERVATIONISTS IS INCOMPLETE WITHOUT IT.

In order to submit a trophy into Boone and Crockett Club's Awards Programs, you must first have it scored by a B&C Official Measurer. You can obtain a list of measurers in your state or province, as well as a list of minimum entry scores, by calling the Club's headquarters in Missoula, Montana, at 406/542-1888 or visiting our web site, www.boone-crockett.org.

If your trophy meets or exceeds the minimum score for your category, the Official Measurer will provide you with a list of entry requirements and assist you in submitting it to B&C for listing in records book. This chapter includes a complete list of entry requirements with tips for streamlining the process.

SCORECHART

The most obvious and basic item needed to enter a trophy is a fully completed, current, original score chart, signed and dated by an Official Measurer appointed by the Boone and Crockett Club. Photocopies of score charts, as well as incomplete score charts, are unacceptable. Entries submitted on Pope and Young Club score charts, or on outdated score forms, are also unacceptable. When an entry is not submitted on the correct (and properly completed) score chart, all other processing steps must wait until a correct and accurate original score chart is received.

ENTRY FEE

A check or money order for $40 in U.S. funds must accompany each entry to cover the entry fee. If the entry fee is not included with the entry materials, or if the incorrect amount is tendered, the trophy owner is notified that the proper entry fee is needed.

ENTRY AFFIDAVIT

Another item of importance that must be submitted with each hunter-taken trophy is an original Entry Affidavit properly signed and witnessed. The correct Entry Affidavit is on the back of all current score charts. The hunter's signature on the Entry Affidavit needs to be notarized by a notary public, or witnessed by an Official Measurer. Once a trophy has been measured that makes the minimum score, the Official Measurer should give the trophy owner an opportunity to read the Entry Affidavit on the back of the score chart. Once the hunter is satisfied that he/she understands and meets all aspects of the Entry Affidavit, he/she should sign it in the presence of the Official Measurer who should then witness the hunter's signature by signing and dating it in the spaces provided on the score chart.

Please note that the Official Measurer's signature witnessing an Entry Affidavit on the back of the score chart is in addition to the Official Measurer's signature on the score chart verifying his/her measurement. The Official Measurer must actually be present and see the hunter sign the Entry Affidavit before the measurer signs it, or the Entry Affidavit is unacceptable.

The notary public is still required in cases where trophy owners have no direct contact with an Official Measurer. For example, measurers frequently do not meet trophy owners when they are scoring trophies for big buck contests, or when a friend, taxidermist, or other individual delivers a trophy to a measurer for the hunter. Canadian trophy owners only can also have their signature witnessed by an employee of a fish and game department, in lieu of the notary's or Official Measurer's signature.

PHOTOGRAPH REQUIREMENTS

All bear and cat entries must be accompanied with clearly focused, close-up photo prints (black and white or color) of the front, left side, right side, and top of the clean, dry skull. All trophies with antlers, horns, or tusks must be accompanied with clearly focused, close-up photo prints of the front, left side, and right side of the trophy, preferably with a plain background. Slides are unacceptable.

Field photograph submissions are highly desired but not required for trophy acceptance. We accept any submissions and publish photos showing the hunter with the animal in the landscape where the hunt occurred, excluding vehicles or structures. Please note that not all field photos will be published.

Digital photographs, which were previously unacceptable for many reasons, are now acceptable in place of regular print photographs. The primary reason is technology to make and reproduce high quality digital photographs needed to guarantee and protect the integrity of the Club's archives is now adequate to meet our needs. Many digital photographs we receive are printed with poor resolution and/or are printed on plain copy paper. Such photographs are unacceptable because they cannot be reproduced in B&C publications and are highly susceptible to damage. The Club needs high-quality photographs that will last forever with each trophy entry. The photographs, especially field photographs if available, need to be high quality to be reproduced in books and magazines.

Digital photographs submitted for acceptance into the Club's Awards Programs, must comply with the following criteria:

A. Camera quality - the resolution level of the image must be 2 mega-pixels and above.

B. Printer - digital photographs must be printed at 1,200 DPI or better.

C. Paper - digital photographs must be printed on glossy, photo-grade paper.

D. Photo size - 3"x4" or 4"x6" singly or three or four photographs per page on 8"x10" or 8.5"x11" glossy photo paper.

HUNTER, GUIDE, AND HUNT INFORMATION FORM

Each entry that was taken by a hunter must also include a completed Hunter, Guide, and Hunt Information (HGH) form, even if the services of a guide were not employed on the hunt. The hunter simply needs to complete the parts of the HGH form that apply to his particular trophy. The HGH form, and all other required forms, are available from the Official Measurer, and from the Records Office. The same forms can be downloaded from the Club's web site.

LICENSE AND/OR TAG

A photocopy of the appropriate hunting license (and/or tags, if applicable) must accompany each entry that was taken by a hunter. If a copy of the license and/or tags is no longer available, the Club will accept a statement from an appropriate Game and Fish Department official who will certify that a license (and any required tags) was possessed by the hunter at the time the trophy was taken. If the Game and Fish Department no longer has records at its disposal to verify the purchase of a license, a written statement, on official letterhead, from Game and Fish personnel stating the fact that the license information is no longer available is acceptable. The hunting license copy requirement will then be waived.

The last three items listed above, the Entry Affidavit, Hunter Guide and Hunt Information form and the hunting license copy, are only required for trophies that are known to have been taken by hunters. Trophy owners submitting picked-up trophies, trophies of unknown origin, or trophies taken by deceased hunters are not required to submit these items to complete the entry. However, entry materials of picked-up trophies and trophies of unknown origin, must be accompanied with a narrative that tracks its origin and history.

In addition to all of the items previously mentioned, there are several other items or pieces of information requested for each entry. The first item is an accurate location of kill for each entry. In most cases the office simply needs the county or geographic location (e.g., river, mountain, etc.) and state or province where the trophy was taken. All trophies from the lower 48 states are listed in the records books by county and state, while all trophies from Canada and Alaska are listed by geographic location and state or province. Trophies from Mexico are listed by state and country. In cases where a trophy is harvested near a category separation boundary (e.g., mule deer/blacktail deer; grizzly bear/ Alaska brown bear; etc.) the exact location of kill, pinpointed by marking an "X" on a map, is required.

Finally, if available, the Club would like to obtain the age of each trophy entry if the age was determined by a competent authority. The Club also would like to record the rack or tusk weights (in pounds and ounces) for walrus, caribou, elk, and moose. Complete details for providing this information are given on the back of each Hunter, Guide and Hunt Information form that must be submitted with each hunter-taken entry. The age data will likely be useful in managing big-game populations for trophy animals, as well as supporting the case for trophy hunting. The rack and tusk weights can be used to make comparisons between various North American big-game species, as well as comparisons with their counterparts in other parts of the world.

Incidentally, up to four people can be listed in the records book as the hunter for a single trophy. However, in order to list more than one person, each hunter must submit a signed and witnessed Entry Affidavit, as well as a copy of his or her hunting license/tag, for the trophy being entered. There are no special requirements to list more than one owner.

RECOGNITION ITEMS

Once your trophy has been processed and passed the Club's due-diligence process, it will be accepted and you will be a sent a handsome acceptance certificate with an image of Theodore Roosevelt on it. In addition, your trophy will be listed in one issue of B&C's *Fair Chase* magazine, and a copy of the Awards Period records book, as well as the next edition of the all-time records book, if it exceeds the all-time records book minimum entry score. Finally, you can obtain several special recognition items to memorialize your accomplishment. These items include a shadow box, a laminated certificate plaque, a belt buckle, and a ring with the category and score of your trophy. 🦌

CATEGORY	AWARDS MINIMUM	ALL-TIME MINIMUM
BLACK BEAR	20	21
GRIZZLY BEAR	23	24
ALASKA BROWN BEAR	26	28
POLAR BEAR*	27	27
JAGUAR*	14-8/16	14-8/16
COUGAR	14-8/16	15
ATLANTIC WALRUS	95	95
PACIFIC WALRUS	100	100
AMERICAN TYPICAL ELK	360	375
AMERICAN NON-TYPICAL ELK	385	385
TULE ELK	270	285
ROOSEVELT'S ELK	275	290
TYPICAL MULE DEER	180	190
NON-TYPICAL MULE DEER	215	230
TYPICAL COLUMBIA BLACKTAIL	125	135
NON-TYPICAL COLUMBIA BLACKTAIL	155	155
TYPICAL SITKA BLACKTAIL DEER	100	108
NON-TYPICAL SITKA BLACKTAIL	118	118
TYPICAL WHITETAIL DEER	160	170
NON-TYPICAL WHITETAIL DEER	185	195
TYPICAL COUES' DEER	100	110
NON-TYPICAL COUES' DEER	105	120
CANADA MOOSE	185	195
ALASKA-YUKON MOOSE	210	224
SHIRAS' MOOSE	140	155
MOUNTAIN CARIBOU	360	390
WOODLAND CARIBOU	265	295
BARREN GROUND CARIBOU	375	400
CENTRAL CANADA B-G CARIBOU	345	360
QUEBEC-LABRADOR CARIBOU	365	375
PRONGHORN	80	82
BISON**	115	115
ROCKY MOUNTAIN GOAT	47	50
MUSK OX	105	105
BIGHORN SHEEP	175	180
DESERT SHEEP	165	168
DALL'S SHEEP	160	170
STONE'S SHEEP	160	170

* MUST BE TAKEN AND/OR POSSESSED IN FULL COMPLIANCE WITH THE MARINE MAMMALS ACT/ ENDANGERED SPECIES ACT AND/OR OTHER FEDERAL AND STATE LAWS.

** FROM LOWER 48 STATES, ELIGIBLE ONLY IF RECOGNIZED BY STATE AS A GAME ANIMAL, WITH HUNTING SEASON AND LICENSE SPECIFIED.

Acknowledgments for
Legendary Hunts II

Stories selected from the Boone and Crockett Club's Awards book series – 18th Awards through the 27th Awards – by:

Jim Arnold

Keith Balfourd

Mark O. Bara

Richard T. Hale

Julie T. Houk

Kyle C. Krause

Remo Pizzagalli

Jack Reneau

Justin E. Spring

Mark B. Steffen

Cover Photograph by:

iStockPhoto.com / Olaf Loose

Legendary Hunts was designed by Julie T. Houk,
Director of Publication, Boone and Crockett Club
using Adobe Caslon Pro typeface.

Paperback printed and bound by Sheridan Books of Ann Arbor, Michigan
Limited Editions bound by Roswell Books of Phoenix, Arizona